François Mauriac

on Race, War, Politics, and Religion

François Mauriac on Race, War, Politics, and Religion

THE GREAT WAR THROUGH THE 1960s

Translated and Edited by

NATHAN BRACHER

THE CATHOLIC UNIVERSITY OF AMERICA PRESS
Washington, D.C.

The paper used in this publication meets the minimum requirements of American National Standards for Information Science—Permanence of Paper for Printed Library Materials, ANSI Z39.48-1984.
∞

The Catholic University of America Press gratefully acknowledges a grant from the Mission Culturelle et Universitaire Française aux Etats Unis that supports publication of this volume.

Photographs: page 1: postcard of Antwerp on the Schelt, c. 1930. Courtesy of Wikicommons; page 35: Waldenberg, German, 1945. Courtesy of Wikicommons; page 97: Athens, Greece, mine, ca. 1948. Courtesy the National Archives; page 149: Warships in Algiers, Algeria. Courtesy of Wikicommons; page 193: Charles de Gaulle, Cherbourg, France. Courtesy of the National Archives; page 246: Nikita Khrushchev, East Berlin, 1957. Courtesty of Flickr.

Cataloging-in-Publication Data available from the Library of Congress
ISBN 978-0-8132-2789-4

CONTENTS

ACKNOWLEDGMENTS

I am grateful to three grants from Texas A & M University: a High Impact Research grant from the Department of International Studies allowed me to initiate this project, while a Seed Grant from the College of Liberal Arts, together with a Research Fellowship grant from the Glasscock Center for Humanities Research, not only sustained my translation and commentaries but also allowed me to secure the requisite copyright permissions. I would also like to thank the following journals for permission to adapt parts of my previously published articles for these commentaries on Mauriac's editorials: *Christianity and Literature* for "The Cold War Christian Humanism of François Mauriac," vol. 52, no. 3 (Spring 2003): 387–408; *Contemporary French Civilization* for "A Not So Distant Mirror: Mauriac's Image of America," vol. 30, no. 2 (Summer/Fall 2006): 17–43; and the *Journal of European Studies* for "Facing History: Mauriac and Lévinas on Nazism," vol. 23 (1993): 159–77. Specific borrowings from these articles are indicated in footnotes to a number of chapters.

Laurence Marie of the Book Department of the French Cultural Services generously assisted me in securing copyright permissions from the French publishing houses. Jean Mauriac graciously gave me permission not only to consult his father's original manuscripts at the Bibliothèque Jacques Doucet in Paris, but also to translate the World War I–era editorial "The Americans in My Town."

Finally I am indebted to my friend and colleague Patrick Henry for his advice on key aspects of the manuscript; to my sons, Christoph, Benjamin, and Andrew, for their inspiration; and most of all to my wife, Françoise, for her unfailing support and encouragement from beginning to end.

INTRODUCTION ❧ THE ARTIST AS POLITICAL PUNDIT

François Mauriac, winner of the Nobel Prize in Literature in 1952, is most widely known for his lyrical, yet socially corrosive novels starkly depicting the ruthless greed, sexual hypocrisy, and relentless infighting of the provincial Catholic bourgeoisie in the Bordeaux region. But he was also one of France's most notable public intellectuals, who penned hard-hitting editorials in prominent venues of the Parisian press. Mauriac had indeed become active in the heated public debates over politics, culture, and society as orchestrated by the major Parisian daily papers and weekly news magazines as early as the World War I era. His editorial activity continued to intensify throughout the next five decades, and among the many other literati also active in journalism, Mauriac is now widely considered to have been France's most accomplished and influential polemicist of the mid-twentieth century. Accordingly, the entire corpus of his newspaper and magazine articles is studied by scholars as his most important contribution to French politics, culture, and society.

Indeed, the impressive number of high-quality scholarly works on his journalism that have been published in recent years testifies to the current and enduring scholarly interest in a career that spanned the most dramatic events of the century. This renewed interest in Mauriac's journalism first became evident in the early 1990s, with the republication in the prestigious "Points-Seuil" collection of the entire five-volume set of his *Bloc-notes* or "Notepad," suggesting reflections jotted down from one day to the next, relating matters personal and quotidian to momentous events and crises of society, politics, and international affairs. The last few years have seen another flurry of newly edited collections of his articles.[1]

1. Jean Touzot published annotated editions of Mauriac's *La Paix des cimes* (Paris: Bartillat, 1999), a set of chronicles dating from the nascent Cold War era, and *D'Un Bloc-notes à l'autre:*

In this context, there is a pressing need on this side of the Atlantic to highlight Mauriac's distinctive role in the turmoil of political and cultural controversy in the Parisian press throughout the interwar years, the Occupation, the postwar upheavals, the Cold War polarization, and the decolonization period. At the same time, it is equally urgent to make François Mauriac's most powerful, eloquent, and influential editorials available in English. Selected from a total production of some two thousand articles, this collection of ninety-four of Mauriac's most important editorials is devoted precisely to that end. The titles and sequence of the chapters herein highlight pivotal events and crises of the mid-twentieth century, while at the same time underscoring Mauriac's incisive, yet balanced and insightful responses.

Now accessible to anglophone readers, these articles highlight Mauriac's intellectual itinerary as he responds to major events over six decades of the mid-twentieth century. From the rise of Fascist powers and the Spanish Civil War in the 1930s to France's harrowing experience of the World War II years, on to the Cold War era, the colonial wars in Vietnam and Algeria in the 1950s, which ushered in the "reign" of Charles de Gaulle in the 1960s, Mauriac's impassioned commentaries on France's politics, scandals, tragedies, trends, books, and performances provide a rich chronicle, while at the same time testifying to his persistent preoccupation with remembering a criminal past, American superpower, and the vexing interface of history and theology.

Amid the conflicts and controversies spawned by those momentous decades, Mauriac played a distinctive role as France's preeminent outspoken Catholic intellectual in a nation that more than many others lends an ear and offers a public forum to its literary authors. Recognizing the key role

1952–1969 (Paris: Bartillat, 2004), a previously overlooked set of editorials from the 1950s and 1960s. Then Touzot edited "*On n'est jamais sûr de rien avec la télévision*": *Chroniques 1959–1964* (Paris: Bartillat, 2008), a previously forgotten set of Mauriac's incisive press commentaries on French television during the ferment of the 1960s. In the same year, Laurence Granger and Jean Touzot, in collaboration with Jean-Luc Barré, published *Journal: Mémoires politiques* (Paris: Robert Laffont, 2008), a one-volume collection of hundreds of Mauriac's newspaper articles dating from the 1930s, 1940s, and 1950s, and previously scattered among several volumes long out of print. Jean-Luc Barré penned a widely acclaimed two-volume biography of Mauriac (*François Mauriac. Biographie intime, 1. 1885–1940* and *2. 1940–1970* [Paris: Librairie Arthème Fayard, 2009 and 2010]), while Jean Touzot and Caroline Casseville are editing a Mauriac dictionary for Honoré Champion.

played by writers, artists, and intellectuals as editorialists and reporters is indeed crucial for understanding the evolution of French politics, culture, and society from the French Revolution of 1789 right up until today. This situation constitutes a distinctive feature of public life in France and contrasts sharply with the United States, where literary figures, philosophers, and professors are commonly relegated to their proverbial ivory towers and (erroneously) considered to be hopelessly out of touch with the gritty reality of everyday life in a workaday world and the rough-and-tumble realm of politics. French writers, artists, and intellectuals have, on the contrary, often ventured into politics by writing editorials for major daily newspapers and weekly news magazines. Intellectual expertise, cultural sophistication, and eloquence are explicitly valued as gauges of prestige: such qualities have not only helped major figures in French arts and letters achieve star status, but have also given them considerable clout in championing social or political causes. Conversely, writers, artists, and intellectuals have often taken advantage of this situation to throw themselves into the political fray by becoming active in the press, which has proved to be highly influential in public affairs ever since the Revolution of 1789.

The capacity to influence public affairs or to champion a social cause in France accordingly hinges on the ability to articulate informed, eloquent, and persuasive discourse. That is why the most influential voices of the French press have most often not been investigative reporters, but writers and philosophers whose erudition and linguistic prowess command the respect of a public that for generations has revered artists and writers as heroes, and occasionally traitors. Such was dramatically the case after the trauma of war and occupation in 1944 and 1945: Sartre, Camus, Éluard, and Aragon, among other writers, were catapulted into stardom not for taking up the sword but for wielding their talented pens in the clandestine press of the Resistance (and risking arrest, torture, deportation, and death in doing so). Conversely, Robert Brasillach was executed by firing squad for his open strident support of the Nazis and their French collaborationist cohorts in the Fascist newspaper *Je Suis Partout*. Where else but in France does a philosopher, Bernard Henry Lévy (who has incidentally published books such as *American Vertigo* and *Who Killed Daniel Pearl?* that have been translated into English),[2] enjoy star status; write a weekly op-ed borrowing the name introduced by Mauriac, "Bloc-notes," in one the country's major weekly news magazines, *Le Point*; and even enjoy the privilege of private conversations with France's president at the time, Nicolas Sarkozy, thus conspicuously and effectively spurring the French government to intervene on behalf of the rebels in Libya? Clearly, intellectuals still play a crucial role in the French press.

The press moreover serves as a kind of bellwether for politics, culture, and society in France, as Albert Pierre observes: "As archives of the everyday, newspapers are the most complete, and in their diversity, the most objective source of general history."[3] Jean Lacouture's assessment of Mauriac's editorial production during the immediate postwar period in the fall of 1944 provides a striking case in point. From de Gaulle's triumphant procession down the Champs-Elysées on August 25 until the end of that year, Mauriac penned more than fifty articles for the columns of the Parisian daily *Le Figaro*. His commentaries on the liberation, the ongoing war effort, and the beginning of the purge in France were central not only to the French public's political disposition but also to its impassioned experience of "the most highly politicized period of contemporary history."[4]

Like others who write newspaper articles, Mauriac moreover played a double role. Documenting events, his commentary provides a chronicle of the time. For us today, delvingback into dusty collections of the articles devoted to the seemingly bygone concerns of yesteryear thus constitutes an intellectual venture rich in pleasure, "that of having restored contact with the daily preoccupations of past generations and the passionate involvement of journalists."[5] Mauriac's talent as a memorialist clearly shows in his many deft and savory sketches of the people and events of the day. At the same time, his power as a polemicist is equally evident in pithy commentaries on the stark choices so often confronting France in the mid-twentieth century. Assessing what is at stake and articulating a stance, his

2. Bernard Henry Lévy, *American Vertigo* (New York: Random House, 2006), and *Who Killed Daniel Pearl?* (New York: Melville House, 2003).

3. Pierre Albert, *Histoire de la presse* (Paris: Presses Universitaires de France [Que sais-je?], 1996), 4.

4. Jean Lacouture, *François Mauriac. 2. Un citoyen du siècle* (Paris: Éditions du Seuil, 1980), 177.

5. Albert, *Histoire de la presse*, 4.

editorials, like those of his counterparts, influence public opinion and so participate actively in the life of the nation.

There are a number of compelling reasons why press articles published by François Mauriac over the course of six decades of the twentieth century offer informative, enlightening, and pleasurable reading for us now, in the twenty-first century. To begin with, Mauriac's editorials chronicle the most momentous decades of twentieth-century France and Europe when, in contrast to today, the print media were still at the height of their prestige. While offering a rich panorama of these times, Mauriac's articles also link the experience and convictions of the author to the vicissitudes of history, politics, society, and culture. Fully capable of stepping back and understanding people and events from a wider perspective over the *longue durée* of human history, Mauriac does not, however, just survey the situation from some lofty promontory. He plunges into the fray, taking sides, and participating in the skirmishes of his times. He nevertheless manages to avoid the doctrinaire perspectives of either the Left or the Right, offering instead a series of rich, subtle, complex, and nuanced analyses that defy ready-made categorization.

Mauriac also presents a noteworthy case of a Catholic intellectual all the more interesting because he does not fit into any ideological pigeonhole. Though not without distinct values and orientation, he has a keen eye for the subtle, poignant human implications of a wide range of vexingly complex issues arising not only from such momentous events as the trauma of war, but also from seemingly mundane realities of everyday life and common people. Finally, beyond "reporting the facts" and "analyzing" the situation, Mauriac was a consummate artist whose editorials testify to his talents as a poet, novelist, and playwright. A number of these pieces can be read as Montaigne-like essays, others as veritable prose poems, and still others as metaphysical dramas set in the form of dialogues. Here again, Mauriac succeeds in tying the topical and the ephemeral to the universal and the timeless.

While going well beyond the particular debates of the mid-twentieth century, many of these editorials nevertheless provide timely insights about issues looming large on our horizon in these beginning decades of the twenty-first century. As someone who unconditionally condemned the use of torture in the face of terrorism, decried the faceless power of entrenched economic interests blocking urgently needed reforms, denounced the wanton pillaging and destruction of our habitat and natural resources, and lamented the unbridled vulgarity of consumerist society, Mauriac offers fruitful avenues of reflection in our own time. His editorials invite us to ponder what we share as human beings, within or without our respective national borders, regardless of the various religions, ethnicities, and pigmentations that could divide us. In sum, they ask us what sort of beings we want to become in the face of all that would deny or even destroy our fundamental humanity. In this first quarter of the twenty-first century, as one crisis after another—and in particular, acts of terrorism, torture, and war—confront us with acutely ethical questions for our individual and shared humanity, Mauriac's unique editorial voice resonates more powerfully than ever.

François Mauriac

on Race, War, Politics, and Religion

1 ∽ THE GATHERING STORM OF CONFLICT IN THE 1930s

Hitler, Mussolini, and the Rise of Fascism

Among the numerous eras of conflict and crisis that have characterized the long, rich, and tumultuous history of France, the decade preceding the Second World War is by no means the least dramatic. The early 1930s prove critical not only for France and the world, but also for François Mauriac's career as an editorialist. Without revisiting the entire set of that era's momentous events, we can most usefully recall four pivotal developments: Hitler's accession to power in 1933; the massive march on the French national assembly on February 6, 1934, nearly resulting in an extreme right-wing coup d'état; Mussolini's invasion of Ethiopia in the fall of 1935; and the outbreak of the Spanish Civil War in July 1936.

To borrow from Thomas Paine, these were indeed times that tried people's souls. Amid widespread dissatisfaction with the endless maneuvering and fragile coalitions in France's National Assembly, many not only saw the democratic institutions of the Third Republic as irremediably ineffective and obsolete, but even thought that the future would belong to more "modern" regimes, modeled either after Mussolini's Italy, Hitler's Germany, or Stalin's Soviet Union. Extremism and bitter invective thus heavily influenced the French political scene. Moderation, cool reason, and lucid analysis of the highly dangerous international situation were sorely lacking on all sides. Michel Winock points out that on the Left, the intellectuals who after the February 1934 riots banded together in the Comité de Vigilance des Intellectuels Anti-fascistes intent on blocking a coup, saw matters in terms of French domestic politics and had no interest in opposing Hitler with a show of military force.[1] Their enemies were the pillars of established order: the bourgeoisie, the army, authority, and nationalism.

Like many others on the Left, they were moreover aligned with and guided by the Soviet Union: Comintern operatives Willie Muenzenberg and Ilya Ehrenbourg served as key organizers for the writers who convened in Paris in 1935 to denounce the Fascist threat. Many, like philosopher Alain (Émile Chartier), saw war as the greatest evil, to be avoided at all cost. Others, such as the Surrealist writer André Breton, made no distinction between what they saw as a capitalist imperialism in France and a remilitarized, Nazi Germany violating international treaties and clamoring for more territory. Breton even championed German culture and philosophy as the "only effective antidote against the positivist rationalism that continues to exert its ravaging force here [in France]"[2] and, with Georges Bataille, published a tract advocating "a vast composition of disciplined and fanatical forces, and an intransigent dictatorship of the common people in arms."[3]

It is precisely because of the highly volatile context of national and international politics and the vehement debate in the press that we would do well not to underestimate the importance of Mauriac's editorials, as imperfect—and sometimes severely flawed—as their politics clearly were. His voice would become increasingly audible in this raucous debate, finding a wider audience and deeper resonance outside the comfortable confines of the Catholic bourgeoisie for whom he had so often written

1. Michel Winock, *Le Siècle des intellectuels* (Paris: Éditions du Seuil, 1997), 244–62.

2. Ibid., 256.

3. Ibid., 261.

in *L'Écho de Paris* as well as in the more centrist paper *Le Figaro*. If the editorial prompted by Franco's attack on the Spanish Republic displays Mauriac's deep-seated suspicion and even latent hostility toward Premier Léon Blum, it is because he remained even in 1936 decidedly less than sanguine about the merits and viability of the parliamentary democracy of the Third Republic, whose institutions had nevertheless weathered numerous storms since its origins in 1870, including most notably the Dreyfus affair and the First World War.

As a staunch Catholic still stinging from the 1905 separation of church and state that had driven religion out of public schools, Mauriac saw France pursuing a special vocation as "la fille aînée de l'Eglise" ("the eldest daughter of the Church") and a beacon of Catholic civilization. He accordingly remained highly wary of the anticlerical tendencies of a regime that championed secularism in government, public affairs, and social institutions. As a landowner from the rural provinces, Mauriac was fiercely attached to his ancestral dwelling and vineyard at Malagar, which he regarded as the sacred, inviolable patrimony of a well-to-do bourgeois family intent on living from the proceeds of their land and avoiding the socioeconomic status of those who have to work for others. Always anxious about harvests, plant diseases, market prices, interest rates, and banks, Mauriac was bitterly opposed to what he saw as the scheming, corrupt, incompetent party politicians of the Third Republic, who he feared would endanger this family heritage and social status.[4]

In the face of the nascent Fascism that was transforming two neighboring European powers, Mauriac displays a rather discomfiting ambivalence emblematic both of that specific historical context and of the conservative character of his political views in the first half of the 1930s. As was the case for many of his compatriots in the 1930s, Mauriac yearned for a national synthesis that could overcome the bitter rancor of deep social and political divisions that were paralyzing France at the very moment when it faced an acute economic crisis and grave international threats.[5] As he would insist after Charles de Gaulle returned to power in 1958, ushering in a new constitution based on a newly empowered independent executive branch,

4. Barré, *Mauriac. Biographie intime, 1. 1885–1940*, 482–85.
5. Winock, *Le Siècle des intellectuels*, 233–37.

he persisted in believing that only a strong patriotic leader could put an end to the dithering, incoherent party politics of the National Assembly and live up to France's presumed vocation as the beacon of civilization and enlightenment. That is doubtless why Mauriac accepted the invitation to serve as the official sponsor for the inaugural issue of the Fascist-leaning Belgian Catholic monarchist journal *Rex*. From April 1933 through November 1934, he was for all practical purposes a fellow-traveler with Léon Degrelle,[6] the publisher and party activist who would later join the Waffen-SS and fight on the eastern front. At the same time, however, the Mauriac of the early 1930s that we find in these editorials was also guided by his deep conviction that a Christian must first and foremost remain loyal to Christ.[7]

Only six months after Hitler had assumed power, we find Mauriac writing an editorial on the question of authoritarian leaders and recoiling before what he perceives as "the terrifying face" of the Fascist dictatorships imposed by Hitler and Mussolini, pointing out that these strongmen have above all been "skillful in utilizing the economic suffering of a generation, the hungry bodies of twenty year old men, the rancor in people's hearts, [and] despair." The French see themselves, as does Mauriac, as a "civilized people par excellence," as Minerva shocked by the cluster of snakes displayed by this new Medusa: while Medusa may be "throbbing with life," it remains a monster having emerged from the "forces of darkness," a beast that is visibly "disturbed and feverish," totally unsuited for a people priding themselves in following Montaigne's level-headed, reasoned, and measured approach, which he identifies as "our wisdom." In the end, Mauriac clearly designates the Fascism visible in Nazi Germany and Mussolini's Italy as a manifestation of "barbarity" whose "seduction" must be resisted and whose danger must be eliminated: hence his concluding reference to a Perseus who, shunning fear and subservience, summarily beheads the brazen Medusa.[8]

Mauriac was clearly heading in a new direction that would distance him more and more from the arch-conservative, ultra-nationalist right-

6. Barré, *Mauriac. Biographie intime, 1. 1885–1940*, 486–87.

7. Ibid., 493.

8. François Mauriac, "L'homme qui ne vient pas," in *Journal. Mémoires politiques*, 685–89.

wing ideology inspired by Maurice Barrès and Charles Maurras. Rather than a sudden, dramatic redefinition reminiscent of some road to Damascus experience, his change of perspective followed a gradual progression over several years. On February 6, 1934, in the wake of the Stavisky affair, an angry mob of demonstrators almost succeeded in invading the National Assembly and staging a coup d'état.[9] Mauriac, although opposed to any violent overthrow, depicts the rioting crowd as the true embodiment of the French people, bringing together students, war veterans, shopkeepers driven out of business, even the working class that a number of intellectuals were claiming to defend.[10] And when, in January of 1935, the newspaper *Le Journal* sends him to Rome with French Foreign Minister Pierre Laval to report on the latter's diplomatic visit to Mussolini and the Vatican, Mauriac delivers a relatively favorable, if reserved, ironic, and inconclusive assessment of Italy's *duce* after meeting him in person.[11]

Mauriac's reaction to Mussolini's invasion of Abyssinia (Ethiopia) in "A Cartoon by Sennep" therefore represents a highly significant, if hesitant step in a new direction for the bourgeois Catholic novelist and member of the Académie française who up until then had seemed to be such a stalwart and intransigent defender of all that was associated with order, tradition, national pride, and European "civilization." Mauriac's stance on the Ethiopian question, however, is not as straightforward as it might first appear to us now, some eight decades later. The Ethiopian crisis of 1935 further complicated the delicate—if ultimately illusory—balance of power pursued by French diplomacy in hopes of preventing another war on European soil. Ethiopia was a full-fledged, completely independent state, virtually the only such nation in Africa at the time, and had moreover been unanimously admitted to the League of Nations in 1923. Italy was present in neighboring Eritrea, which it claimed to "possess." The Italians had unsuccessfully tried to conquer and colonize Ethiopia in 1896: now, in 1935, Mussolini was first and foremost interested in displaying the power and prestige of his Fascist Italian regime. He thus used a border incident

9. The infamous Stavisky affair had exacerbated hostilities toward the parliamentary regime of the Third Republic, since a number of high-ranking police, administrative officials, members of parliament, and governing team were implicated in the murky network of bribery and swindling.

10. Barré, *Mauriac. Biographie intime, 1. 1885–1940*, 400.

11. Lacouture, *Mauriac. 2. Un citoyen du siècle 1933–1970*, 37–39.

to mass his troops in Eritrea and invade Ethiopia on Oct. 2, 1935. Thanks to diplomatic irresolution and military pusillanimity on the part of France and Great Britain, who could have forced Mussolini's hand with a solid display of their overwhelming naval power but who were intent on maintaining an alliance with Mussolini in hopes of containing Hitler, the naked aggression went unpunished: sanctions were voted in the League of Nations, but soon lifted in 1936.[12]

Mauriac does not actually address the question of Mussolini's colonial conquest itself. He states that it is not for him to decide the question, and even more disturbingly alludes to Mussolini's "grandeur," admitting that he is impressed by arguments supporting the invasion. Yet for these two steps backward, as it were, Mauriac takes several important strides forward. Perhaps the most crucial step in the direction of greater justice consists of a reversal of perspectives: Mauriac invites his readers to put themselves in the place of the Ethiopians, in order to empathize with those subjected to a brutal invasion and to mockery that would deprive them of their human dignity. As Montaigne had pointed out some 350 years before in his essay "Of Cannibals," Mauriac observes that what some tout as "civilization" manifests itself as unmitigated barbarity. He further offers one of the many lessons of history that will be so prominent in his future editorials: the very same event takes on dramatically divergent meanings for those who observe it from varying perspectives and relate it to different contexts. Such is certainly the case, he points out, for the Africans from French colonies who were massively and sometimes forcibly recruited from their homelands many thousands of miles away to come and fight for France during the Great War: though they experienced first-hand the unprecedented carnage and destruction (out of some 500,000 colonial troops engaged by France in the conflict, some 70,000 lost their lives on French soil), they are not likely to have much enthusiasm for the "civilization" that still considers them to be inferior even though many of them had given their lives in its defense. While Mauriac remained fearful that criticism of the brazen violence and injustice of Mussolini's invasion would offer powerful arguments for his political enemies on the Left in

12. Winock, *Le Siècle des intellectuels*, 263–64.

France, he was clearly determined to defend the dignity and worth shared by all human beings, but scorned by Sennep.

Michel Winock points out that between the two major rival factions of French intellectuals in the mid-1930s, Mussolini's invasion of Ethiopia gave rise to an ideological confrontation of an intensity unseen since the Dreyfus affair.[13] When, on October 4, 1935, Henri Massis writes "Manifeste pour la défense de l'Occident" (later renamed "Manifeste des intellectuels pour la paix en Europe et la défense de l'Occident"), subsequently signed by sixty-four intellectuals and published in *Le Temps*, Mauriac goes beyond his rebuke of Sennep to condemn the invasion outright. Henri Massis had sneered at the integrity of Ethiopia as an independent nation in particular, charging that the country was nothing but a collection of illiterate, backward tribes, scoffing at the notion of the equality of all nations in general, and stressing the prerogatives of the supposedly civilized, superior nations over the barbaric, inferior ones. Massis had thus prompted a number of prominent Catholic intellectuals to protest by publishing their own manifesto, "Cas de conscience" ("A Case for Soul-Searching"). The counterdeclaration was then written by Georges Bidault and Maurice Schumann, but inspired by Mauriac: the declaration adamantly condemned the notion of racial inequality, refused any "need" for territorial expansion, and denounced the hypocrisy of claims to spread the benefits of Western civilization with a brutal invasion that violated international law.[14]

Mussolini Invades Ethiopia: A Political Cartoon by Sennep

Le Figaro, September 24, 1935

The desert. At the foot of a coconut tree, a sign reads "Royal Palace." Perched in the palm branches are two monkeys and the Black sovereign of Abyssinia.

That's very funny and I should laugh. But my profession has given me the habit of putting myself in the place of others. What might this

13. Ibid., 263.
14. Lacouture, *Mauriac. 2. Un citoyen du siècle 1933–1970*, 46–48.

cartoon have conjured up in the mind of the Blacks who have seen it, or who will see it when Sennep's newspaper has gone overseas?

I can imagine a young man of color, whose father or older brother has been resting in peace for twenty years somewhere between the English Channel and the Vosges Mountains. I submit that in Sennep's cartoon there is what it takes to stir up a hatred powerful enough to last a lifetime in his candid heart.

All that has nothing to do with the crux of the matter in the conflict between Italy and Abyssinia. Those who approve Italy's position have impressive arguments. But that in no way justifies heaping scorn on the one who inherited his throne from one of the wisemen in our childhood nativity scenes ... Not even Mussolini, who has grandeur, asks as much. No, he isn't asking the French people, who have contracted with the Black people a debt whose sum only God knows, to do that.

Moreover, whatever the wrongs that the "savages" may have committed in this matter, they are nonetheless about to see the squadrons of the civilized appearing in their skies. This will be no more of a laughing matter for them than it has been just recently for us. Why laugh and mock those who are about to die? There will soon be unmitigated suffering and death in this country of slaves that, for a few more days yet, rainfall is protecting from its liberators.

It is not for me to decide whether this war is a just war. But I must confess that the lack of imagination on the part of some of my counterparts here in the French press, particularly those who put patriotic duty above all else, is simply astounding.

The Abyssinians are naive enough to believe that they are within their rights. They don't feel themselves to be barbarians. We cannot demand that they have as clear an awareness of their own barbarity that the Italians so unmistakably are seeing. And just what is a barbarian these days? In any case, love and faith are creating an equality between the Italians and the Abyssinans, since there is no greater love than to give one's life, and since there are not two different ways of dying for one's native land while invoking the name of Jesus.

In Sennep's next cartoon (the rainy season will soon be over ...), the Ethiopian will no longer be perched up in a coconut tree between two monkeys, but perhaps will be stretched out on the sand, with his arms spread apart, his face pointing up toward the sky.

Sennep has placed a newspaper in the Black sovereign's hands: *L'Humanité* ... And that also gives us pause. Ever since the Dreyfus affair, the forces of disorder and destruction know how fearful a weapon a just cause can become in their hands. And we Christians should remember that. But we have forgotten.

The Spanish Civil War

Mauriac's editorial forays into public controversy were not exercises in rhetoric: that Maurras's paper *L'Action française* mounted an attack on Mauriac in response to the declaration opposing Mussolini's invasion of Ethiopia clearly demonstrates the importance of Mauriac's voice in the political arena. Such public expressions of hostility toward Mauriac the editorialist were only to increase during the Spanish Civil War that began in mid-July 1936, only two months after Socialist Léon Blum had become the French premier with the victory of the Popular Front in legislative elections, to the point of making him "France's most insulted editorialist" once he had clearly sided with the anti-Fascists and the Spanish Republicans.[15]

As was the case with many other French citizens, Mauriac was disgusted with what he saw as the inept, career-minded politicians of the Third Republic. For the ultimate "victory" over Germany in World War I had required not only massive aid from Great Britain and the United States (to whose troops in Bordeaux Mauriac had devoted a noteworthy article that can be found in chapter 6), but a frightful tribute in blood: more than 1.3 million, many of whose remains would never be found, had lost their lives, while hundreds of thousands were left terribly disfigured, maimed, and incapacitated. The Mauriac that we see here warning Blum not to provide arms to the Spanish Republicans was moreover the novelist who had on June 1 of that same year just secured a highly coveted place of national prestige and honor by winning a seat in the Académie française, largely dominated at the time by strongly reactionary attitudes not

15. Barré, *Mauriac. Biographie intime, 1. 1885–1940*, 540.

only in matters of literature and language but also in culture, politics, and society.

News of Franco's assault on the Spanish Republic reached Mauriac vacationing in the provincial town of Vichy, long celebrated as a mineral water spa that attracted high-ranking military and administrative officials from the French colonies along with the wealthy elite from all over Europe. Like so many of his compatriots, Mauriac feared that the conflict in neighboring Spain foreshadowed an upcoming civil war in France, particularly since the name of the party in power, the Frente Popular, was erroneously seen as a mirror image of the Front Populaire that had just won a majority in France.[16] Fearing moreover that the Catholic church was under assault by the Spanish Republicans aided by the French government, Mauriac hastened to compose an impassioned editorial on July 24 and phoned it in to the Parisian daily newspaper *Le Figaro* to expedite its publication the following day, when it would appear on the front page with the headline "The International League of Hatred."[17]

In words that only thinly veil his bitter resentment of the Popular Front, his disdain for the Socialist Léon Blum, who just a few weeks prior had become France's first Jewish premier, and his fear of what Blum's administration might do for its presumed friends in Spain and in Moscow, Mauriac vents his apprehensions in unseemly terms that he would later regret and disavow.[18] He charges that Blum is on the verge of unleashing his "centuries-old rancor," speaks of a "stream of hatred [against Blum] that has been welling up within the French people," threatens to hold Blum personally responsible for any "crime" that he would commit in aiding the Spanish Republicans, and ominously warns that such aid "would risk seeing the wisest and best behaved throw their weight behind those who are violent." Such invective provides a stark measure of the hostility stirred up not only by the conflict on Spanish soil but also by an antisemitism and a disdain for the working class deeply ingrained in the French Catholic bourgeoisie under the Third Republic.

16. Winock, *Le Siècle des intellectuels*, 280.

17. Lacouture, *Mauriac. 2. Un citoyen du siècle 1933–1970*, 58. The original French title was "L'Internationale de la haine."

18. Laurence Granger in François Mauriac, "Guerre d'Espagne," *Journal. Mémoires politiques*, 719n.

Mauriac's rhetoric reveals his initial ambivalence toward the Spanish Republicans, which it is important to recognize in order to fully appreciate the considerable evolution of his stance on the war. Depicting himself as fiercely attached to the land of his native Bordeaux region in the southwestern part of France near the Spanish border, Mauriac, albeit without excluding the rest of the Spanish people, explicitly designates the "Fascists" and "Royalists" with Franco as his "brothers." At the same time, he worries openly that the Jewish Socialist Blum might in fact prove to be at the beck and call of the foreigners acting for the Communist International, that is, "l'Internationale de la haine" (the International League of Hatred). Such suspicions sadly echo the perennial notion that Jews were not "rooted" in the land, thus that they were not truly French, meaning that their loyalty was questionable.

Yet the same François Mauriac whom we see venting fears that will in the near future lead many of his compatriots to side with the Fascists and the collaborators remains intent on touching his readers with the image that has so moved him: the two boys lying dead in Barcelona point to the massacre of innocents that had only just begun. Here as before, during the First World War, and as will follow in the succession of conflicts marking French and world affairs from the late 1930s up until the end of the Algerian war in 1962, Mauriac pleads for an end to bloodletting in the name of a Christian humanism, which he sees as "enfolding [all] in the same love, irrespective of political affiliation." All of these various ingredients make for a rather strong, curious, and potentially dangerous cocktail of political inclinations, human sentiments, and historical perceptions that are not necessarily coherent or compatible with the values that Mauriac claimed to profess later—or even then. For that very reason, it would be a mistake to sweep such unsettling aspects under the rug, as did Mauriac in composing his *Mémoires politiques*. Having noted the contrasting ideological and psychological ingredients of this first impassioned editorial on the Spanish Civil War, we can accurately situate Mauriac the editorialist in the summer of 1936 and measure the long intellectual and ethical road that he would follow over the course of the next few decades.

A major transformation is indeed already palpable by the time Mauriac pens "The Demon of Spain" in January 1937. He had already distanced himself considerably from his initial reactions to the outbreak of the Spanish Civil War in July of the previous year: although alarmed by certain atrocities against priests and nuns on the Republican side, he had as early as August 1936 forcefully condemned the brutal massacre carried out by Franco's forces in the little town of Badajoz, in an editorial bearing the town's name as its title. Mauriac was indeed incensed by Franco's claim to be leading a crusade; the Spanish episcopate's embrace of such claims; the ironic spectacle of Muslims wearing the insignia of the cross on their djellabas, enrolled in this war against what the highest Catholic prelate in Spain termed "the Anti-Christ"; and the sight of Catholic bishops parading in front of the tanks and canons sent to Franco by Hitler and Mussolini.[19]

Such brazen attempts to put the Church under the banner of the Axis powers were repugnant to Mauriac, who saw independence from any and all political regimes and ideologies as vital to the Church's integrity. Indeed, Christianity proved central to his political and ethical sensitivity. Hence his portrayal of the war as an eminently spiritual drama here in "The Demon of Spain," where we see the talented hand of the novelist personify Spain in the form of a vivacious cabaret performer whose electrifying dance symbolizes the ordeal of the Spanish people. Mauriac's theatrical portrayal of the cabaret dancer captures all the passion, flare, and beauty habitually associated with the art, literature, and geography of the country. At the same time, it allows Mauriac to cast other nations in personified form, and comment on their attitude and their behavior as would such astute literary observers of humanity as Montaigne, Pascal, or La Bruyère.

One might understandably be wary of a piece that literally stages historical events in the form of a production aimed first and foremost at entertaining a monied, predominantly masculine audience, since, as Walter Benjamin and Theodor Adorno along with many others have warned, aesthetics can so easily distort, mask, and even totally conceal the brutal realities of war and violence. Yet Mauriac's staging of history as a dramatic performance only intensifies the brutal reality of violence and death in this editorial, as his vivid prose suddenly transforms the sensual dance celebrating the joie de vivre into a danse macabre before our eyes. Mauriac shatters the aesthetic illusion by abruptly veering away from the enchant-

19. Lacouture, *Mauriac. 2. Un citoyen du siècle 1933–1970*, 58–63.

ing spectacle of the vivacious young woman to the stark reality of bloodshed and death, as conveyed by the grim reports of battles, bombings, and atrocities in the newspaper on his knees.

At the same time that he dissipates the aesthetic rapture, Mauriac dramatically reverses the perspective: no longer a simple spectator looking in on a drama in view of passively consuming it while remaining detached, Mauriac suddenly finds himself under the gaze of those who are dying. He thus models our perspective as readers: like Mauriac, we are summoned to answer for the violence from which we can no longer remain detached. The consummate art of the novelist paradoxically finds itself employed here to shake off literary charms in order to look squarely at historical events and heed the searching gaze of others, whose eyes beckon us out of passivity and indifference to intervention on their behalf. Mauriac thus uses a reversal of perspectives similar to the one found in "Mussolini Invades Abyssinia: A Cartoon by Sennep." Let us note in passing that Mauriac clearly designates as the prime perpetrators of atrocities the Germans and Italians, who were acting cynically to advance their own strategic interests with little regard for Spain and the Spanish people.

The Demon of Spain

Le Figaro, January 9, 1937

Out of the mist and stupor of the music hall where I have been led this evening, there suddenly emerges a Spanish woman with a bright red carnation over her bosom. She dances as if possessed, then her dance gradually gives way to torpor, resumes its original intensity, and dies out. Is Spain still alive? We haven't heard her breathe for several weeks now. The only thing that was coming across the Pyrenees were echoes of insults being traded in all the dialects of the world: rival human populations were engaged in mortal combat over a cadaver ... And now all of a sudden the dark mantle of death is floating over one of these shows in which the feminine body, while offered to the spectators' gaze, is separated from the mind that was transfiguring it. Among all these young bodies without a soul, the Spanish woman is, for an evening, the only one that is a soul without a body. Since in the end she is absent from the slaughter for which she was the pretext, she has abandoned her body to the executioners. And here we see her dancing for us who love her and are letting her die.

She dances and dances … I have in my lap a freshly printed newspaper, in which just a little while ago I read: "In the morgue of Chamartin de la Rose, in the section of town called Tétouan, fifty bodies had already been laid out at five o'clock in the afternoon. …" Among this crowd of people who have come to be enchanted by the beauty of bodies, how many are there who can see that this young woman in mourning is dancing over a mass grave?

But do the very ones who are killing each other in her name over there feel sorry for Spain? What does she represent in the eyes of these Germans, these Italians, these Anglo-Saxons, these Slavs? There is no country more poorly known nor more disdained by these nations who, using different words, have never adored anything but might in service of matter.

In Madrid, during the last days of the monarchy, I remember having dined at the residence of a member of the royal family, who resembled an El Greco. With his handsome eyes clouded by bile, he was observing the representative of a foreign power who, holding a glass of liquor in his hand, kept talking too loudly with a drunken laugh that kept breaking out over his dark red face: "When I think," the Spaniard said to me in a hushed voice, "that those people consider us to be monkeys!"

Spain never counted much in their view; but now we see it becoming every day farther removed from this battle of nations being waged over her body. She is being trampled by these Gentiles who are incapable of entering into her mystery. These Russians, these Italians, these Germans have come to settle scores in her house, which has been ransacked by a quarrel that does not concern her, and she remains puzzled by the severe abuse that she is suffering at their hands.

The leaders on both sides have been trafficking her soul; both sides have delivered her to wolves who seem to be devouring each other … In reality, they are devouring each other vicariously. They are playing their game hundreds of miles away from their own homelands. What a wonderful field for maneuvers! What an unexpected firing range! They are trying out their tanks and their torpedoes over Spain's trampled body. They are indeed the descendants of the people who used their slaves to test various poisons.

It is less and less to be about the victim. The Spanish are both the most physical and the most spiritual of peoples, for whom every idea is materially embodied, and in whose hearts waves of divine love and human passion are combined indistinguishably. The Spanish people, whose scorched, rocky land stretches out between heaven and hell, and who, in the end, have never vacillated between anything but righteousness and anarchy, now find themselves subjected to what would appear to be the most radically foreign to their character: they are being killed for the sake of systems that they could not even conceive of. And to the nations gathered in a circle at the scene of her torture, Spain casts the fearful, wide-eyed gaze of a bull covered with blood who does not understand what its tormentors want.

Of the demon to whom Spain has been delivered, we could not say that the right hand does not know what the left hand is doing: does it ever occur to the protagonists of this civil war that it is the same Spirit at work in each camp, pitting them against each other? It is a Spirit that is foreign to them, for Spain certainly has its own demon, one that belongs to her alone: one that is cruel and sad, fond of blood and death. But that's not the one that has been tearing it apart for the last six months. Consumed by a sordid demon for which it is no match, Spain is agonizing. The Master of Moscow and Berlin can well tread this people under foot like grapes in a wine press, but he will never possess it from within. He will reign over her by the power of his left fist or his right fist, but he will never take the secret stronghold of the Spanish soul, in which the drama that is playing itself out goes far beyond that of dividing up the wealth, transcending the categories of this era and resounding in eternity.

"Open City" reveals Mauriac's determination to shake the French public out of its apparent indifference in the face of steady newsreel and press reports of suffering and death brought about by what one might view as the first fires of the immense conflagration about to be ignited. Europe would indeed suffer horrifically from the bombing of its civilian populations over the course of the Second World War, beginning with the rape of Poland in the fall of 1939, and continuing on not only to the German invasion of France, Holland, Belgium, and Luxembourg in May–June 1940, but also to the onslaught against Great Britain during the rest of 1940, and even to the final phases of the war, as the Allies swept across France and northern Europe to meet the Red Army in Berlin: in Europe, some 500,000 civilians, including 60,000 in France alone, would die from Allied bombings. The dire warnings that Mauriac issues about the devastating human, not to speak of material, destruction wrought by coldly calculated bombing ordered from the comfort of administrative offices of course were premonitory in February 1938, and they remain pertinent today, as thousands of civilians still perish from bombings, even when the most advanced technologies are implemented.

Once again, we see Mauriac deploying his considerable talent as a writer in hopes of preventing his readers from consuming these events as mere "news items" and thus remaining inured to their horrific violence. Here too we find a paradox, since the very art of his rhetoric could significantly diminish the impact of his appeal to the reader's conscientious empathy. Hence Mauriac's recourse to preterition, the rhetorical device that allows one to advance the very arguments that one says will have to be omitted. Citing the eloquent verses of Albert de Vigny, and representing the violence as the minotaur gorging itself on the blood of sacrificial youth, Mauriac thus insists that one should speak of these events coolly and that the most appropriate response would be silence. Similarly, he cites the exact number of dead children while refusing to get caught up in body counts, and proceeds to anticipate all sorts of objections to his reasoning while insisting that it is useless to argue with those who disagree.

Mauriac's most powerful technique, however, is doubtless once again his stark reversal of perspectives: he points out that all Europeans, including his compatriots, risk suffering the plight of those streets, shops, parks, and homes that have been subjected to aerial bombardment, and of those whom they now view on cinema newsreels. The apathetic spectators of today thus risk becoming the object of a similar newsreel shot once they have endured the same fate. Using the figure of apostrophe to issue a dramatic appeal to Europeans in general, as well as to his French compatriots, Mauriac announces, "Now's the time to shudder, folks," and asks ironically, "You bourgeois in Frankfurt and Cologne, brothers in Milan and Turin, do you think that France will turn the other cheek?"

Open City

Le Figaro, February 2, 1938

It is hard to speak of these things with composure, so that no one might suspect you of sensationalism, nor of having thought, "The bodies of eighty-five dead children! What a fine subject for an article!" And yet, today, who among us does not feel the temptation to remain silent in the presence of others? We would like nothing more than to bemoan the tragedy secretly before God, or if we are not believers, before the trees and under the stars:

> It is fitting for you to harken to the heavy moans of suffering
> That humanity softly exhales with each tired breath ...[20]

It is hard to avoid getting cut off in the middle of one's first sentence by "How about the fifteen thousand priests in Barcelona? ..." and not to immediately fire back with another salvo in the grim battle of body counts. As if each side had opened an account with unlimited credit on death! As if these eighty-five children killed one Sunday noon represented a monthly payment, as if they were legally owed to the minotaur endowed with frightful ubiquity and who gorges himself on blood both in Spain and in China!

Don't try to make your adversaries understand that one cannot compare things that are not of the same nature, that it is futile to claim to establish some connection between the atrocious massacre perpetrated by an enraged people right after a military uprising, and the bombing of an open city that was decreed, decided, and carefully planned in the silence of an office. (One would like to know why they

20. Alfred de Vigny, "La Maison du Verger," III.26: "C'est à toi qu'il convient d'Ouïr les grandes plaintes / Que l'humanité triste exhale sourdement." http://poesie.webnet.fr/lesgrandsclassiques/poemes/alfred_de_ vigny/la_maison_du_berger_iii.html.

chose a Sunday: was it in order to kill fewer people because the streets would be empty, or on the contrary because they were hoping that many people would be out taking a stroll with their families?)

The question of bombing open cities should be addressed in Europe's capitals outside of any polemics, without cries of indignation and without people renting their garments, without mentioning the dead bodies of women and children. That serves no purpose: we see these bodies every day on newsreels at the cinema, between a soccer match and an ice-skating show. Not one outcry, not a single sigh arises from the numbed, overfed crowd.

What we should have this crowd understand is that the minotaur does not have a taste exclusively for Spaniards, Chinese, and Abyssinians: he's practicing, whetting his appetite, fattening up, and gaining strength in view of a feeding frenzy in which we will not be just spectators. What we must keep on telling people is that tomorrow perhaps it is we who will be filmed by the Pathé-Journal's cameraman leaning over a row of bodies and seeking to recognize a face.

If we are only able to let ourselves be moved when our own plight is at stake, now's the time to shudder, folks.

A young German, Ernst Erich Noth, has just published a novel, *La Voie barrée* [*The Blocked Road*], in which the hero, having escaped from Germany, takes refuge in the Provence region and becomes deeply attached to the kind family that takes him in. "At times, he would laugh and joke with them," writes Ernst Erich Noth, "and then all of a sudden his laughter would be shattered when this thought would occur to him: they don't know that fate has already reached its hand out over them."

But this hand is also reaching out over peoples who will lash out at us. You bourgeois in Frankfurt and Cologne, brothers in Milan and Turin, do you think that France will turn the other cheek? Whoever we may be, French, English, Germans, or Italians, whatever we may do for the defense and protection of open cities, we will be doing it for ourselves, for us, our women and our children. That is doubtless the sole argument that is possible for us to use these days in Europe with its unbelievable insensitivity.

Let us make haste, for spring is approaching. It's in a hurry this year, coming ahead of its usual time. The shrubs in the gardens of Auteuil are already greening up. I don't like this impatience of nature, this sly intervention, this complicity of Cybele and the god of the dead … I am wary of this breeze that is too gentle, this warm wind that smells of the earth and of clay, of these puffs of wind that have the smell of fate.

"The Christmas Offensive" is permeated by irony, as Mauriac points out that Franco's forces have found in the supposed celebration of "Peace on earth, good will to men" an opportunity to launch an offensive that makes a mockery of the supposed "Holy Crusade," its "noble crusader," and its theologians mindful not to disgrace Christian charity by favoring the Christmas Day truce that Pope Pius XI had requested both sides to observe.[21] Mauriac remarks ironically that it would have been indeed too much to expect Franco to let his "Holy Crusade" be delayed by the celebration of what Christians regard to be the pivotal moment of human history. Thus noting Franco's remarkable display of Christian charity, Mauriac hardly forgets to hail the "miraculous indifference" of the oh-so-proper high-society women of the day who would not stoop to signing a petition to provide hunger relief for the children of Spanish Republicans. Finally, he notes the determination of the Italians to fight right down to the last Spaniard. Often present in his uncompromising representations of the well-to-do rural bourgeoisie in his native Bordeaux region, such acid portrayals of hypocrisy and indifference proved to be part of Mauriac's stock and trade as an editorialist whose withering rhetoric left no one indifferent.

The Christmas Offensive

Temps présent, December 30, 1938

This Christmas truce that I was requested to advocate in my editorial turned out to be an offensive. It takes the lowly editorialist more time to wrap up his article than it does for the great leader to give the signal to start the music.

21. Granger, in Mauriac, *Journal. Mémoires politiques*, 738n5.

Having learned a lot over these past two years, I had moreover not been in any particular rush. As the years go by, one becomes more reasonable: one no longer fails to see that the birth of the Child that will be crucified can in no way disturb the intentions of the one who is leading the Holy Crusade. Throughout the blessed night, his cannons ended up making more noise than the angels, and tallied stronger results as well.

He has his theologians. He has learned from unquestionable authority that Saint Thomas approves of this offensive carried out in view of the common good. The Tercio's theologians, who are profound, know that the Christmas truce would have constituted an egregious failure to show Christian charity.[22]

Meanwhile, from both armies, both branches of the same people, there arises a chilling cry for peace. And the children of Barcelona are dying of hunger: amid a miraculous indifference, we must dare to say it and write it. One of my friends in a religious order has tried to collect signatures from the wives of prominent figures: he failed. Another call is being drowned out by a good many newspapers ... These are Communist children, of course! But they must not be as red as that anymore, the poor little things!

Let's be fair: it's not General Franco's fault that he's dealing with people who keep on fighting even though they're supposed to be vanquished! You cannot expect anything from enemies who, in bad faith and contrary to all appearances, stubbornly refuse to consider themselves beaten. Nor is it the fault of the noble crusader that when he was making a deal with a foreigner, he did not realize that that particular foreigner had not the slightest yearning for the transaction: he could not guess that the Italians were determined to fight right down to the last Spaniard.

22. Mauriac is referring to El Tercio Extranjero, a rough equivalent of the French Foreign Legion. The elite troops of El Tercio played a key role in gaining a military advantage for Franco.

Hitler and the Specter of a Second World War

The editorials penned on the eve of the Second World War in 1938 offer us rich insights into the crises leading up to the conflict, insights shedding light both on Mauriac's personal connections to the events and on France's collective dilemma. He struggles visibly to balance the various imperatives of national interest, political integrity, and intellectual lucidity in the face of the ever diminishing prospects for the peace that he, like millions of others in France and Europe, desperately wanted to preserve, and understandably so. For one thing, Mauriac like millions of others had experienced firsthand the horrors of the First World War while serving as a medical aide on the front, where so many lost life and limb in the ghastly conditions of the trenches. Now, some twenty years later, he shudders at the prospect of seeing his two sons, Claude, born April 25, 1914, and Jean, born August 15, 1924, being called up into active duty. Just a few months after the war began, his daughter Luce would become officially engaged to an army lieutenant, Alain le Ray, in February 1940.

Observing Hitler swoop down on Austria while Franco continued his brutal onslaught in Spain and Hirohito's forces inflicted mayhem on China, Mauriac avows his dismay and confusion.

> But for us, whose friends and children represent our last remaining earthly hope, what good is it to speak of these things that are beyond our control, that are decided without us, and that moreover we cannot even foresee? It is not our own death, but the death of those we love that we cannot countenance.[23]

Similarly, Mauriac salutes the Munich accords for providing at least a reprieve from the implacable threat of war and concludes by rejoicing that his offspring are, for the moment, safe: "For now, we are entitled to breathe in relief, to bless God, to listen to our children make plans, and to look at their still intact chests and their hands that have yet to shed blood." Later embarrassed at not having taken a hard-line stand against appeasement, Mauriac added a paragraph to the version of that editorial that he chose to include in his *Mémoires politiques*, explaining that he had only approved of the Munich accords out of fears for his sons.

23. See "The Basis for Our Action."

Mauriac may indeed vacillate between the dread of renewed slaughter and the need to oppose Mussolini's pitiless plundering of Ethiopia, Franco's ruthless aggression on his own people in Spain, and Hitler's unbridled expansionist aggression. In all of those aggressions, he sees a brutal, racist ideology threatening not only France's interests and security, but even the fundamental notions of humanity (and in the case of Spain, the essence of Christianity and the integrity of the Church) upon which society should be based. Viewed in the context of the late 1930s in France, Mauriac proves to be one of the most lucid observers of the situation, since the great majority of his compatriots on both the Left and the Right of the political spectrum remained intent on avoiding war with Nazi Germany virtually at all costs, even in the face of Hitler's demands for the Sudetenland and the provocations of Henlein's Nazi party within Czechoslovakia.[24]

The fact of the matter is that most French citizens of all persuasions remained frightfully ignorant of the ominous reality of Nazism. Although Hitler's autobiographical manifesto *Mein Kampf* had been published in French as *Mon combat* in 1934, very few had read it and far fewer yet had measured the gravity of his threat to make France servile to the demands of the German "race."[25] This failure to discern the true nature of Nazism was perhaps due in part to the fact that certain highly revealing passages had been carefully omitted from the edition that Hitler had authorized for the 1938 edition prepared by Jacques Benoist-Méchin, who was destined to be one Pétain's ministers under Vichy.[26] Assessing Hitler's actions in the wake of the Munich accords, Mauriac himself asks whether it was merely a coincidence that "all of the threats concerning us have been carefully expurgated from the edition of *Mein Kampf* sold on the boulevards of Paris."[27]

In any case, France was so bitterly divided that political leaders, ideologues, and intellectuals on all sides tended to see the major threat, be it labeled as "Bolshevism" or "Fascism," as coming not from Nazi Germany itself but rather from domestic admirers and avatars of Mussolini, Stalin, Hitler, or Franco. The most prominent and influential organization of

24. Winock, *Le Siècle des intellectuels*, 315–17.
25. Philippe Burrin, *La France à l'heure allemande* (Paris: Les Éditions du Seuil, 1995), 46–48.
26. Granger, in Mauriac, *Journal. Mémoires politiques*, 751n4.
27. François Mauriac, "La perle sans prix," in *Journal. Mémoires politiques*, 751.

leftist intellectuals, the Comité de vigilance des intellectuels anti-fascistes, whose members included literati such as André Malraux, Jean Guéhenno, and André Gide, along with Surrealists such as André Breton and Paul Eluard, was dominated by figures such as Alain[28] and Roger Martin du Gard,[29] who tended to see the Fascist threat less in terms of Hitler or Mussolini or Franco's military actions, and more in the form the tyrannical authority exercised by the *ordre bourgeois,* the army, and nationalism.[30]

The major forces on the right of the political spectrum offered even less opposition to Hitler, as they lashed out against their fellow citizens with a virulence now difficult to imagine. Cursing France's rapprochement with the Soviet Union in the mid-1930s, Charles Maurras urged his compatriots to seek instead an alliance with Mussolini's Fascist Italy. To the readers of his paper *L'Action française,* Maurras declared that those advocating war with Germany should not be guillotined like common criminals but summarily shot or stabbed with a butcher knife. Upon the election of Socialist Léon Blum as France's first Jewish premier, Maurras wrote that Blum was "human garbage … a man to be shot, only in the back." Maurras and his paper vehemently opposed going to war with Hitler in order to defend Czechoslovakia, asserting, "The French people do not want to fight either for the Jews or for the Russians or for the Free Masons of Prague."[31] Even when, having broken all his promises, Hitler's troops marched in to take command of Czechoslovakia, neither the Left nor the Right in France reacted in any significant way, fixating instead on their ideological and socioeconomic enemies within French borders and persisting in their pacifism.[32]

In the face of such ideological extremes on the domestic front, Mauriac offers an example of equanimity and gravitas as he weighs the grim prospects for peace on the international scene in the aftermath of the

28. Alain was the public name of Emile Chartier, one of the most influential philosophers of the time who taught at the prestigious Lycée Henri IV in Paris.

29. Roger Martin du Gard was the 1937 Nobel laureate in literature, largely in recognition of his novels, such as the series titled *Les Thibault,* depicting individuals caught up in the ordeals of the Great War.

30. Winock, *Le Siècle des intellectuels,* 247–52.

31. Ibid., 324–25.

32. Ibid., 318.

Anschluss, in May 1938.[33] In his meditation on "War," he warns his compatriots that by relentlessly portraying France as a decadent nation weakened by scheming politicians, widespread immorality, and immigrants, the press (mainly the extreme right-wing newspapers such as *L'Action française* and *Je suis partout*) was playing right into Hitler's hands. Mauriac moreover provides a remarkably lucid assessment of Hitler's designs in late May 1938 when he points out that Hitler had set his sights on the sources of food and energy in Eastern and Central Europe needed to engage in an extended military campaign.

In that most unsettling context, Mauriac borrows Hamlet's famed last words, "The rest is silence," for the title of one of his most somber editorials, whose strains echo throughout several other pieces from the same period. Assessing the international crises weighing so heavily on the fate of France, Europe, and the world, Mauriac voices deep anxieties over the approaching war, while at the same time reflecting on the role of human thoughts, words, and deeds in history. Just as Shakespeare's Danish prince uttered his despair and died without learning of the news brought by ambassadors returning from England, so Mauriac expresses a keen sense of the futility of attempting to influence the course of events. Pointing to "the ring of fire [that] is closing in on us," Mauriac harbors few illusions as to either Hitler's intentions or the prospects of avoiding another war; only a few weeks later, he sees armed conflict "directly in the line of destiny," in the editorial bearing precisely that title, "War." In it Mauriac articulates a particularly pessimistic view of history, finding that instead of achieving progress and enlightenment, "from one killing field to the next, humans do not learn or retain anything."

Yet Mauriac refuses to despair, borrowing again from Hamlet in affirming that "there are more things on earth and in heaven that a racist brain could dream of." The expression is more than a witticism: it conveys one of Mauriac's fundamental convictions about human beings and their history. Gloating over his string of successful gambits, Hitler claimed that events proved that God was on his side. Mauriac mocks that pretension

33. On March 12, 1938, Hitler's troops stormed into Austria, completing the annexation by the Third Reich without encountering any opposition either from Austrian authorities or the Western democracies.

by paraphrasing Shakespeare. When the cardinal archbishop of Vienna echoes Hitler's claim in his post-Anschluss pronouncement, Mauriac denounces the statement as having been coerced, and vigorously asserts that the unchecked chain of successful Nazi aggressions in no way reflects the will of Providence.

It is in this light that we can more fully appreciate both "September 26" and a January 6, 1939, editorial, "The Event," in which Mauriac explicitly and forcefully rejects the Pascalian notion of events as coming from the hand of God. We moreover find Mauriac implicitly articulating the same adamant refusal to see history as the translation of the divine will in the editorial appearing in *Temps présent* the week after "War." When Franco, echoed by many on the Right in France, claimed to be leading a crusade against the enemies of the Church, Mauriac would have none of it. Franco, writes Mauriac in "The Basis for Our Action," would have it that "the sound of machine guns announces the coming of the Son of Man and the smell of mustard gas is the sign that His kingdom has come." Far from representing any sort of Pascalian "masters from the hand of God," the events in Spain, Austria, and Czechoslovakia on the contrary bear witness to a brazen will to power: "These events are marked in a human effigy. They are the fruit of a will and a reflection that France must oppose with an equal reflection and a stronger will."[34] The relentless advances of Nazi Germany were neither the work of fate nor that of Providence, but the human-all-too-human product of Hitler and company's ruthless designs, which could and should be thwarted.

When we recall that what today, some seventy-five years after the fact, appears obvious was anything but clear to all but a tiny handful of the most exceptionally perspicacious in France, or for that matter in Europe and the United States in 1938, Mauriac's initial hesitation to advocate unflinching opposition to Hitler's demands is quite understandable. Yet unlike so many of his compatriots who remained preoccupied with domestic politics, Mauriac laments France's inaction and public apathy in the face of the developments that were clearly visible on the international scene in that fateful spring. When Hitler's troops stream into Austria, annexing it

34. François Mauriac, "L'Evénement" [The event], in *Journal. Mémoires politiques*, 752.

into the Third Reich without the least resistance on the part of either Austrian authorities or the democratic allies, Mauriac underscores the ominous link between the Anschluss and Fascist aggression on other fronts, including Mussolini's plunder of Abyssinia in the fall of 1935, the Japanese Rape of Nanking in December 1937, and the air forces of Fascist Italy and Nazi Germany that relentlessly bombed Barcelona just as Hitler's forces were taking over Austria. Although, in his own partisan leaning, Mauriac blames Communism for stirring up the fears and resentment that he sees as largely responsible for the stiff arm salutes given at the tomb of the unknown soldier at the Arc de Triomphe in the French capital, he clearly identifies Nazi Germany as the "the most dreadful" of "the two monsters."

France Has but One Countenance

Temps présent, February 25, 1938

Here we see the error that was the fruit of the Molotov-Ribbentrop pact of non-aggression between Germany and the Soviet Union.[35] It is because in Moscow, they thought that we were not taking sides, because the French were ultimately leaning to the right, that Stalin signed the treaty making the tragedy inevitable ...

My state of mind such as can be seen here was the very same as that which made Stalin decide to do Hitler's bidding.

In spite of the love that they claim to feel for France, a great number of French people on the Right and on the Left err in not accepting their country with the face shaped by centuries of history, that is, in failing to embrace the entirety of this great soul divided against itself.

Many people are also making the mistake of becoming accomplices of a foreign power against the part of the French soul that appears odious to them. We must fight against error wherever it may crop up, but out of our intense commitment, we should first derive a creativity sufficient for composing, and out of so many contradictory

35. The pact dates from August 23, 1939, when Nazi Germany and Soviet Russia penned an agreement that in effect allowed them to divide Poland between them without going to war with each other. The obvious anachronism is due to the fact that Mauriac added these first two paragraphs in retrospect when republishing this article for his *Mémoires politiques*.

components, an image of France one and indivisible, accepted and cherished by all.

We then would see that in spite of its innumerable contradictory and clashing expressions, the face thus obtained does not resemble any of the three masks whose atrocious grimaces are petrifying Europe in 1938. As weak and divided as we may be, as much as we lash out against each other, the world will, as long as France holds up its vainly insulted, suffering face, believe and hope that it still has a chance of escaping the need to choose among the three grimacing gargoyles. No, France will never be joined with Moscow against Berlin and Rome, nor with Berlin and Rome against Moscow. While still appearing to be beaten, France is with each instant achieving a victory in making the killers hesitate as they prowl around the free nations, the daughters of God.

The Rest Is Silence

Temps présent, March 18, 1938

I didn't have the courage to accept the honor of presiding a rally in support of Austrian Catholics. Our Austrian brothers were not in need of words. In their place, I would only listen to such words with anger, perhaps responding with an ironic, desperate "Heil Hitler!"

Some words are deeds; others resemble only caricatures of deeds. As long as France refuses to take any active role, the only thing left for French people to do is lower their heads and keep quiet.

Over Catholic Austria, let us shed the child Abencerage's tears:[36] let us weep like women over the Catholic kingdom that we did not succeed in defending like men.

It is for the French that we must give speeches. They still do not know that the same mindset triumphing in Austria has already triumphed in Spain, Abyssinia, and China. A large number of them are still rejoicing

36. In *Aben-Hamet, the Last of the Abencerages,* René de Châteaubriand recounts the last royal family's sorrowful departure from the kingdom of Grenada. Upon reaching a promontory offering a panoramic view of the kingdom, the sultan said to his son, "Weep now like a woman for a kingdom that you were unable to defend like a man." See http://books.google.com.

over what is happening these days in Spain. The frightful coincidence of Hitler's entry into Austria and the victory of the Italo-German air forces on the Catalonian border is not opening their eyes.[37]

The ring of fire is closing in around us, and Saturday, the day of the Anschluss, there were people standing in front of the Arc de Triomphe and giving the Nazi salute to the flag that flew over Verdun!

Because of the horror it arouses, one of the perversities of Communism is to have made a large part of the European bourgeoisie an accomplice to the rule of dictators. The latter have made a fine use of such horror and disgust! Are we aware of that reality? We should be by now. Alas!

Yet there are more things on earth and in heaven than a racist brain can dream of. And *Mein Kampf* will not forever coincide with the will of Providence.[38]

The Basis for Our Action

Temps présent, March 25, 1938

From time to time, I manage to get a friend who shares none of my political opinions to acknowledge that *Temps présent* has placed itself at the front lines of Catholicism in what some would say a rather risky position that must, however, be held at all costs.[39]

More than any open attack of hatred, what the Catholics at *Temps présent* dread are all these hands on the Right and on the Left reaching out toward Christ in order to draw him over and hold him on one side of the barricade, where he would be reclothed by the soldiers of

37. The most intensive bombings of the city of Barcelona took place from March 16 through March 19, 1938, at the very moment of the Anschluss.

38. Since he had not been stymied on any front, Hitler was claiming that his policies had the favor of Providence.

39. Mauriac was spearheading the liberal Catholic intellectuals who had just found the periodical *Temps présent*, a sort of continuation of *Sept*, which had been put out by the liberal Latour-Maubourg Dominicans in Paris, but which the Vatican had shut down. Since it was edited and funded by lay people outside of the Church, *Temps présent* enjoyed the autonomy and intellectual freedom that had been denied to *Sept*, which had incidentally carried the subtitle, "hebdomadaire du temps présent" (weekly magazine for the present times). See Lacouture, *Mauriac. 2. Un citoyen du siècle 1933–1970*, 70–75.

the cohort, not in a cloak of ridicule, but in a uniform, with a brown, red, or black shirt.

Temps présent has no reason for being other than to lay out all the issues and try to resolve them in light of the Gospel. Not that it believes itself to be infallible or immune to error. It is not written by pure minds. Each one of them has his preferences and whether he likes it or not, carries within the spirit of partisan politics.

That is why the basis for our action must be an inner victory, one that we shall win over the leftist or the rightist that is active within.

Is that to say that we soar above political parties with the sole concern of maintaining an equal balance between them without choosing one over another? No, we believe on the contrary that there is a Christian solution to the problems presently dividing nations. We believe that the world covers itself in blood to the extent that it returns to idols.

Everything taking place in the world today almost seems to suggest that God were trying, by the means of concrete images, to give humans a foretaste of this hell into which the worship of idols will lead them, already here on this earth.

In Moscow, we can see what those who worship humanity are doing to that humanity after twenty years of revolution. And we can see elsewhere that race is a goddess more dreadful than those that, under the ancient law, liked the smell of human sacrifices: this new idol demands the immolation of entire peoples.

We who, in the brief span of our earthly life see only one episode of the eternal fight between the two banners, must indeed confess that we have the impression of being defeated and crushed. What to do, if not persevere in our effort to ensure that whether he be on the side of the victors or the vanquished, every human being should know that Christ is not under the orders of any leader of an army or nation, and that he does not look upon those who have fallen on one side as if they were rogues. We believe that the priests and the nuns that were massacred, but also the victims that were summarily judged, the innocent people machine-gunned on the threshold of their homes by foreign aviators have an equal right to his love and mercy, and that the perpetrators of these crimes—all of the perpetrators, even those who invoke his name—come under his justice as well.

We shall repeat and shout this out more obstinately than ever when the hour of crushing humiliation has come to these suffering people upon whom Christ had pity in more than one place in the world: condemned to despair and hatred, these are people from whom all has been taken and confiscated, even Christ. For on the Left, his masters have locked him up in this materialist prison in which the light of heaven no longer penetrates. And on the Right, alas, they make sure that he knows that the sound of machine guns announces the coming of the Son of man and that the smell of mustard gas signals that his kingdom is approaching.

We lay people must say these things all the more forcefully, since we are only committing ourselves without compromising anyone, and since, in a good number of countries, the spiritual leaders are no longer free: they are required to remain silent when they are not forced to speak. Do you believe that it was of his own volition that, on the very day when, after being assassinated, Austria disappeared from the face of the earth, the cardinal archbishop of Vienna published the following declaration: "Priests and the faithful will have to support unreservedly the German state and the Führer whose fight against Bolshevism and for the honorable power and unity of Germany corresponds to the views of Providence."

We are not giving ourselves over to feeling nor do we dream of a politics of the heart or a politics of adventure.

I would not want my words to create any misgivings on this point. As far as I am concerned, it seems to me that France, not having acted when it still had the power to do so without spreading the fire to all of Europe, cannot now act when it is isolated and threatened on three of its borders as well as in North Africa . . .

But for us, whose friends and children represent our last remaining earthly hope, what good is it to speak of these things that are beyond our control, that are decided without us, and that moreover we cannot even foresee? It is not our own death, but the death of those we love that we cannot countenance.

But even striving to put aside these reasons of the heart, it seems to me that we can do nothing more today than to work at reconstructing France, rebuilding French unity in a newfound awareness of its mission. In the face of Marxism and racist ferocity, France would already be accomplishing a great deal if it kept intact the collection of the Christian values cherished by all, believers and unbelievers.

And above all, we shall continue to watch over the wellspring of living water in order that it not be captured nor hijacked nor fouled by the apostles of terror and might, and so that the throng of those who are heavy laden and overwhelmed, as well as all those having suffered defeat may some day find the way.

Dear friends, I would like to conclude on a hopeful note and, in these days of humiliation, give you a reason not to lose heart. The leaders of the new Reich excel in the art of blending audacity and cunning tricks. But perhaps the time is drawing near as it always does for Germany, whoever its leaders may be, when it overplays its irremediably heavy hand. Assassinated countries do not die without a cry. Austria is struggling under its gag: already, we know, prisons and concentration camps are overflowing. Amid the universal anxiety stemming from the aggressions of brute force, all the peoples of the earth are turning toward this divided, paralyzed, haggard French nation that seems absent from itself. They are whispering France's role in her ear, and at times they slap her in the face with a contempt stemming from their jilted love, a contempt that we are sure will awaken her, and which has already awakened her. They are recalling to this humiliated nation her vocation as the daughter of God.

War

Temps présent, May 27, 1938

What good would it do to blind ourselves to the facts? War is now directly before us on the road of destiny. Between us and war, there is no longer anything but the calculations of the man holed up at Berchtesgaden questioning his military advisers and weighing his chances.

He would like to be sure that France is as ailing and divided as the French press suggests. Nary a doubt lingers in the mind of a German who observes "the rotten nation." And how could he not believe the French themselves on this subject?

There remains England, the obstacle that he is still hoping to surmount. He is just waiting for the opportunity, the opportunity that his old buddy Stalin has been trying in vain to create with regards to Spain: if there were the tiniest crack in the block formed by France and England, the German axe would wedge its way in.

Hitler is waiting for that to happen: he thinks it inevitable, and as far as he is concerned, what difference does it make to wait since time is on his side? Time is on his side and not ours. As much as we may arm ourselves, he will arm himself still more. But above all, he will without firing a shot get his hands on everything he still needs to sustain a long war.

That is what Mr. Eden understood. England and France could have without risk held at bay a Germany that knows it is equipped only for quick military strikes. Our weakness is going to put Germany in a position to have enough oil and wheat and everything else necessary for a large nation engaged in a war of attrition. And then that will be the day of reckoning …

But we should be completely frank. Can there not be found in our government ministries men who conclude from this state of affairs that it would be better to take our chances right now? Alas, war always breaks out from such convergence of wills on both sides of the border …

Such is the naked truth. From one killing field to another, humanity neither learns nor retains anything. The new war is always the stupidest, and the least excusable. We are running straight toward it with our eyes wide open.

September 26

Temps présent, September 30, 1938

Today, Monday, September 26, the harm is not yet irreparable, and that is our only reason for not losing heart. Since the die has not yet been cast, we continue to hope against all hope. If, as Pascal says, events are masters from the hand of God, we will refuse to recognize the master of war as long as he has not yet tightened his grip on our necks, and as long as our children remain by our sides.

But even if the threat of war has once more subsided, the mere appearance of the hideous scourge of war on the horizon twenty years afterward is judgement and condemnation for us, the survivors of the Great War. Last July, I had my youngest son make a pilgrimage to Verdun.[40] Twenty years have hardly changed a thing in the appearance of the Mort-Homme battleground.[41] The earth there is still in agony. And already, we might have to do it all over again!

In addition to our individual responsibilities, there exists a collective responsibility for our entire generation. The League of Nations is falling into a ridiculous irrelevance that illustrates the failure of the hope that we inherited from those who died at Verdun.

But now what good does it do to talk? I ask my readers to forgive me: if the signal to start the slaughter were given, I wouldn't even be good for "raising morale." Even writing already seems criminal to me: lining up words, arranging sentences … I managed to let myself go ahead with it when it concerned other nations. But today "the rest is silence …" No! Let's correct Shakespeare's line and say: "the rest is prayer …"

40. The Battle of Verdun raged on for over nine months, from February 21 until December 15, 1916, and has remained the symbol of the unprecedented human and material destruction brought about by the Great War. It was at Verdun that flamethrowers and poison gas were first used: the death toll ultimately rose to more than 500,000 men.

41. The Mort-Homme, literally "death of man," was a hill that had carried its name long before the events of the Great War made it famous. In initiating the Battle of Verdun, the Germans had wanted to take the site at all costs. The hill remained at the center of the devastating artillery bombardments throughout nine months of combat.

The Nightmare Has Vanished

Temps présent, October 7, 1938

I know quite well that we shall awake from this joy and that beyond this great wall of the Versailles treaty struck down by Germany's strong hand, an unknown road often open to ambush is stretching out before us. But the fact remains that the danger of war has subsided and that the Beast has been brought under control at the very moment it was getting ready to pounce.

The determination of a few men proved to be stronger: a few men for democracy. They did not resort to any of the idols commonly attributed to democratic states. They did not wield any words with capital letters. They did not speak of either Law or Justice. They were simply human.

Within their adversaries who seem so totally lacking in compassion, perhaps they even stirred up an emotion, some obscure remorse, pity for these millions of children of the men who are already marching with docility toward the slaughter …

The outbreak of joy in these poor docile nations is indeed touching. The same joy in Berlin, Paris, and London! They are all powerless to hate each other! Yes, war, in failing to make this final leap ahead, has in the end revealed the unity of the human family.

But on this score, our task will be hard: our political parties are challenging each other and are each demanding that the other be held accountable.

War reigns still, and more so than ever in our hearts and minds.

Beginning tomorrow we will renew our efforts for the cause of peace. For today, we have the right to breathe easier, bless God, and listen to our children make plans and look at their chests that are still intact and their hands which have not shed blood.

I therefore approved Munich at the time, but without any illusions, as can be seen by the editorial that I wrote a week later.[42] In reality, I was thinking of my two sons and it was the momentary appeasement of that anxiety that was my first inspiration.

42. Mauriac added these lines to the article as republished in 1967 in his *Mémoires politiques*.

2 ∽ THE SECOND WORLD WAR

The Outbreak of War and the Fall of France

From Hitler's invasion of Poland and France's ensuing declaration of war at the beginning of September 1939, through the long, relatively uneventful and highly misleading months of the so-called phony war, to the Wehrmacht's brutal May 10, 1940, invasion and relentless prosecution of their latest blitzkrieg, the French experienced one of the most eventful years of their long history. Six weeks sufficed for the Germans to inflict a humiliating military defeat that was accompanied by a severe disruption of France's infrastructure, causing extreme suffering and confusion among the civilian population. The resulting implosion of the Third Republic set the stage for the creation of the Vichy regime, which from July 10, 1940, would quickly implement policies of state antisemitism and collaboration with Nazi Germany.

Mauriac provides a particularly valuable window on these pivotal events, which were only the beginning of France's long, bitter, and highly divisive experience of the German occupation. As a well-known Parisian socialite, a prestigious novelist, a member of the Académie française, and a widely read editorialist acquiring an ever larger audience, Mauriac frequented writers and intellectuals serving as military officers. Maurice Schumann, for example, was destined to become the voice of Charles de Gaulle's France Libre on the BBC, while André Chamson was a Popular Front activist who founded the left-leaning weekly magazine *Vendredi*, and who would be charged with evacuating and safeguarding the artistic treasures of the Louvre during the war. Mauriac also dined with diplomatic and political officials such as American ambassador William Bullitt and French government minister Georges Mandel, who would be targeted as a Jew and infamously assassinated by collaborationists of the French Milice in July 1944.[1] Circulating among France's intellectual and political leaders thus afforded Mauriac a privileged perspective on matters of state.

For contemporary readers looking back on that early phase of World War II in France, Mauriac offers a rich array of insights into that highly unsettled time, into his eminently French experience of the events, and into the deeper lessons that he strives to draw from this pivotal moment in history. It is as if three writers had synthesized their contributions into one set of texts. His editorials provide the political commentary of a journalist, while at the same time, in a manner somewhat reminiscent of Montaigne, relating these momentous events to his own multifaceted thoughts and feelings, not only as a man of letters deeply attached to France's soil and cultural heritage, but also as a father who, in the form of his two sons, had "skin in the game." Added to that are meditations on ethics, spirituality, and human destiny articulated by a writer steeped in French Catholicism and mindful of incorporating his faith into his concrete, daily existence as well as into his intellectual production.

Mauriac's attention to the deeper metaphysical questions posed by France's return to the state of war is evident in the words he inscribed in the "Livre de raison" (literally, Book of Reason, a sort of family ledger) at Malagar for September 1, 1940:

> But from the beginning, from Cain to Hitler, the realm of nature is the murder of the weakest. All plant and animal life comes down to a mutual destruction. The Kingdom of Jesus is not of this world. He told us so. But we have not understood

1. Lacouture, *Mauriac. 2. Un citoyen du siècle 1933–1970*, 99–108.

... But if it begins, this infamous massacre will plunge us deeper than ever into the abyss, such that our last hope resides at the very heart of human despair.[2]

Here again, an acute sensitivity to the cruelty and aggression that all too often prevail in human events proves to be one of the hallmarks of Mauriac's writing, as notably expressed in his outcry against Sennep's mockery of the Ethiopians about to be slaughtered by Mussolini's colonialist aggression, later during the Algerian war, and throughout the 1960s. It also undergirds each of these editorials from the first phase of the war, as announced by the somber reflections that conclude his public meditation "For the Time of War," published in *Temps présent* three weeks later:

The great spiritual trial of war is that it forces us to face and confront an obstacle that we constantly avoid during peacetime: settled into our happiness, we hope we can forever honor with our outpourings of sentiment this God who "is agonizing until the end of the world." We must now watch with Him, admitting and accepting this unimaginable permission that love grants to the power of darkness: "The Lord said to Satan, 'From where have you come?' Satan answered the Lord, 'From going to and fro on the earth.'"[3]

Far from denying or camouflaging the pain and destruction that his compatriots were on the verge of suffering and inflicting on their fellow human beings, Mauriac cites these words from the biblical narrative of a blameless man delivered into the hands of the Prince of Darkness to express spiritual tribulations that are not particularly reassuring: though Mauriac implicitly summons his readers to courageous lucidity, his quotation from the book of Job provides no epilogue to the picture of evil enjoying a free reign over the earth.

Instead of offering spiritual consolation or a teleological vision of events leading to some "happy end," the editorial "Touch the Earth" contemplates the age-old beauty of the countryside, the familiar rhythms of tending the vineyard and gathering the grape harvest that from Mauriac's childhood days had been engrained in his sensibility. Similarly, at the end of this piece we see him contemplating the beauty of the sky and the landscape that have retained their beauty throughout the horrors of the past

2. Cited by Barré, *Mauriac. Une Biographie intime, 1. 1885–1940*, 565.

3. François Mauriac, "Pour le temps de guerre," in *Journal. Mémoires politiques*, 260. Mauriac is quoting from the book of Job I, 7.

(such as the religious wars), and which promise to endure the present conflict. As indicated by the title of this article, published exactly three weeks after Hitler had invaded Poland on September 1, 1939, Mauriac invites his readers to follow his example and "touch the earth to regain the strength to believe in a world that is good and blessed." The point is not to turn away from the stark reality of events at hand, but rather, refusing anything that might come close to the chauvinist bravado or nationalist strutting found in some of the early propaganda of the First World War, to remain as "human as possible," even faced with "the inhuman ordeal in which Germany has engaged" France. Shunning the illusory swaggering of individual and collective invulnerability, Mauriac offers a rare word of praise for a leader of the Third Republic's parliamentary regime, lauding Daladier for speaking explicitly of tender affection for soldiers called into battle. Seeking openly to regain his composure and to prove fit for the ordeal, Mauriac also pledges to respect a certain modest humanity in his editorials by refraining from pontifications and contenting himself with the unadorned truth, while alluding to all which, though left unsaid, is secretly tormenting him.

Touch the Earth

Temps présent, September 22, 1939

In the evening, the smoke from burning grass is slow to spread itself about in the countryside. This motionless haze allows us to gauge the peace that the fields have not lost. On the side of their trunks not facing the burning sun in the west, the trees are black. But the brightened meadows absorb the light. Now that the tilling is done, all that remains is to strip the vines of their leaves so that nothing separates the sun from the clusters of grapes. From the rows of vines arise the same voices that, since my childhood, I have always listened to in the waning hours of a September day. Except for the flocks of pillaging sparrows that swoop down on the grape harvest, the birds are planning their travels and keeping quiet.

Why now talk about these things that are inseparable from the joy of being alive? Because they are, because they exist, and I can see, hear, and touch them. I am thus practicing saying nothing and writing nothing over the course of this war that is not true and evident for all, nor expressing any emotion that I am not sure of feeling myself. I am touching the earth in order to regain the strength to believe in a world that is good and blessed.

In the same manner, Emily Brontë would sometimes write down on paper the exact time on the clock, indicate the room where she was, the task that she had just left off, and what at the same instant her father, her sister Charlotte, her brother Branwell, the servant Tabitha in the kitchen, and even the dog sleeping with its nose on its paws were all doing in this parsonage whipped by the winds where she was suffering. She revealed nothing of her secret torment but stroked the humble face that life presented to her at that precise moment of the day.

Since our present duty, people insist, is to continue playing ball, and since the ball I play with is the written word, I shall at least refrain from raising my voice: being unable to express everything that I am feeling, I shall invent nothing in what I do express. At certain times, the weak need other weak people. Perhaps I shall manage to help some of them to the extent that I strive to remain myself and do not attempt to add one little centimeter to my height.

Germany has led us into an inhuman ordeal: may we French remain as human as possible. From the very first day, Premier Daladier told the thousands of combatants listening to him that he thought of them *with tenderness*. Spoken at such a moment, the word went far beyond all eloquence. Yesterday evening again, he repeated this word *tenderness*.

The last war stripped us of pomposity and overly harsh attitudes. It is no offense to the long shadows of Poincaré the legal expert and tough-minded Clemenceau, whose lack of sentiment was doubtless only an appearance, for us to prefer the university professor of today who talks like a farmer and is not ashamed of his heart.

We are not ashamed of our heart. We shall only be hardhearted in spite of ourselves. Our enemies have condemned our people to utilize the bloody apparatus of war as well and better than they use it themselves, but it is not up to them to create within us a soul in their image. "I reread the *Discourse on the Method*," writes one soldier in his letter to me, "and that does me spiritually and morally deep good. What a joy to be able to cling to these values that nothing, not even war, can threaten! If you want to enter a little into my life, read the page 'There is nothing that is entirely within our power except for our thoughts. . . .'" The strange thing is that it was a young Catholic who confided this reflection to me at the time when, as an elementary school teacher serving as a lieutenant on the front line, he found in his studies, and through marvelous grace, faith in the Father and in this love that will never pass away.

But I am already failing to live up to my promise: among the letters that I have received, I am seeking out those that can serve my ends . . . I must therefore come back and touch the earth. The sky has clouded over as I was writing. A whispering over the leaves announces the rain that will release the strong smell that I love. Is my anxiety not so strong as to prevent me from expecting this pleasure?

Vigny writes in his *Journal* that he walks through his heart twenty times a day. And so do I, twenty times a day, beginning with my son, I go from face to face within me, dwelling on those that I believe to be in danger. But the unreflective side of me pursues its habits, seeks its pleasures, and sniffs with great pleasure the smell of leaves and of the wet clay soil.

Let us not forbid ourselves these pleasures. I remember the words of one Jewish soldier who died in combat and whom Barrès quoted during the Great War: "How pleasant is the coming of daylight to the world, oh my God. . . ." When we look out over these hills of the Guyenne region that since the Religious Wars have had the time to forget that men kill each other, should we blush at feeling what this young French soldier who was already doomed felt when he was in the trench looking out over an apocalyptic landscape? I believe on the contrary that we should accept it and that we must remain attentive for a lesson that we shall learn another day, given to us by these meditative meadows and these hills slumbering under the first rain of autumn.

In "Everywhere or Nowhere," the now open war with Nazi Germany once again leads to a searching of soul and conscience. Inspired by medieval philosophy's description of the deity's paradoxical presence everywhere and nowhere,[4] Mauriac links the temporal to the intemporal, the here-and-now to the universal and timeless, and finally the present conflict between Nazi Germany and the Allies to the wars that have pitted one nation against another since the beginning of humankind. Thus the war that has just begun in September 1940 participates in what Mauriac often depicts as the endless cycle of predatory greed, aggression, and retribution that, borrowing from Goethe, he laments as "the tangled mess of errors and violence" of human history.

Once again inviting his readers to follow his example, Mauriac shares his sense of personal implication in the bloodshed that the French will now both perpetrate and suffer in their own flesh. Though articulated in the confessional mode, Mauriac's reflections are not self-enclosed, for instead of confining his attention to his own thoughts and feelings, he places himself in relation with worldwide events of the moment, mindful of his own responsibility in the collective drama that is unfolding. He thus denounces individual and collective isolationism as an intellectual illusion if not a lie, as a grave political error, and as an ethical failing, pointing out that the horrors he and his readers have for several years been viewing on cinema newsreels may soon be visited on them and the rest of Europe.

Mauriac had indeed warned that the violence of war that cinema-goers were viewing on the screen would ultimately concern everyone: as we have seen, his January 1937 article "The Demon of Spain" had deplored the use of Spain and its people as a testing ground for the weapons and tactics of Hitler, Stalin, and Mussolini, while his January 1938 editorial "Open City" had condemned the aerial bombardment of defenseless civilians in a coldly calculated use of military terror: "tomorrow," warned Mauriac, "perhaps it is we who will be filmed by the Pathé-Journal cameramen leaning over a row of dead bodies and seeking to recognize a face." Mauriac was even

4. "God is a circle whose center is everywhere and whose circumference is nowhere" (Dieu est un cercle dont le centre est partout et la circonférence nulle part). Nicolas de Cues, followed by Giordano Bruno and others, applied the same terminology to suggest the infinity of the universe and of space. See http://expositions.bnf.fr/ciel/arretsur/sciences/grec/index8.htm.

more insistent in his February 1938 article "Contre la guerre 'CRIER' est un devoir" ("Against War, It Is a Duty to Cry Out") deploring the French public's apparent apathy in the face of the deliberate slaughter of civilians in the Spanish Civil War and in Japan's invasion of China.

In movie theaters, the horrific images of cinema newsreels do not create the slightest stir among the sleepy crowd. On the screen, a Chinese woman and a lady in Catalonia stand amidst the rubble and seem to look with poignant reproach at these masses of Europeans smoking and keeping their silence.[5]

As Jean Lacouture remarks, few were perspicacious enough to understand that such images were indeed to be the precursor of a Second World War.[6] Nor should we forget that the Allied bombardment of Germany and Japan made heavy use of similar tactics, notably in the fire bombings of Dresden and Tokyo, not to mention the nuclear weapons unleashed on Hiroshima and Nagasaki.

Everywhere or Nowhere

Temps présent, October 13, 1939

War seems so surprising to us only because now we are the ones afflicted by it. Throughout these last few years, I kept striving to alert myself even more than others with calls and shouts. My own indifference, my insensitivity made me ashamed and horrified.

We spoke of the Chinese, Abyssinian, and Spanish bodies, and at times we even saw images of them in magazines and at the cinema. But how many among us did not even recoil as do animals passing by a slaughterhouse?

The world must either make up its mind to tolerate war nowhere or else accept it everywhere. Today we are the victims of the same fire that for years we had watched as it kept burning, dying out in one place, then flaring up in another. "Let's not get mixed up in the quar-

5. François Mauriac, "Pour le salut du monde: contre la guerre, crier est un devoir," *Paris-Soir*, February 9, 1938, 2.

6. *François Mauriac un journaliste engagé. Jean Daniel, Jean-Claude Guillebaud, Francis Jeanson, Jean Lacouture, René Rémond, Jean Touzot*, Propos recueillis par Gilbert et Nicole Balavoine ([Bordeaux:] Centre François Mauriac de Malagar: Editions confluences, 2007), 53.

rels of others," was the conventional wisdom of many people, and doubtless they were right in the short term. And perhaps we were not able to act otherwise than what we did.

The fact remains that even if the bankruptcy of the League of Nations is discouraging the peoples of the world from reconstructing it, given the mistakes that it has made, let us no longer talk of the last war, nor of the next to last war, nor of the war that will come after this one, for there never was and will be but one single war: the war that began with the human species. The reintensification of this war will mark the beginning of the last days.

In "What an Artist!" Mauriac delivers a highly original portrayal of Hitler. Rather than the facile caricature or patriotic diatribe that one that one could so readily expect now that France was at war with Nazi Germany, Mauriac borrows from Suetonius's description of Nero repeatedly uttering "*Qualis artifex pereo*!" to place Hitler against the backdrop of human history and to reflect on the nature of dictatorial violence and aggression.[7] He thus depicts Hitler as the legendarily cruel and perverse Roman emperor, since both tyrants view history as a medium for realizing their own personal aesthetic: in other words, Hitler engages in politics as one would conduct an artistic project, seeking both to hold the masses under the sway of spectacle and to satisfy the idiosyncratic cravings of the would-be artist within him.

Like the philosopher Emmanuel Lévinas, Mauriac perceives behind the grotesque spectacle of Hitlerism a fundamental attitude of the self toward history, one that can be analyzed and placed into a larger context. Mauriac's antonomasia (making a proper name into a noun by the use of the indefinite article, as in "a Nero, a Robespierre sculpted in human flesh") depicts Hitler not as a freak, but as a certain type of ruler. In characterizing the Führer as a leader treating people and events with the license of an artist intent only on creating some objective correlative to his own obscure quest, Mauriac's analysis parallels Walter Benjamin's famous as-

7. "What an artist perishes with me!" Mauriac's original French text uses the Latin. For the source of this expression, see Mary Francis Gyles, "Nero: Qualis artifex?" *Classical Journal* 57, no. 5 (February 1962): 193.

sessment of the Fascist tendency to aestheticize politics: "'*Fiat ars—pereat mundus*,' says Fascism, and ... expects war to supply the artistic gratification of a sense perception."[8] Mauriac thus sees the violence perpetrated by the would-be artist as a consequence of the latter's failure to recognize any discontinuity between the self and other, and of the artist-dictator's concomitant refusal to acknowledge any constraint on his action. For Mauriac as for Lévinas, violence corresponds to a fundamental failure or refusal to recognize the separate and thus partial status of the self. Ignoring the isolated, fragmentary character of human existence thus entails refusing to take heed of all that which remains exterior to the self, that is, that which transcends its domain, remaining exempt from its claims and free of its grasp: "What is violent is any action in which one acts as if the rest of the universe were there only to receive the action."[9] In both Lévinas's philosophical analysis and Mauriac's sketch of Hitler, we find that violence is committed by a particular being that ignores its status as creature and behaves as if it were of one substance with the rest of being.

Mauriac's characterization of the paradigmatic violence of Hitler's politics thus offers striking parallels with Emmanuel Lévinas's analysis of the inherently violent nature of Hitler's doctrine of blood, race, expansionism, and war that the philosopher, one of the rare French intellectuals alert to the grave dangers specific to Nazi ideology, laid out in his essay "Quelques réflexions sur la philosophie de l'hitlérisme" published in the November 1934 edition of *Esprit*.[10] On a more anecdotal level, it is noteworthy that the spectacularly tragic "Shakespearean ending" that Mauriac foresees for the Führer turned out to be a rather accurate anticipation of his demise, as did his grim expectation that Hitler would not disappear from the scene before having occasioned the deaths of millions.

8. "Let there be art, and let the world perish." Walter Benjamin, *Illuminations* (New York: Schocken Books, 1969), 242.

9. Emmanuel Lévinas, *Difficile liberté* (Paris: Albin Michel, 1963), 18.

10. Cf. Nathan Bracher, "Facing History: Mauriac and Lévinas on Nazism," *Journal of European Studies* 23 (1993): 164, 166–67.

What an Artist!

Le Figaro, November 17, 1939

"Although Herr Hitler had spoken of his artistic tastes and of his ardent desire to satisfy them," wrote Sir Neville Henderson in his definitive report on the circumstances that brought his mission in Berlin to an end, "I had the impression that this corporal from the last war was even more eager to demonstrate what he would be able to do in the next war, as a conquering generalissimus. . . ."

An artist or an unfulfilled artist, or frankly speaking a failed artist, is making Europe pay dearly for his failure. Among the masters of the world, the most dreadful belong to this species: a Nero or a Robespierre sculpt out of human flesh a work that would not have had to be bloody. Poetry is a deliverance. One must be wary of those who have been touched by its fire and, for lack of genius, have not delivered themselves from it. If Hitler had been able to get himself caught up in his own artistic creation, he would not have been the renovator of German borders, he would not be today prowling around the last few little nations that he has not yet violated. He would not be treating the material of humanity the way he would have treated colors and forms or ideas and dreams if he had been a great artist.

A great artist is not tempted by politics. I am wary of those who envy conquerors. Was Beethoven jealous of Napoleon? Chateaubriand was: not a good sign for *Les Natchez* and for *Les Martyrs*. Barrès was seeking to find in the National Assembly what he no longer expected to achieve through his writing.

As for Hitler, he did not have the choice. Incapable of expressing himself in his first calling, he found it easier to exercise control over human beings than to master the appearance of things. But even if he had not admitted the fact to Neville Henderson, we would know that the artist was still alive in the Führer of eighty million Germans.

The artist within the leader can be discerned by two signs, and first of all by the very character of his politics. His policies seek to turn mental constructions into material realities, and only insurmountable obstacles make him adapt these policies to the circumstances. These policies seek to reproduce at any price a work that he has pondered for a long time and whose model he carries within himself. The other sign is that the life of an artist who has gotten lost in history makes for a spectacle. He lives the life that he was not able to write, and the tragic image that he was not capable of making into a work of art becomes that which he himself proposes for the world. But the living matter with which he is working cannot tolerate everything in the manner of clay, colors, or blank pages. In politics, audacity and contempt for rules cost a lot of blood.

Hitler the painter might have died impoverished or abandoned like Mozart, or insane like Nietszche. Such deaths would have been sinister but not spectacular, and would have only been the stuff of bad films. As the head of a party, the chancellor of the Reich, and conqueror of defenseless nations, Adolf Hitler the Führer will have a Shakespearean ending of the type that was almost his fate the other evening in Munich. He already belongs to the realm of theater, and we listen to him as we do the main character of a tragedy whose minor characters, regrettably, are not killing each other for fun.

From the first words that he pronounced on the evening of his attempted assassination, we identified this awful voice, which is more familiar than the voice of one of our friends. For when we listen to someone speaking over the radio, we sometimes wonder: "I believe that's Duhamel speaking. Isn't that Maurois? Are you sure it's Giraudoux?" But when it's Hitler, we don't mistake him for any of his disciples, we recognize him right away: "That's him for sure!" From the reactions of his audience, we discerned that he wasn't addressing a large anonymous crowd, but faithful followers. What obsequious laughter! What fond cries! It was like Robespierre in the Club des Jacobins, defending his actions, accusing the wicked and delivering his heart. Hitler and Robespierre are the heroes of the work of art that they were not able to give to the world. The Führer's voice sounded like it was amplified by the mask of Greek tragedy. He was speaking fast. He knew that he had to hurry. His daemon made him vaguely aware of the hidden clockwork over his head, with a slowly unwinding spring. His hour had not yet come. It is not time for him to exit the stage. His role involves other retorts and other gestures. Millions of men are still breathing, and Hitler has not fulfilled his destiny.

For all his lucidity on the sinister implications of Hitler and Nazi politics, Mauriac was neither sheltered from the war's hardships and dangers, nor entirely immune from the illusions, misgivings, and hesitations that abounded during that trying era, and which now, some seven decades later, are often clearly visible. Shaken to tears by Hitler's invasion of Poland, since it meant war with Great Britain and France,[11] Mauriac continued to believe that Germany could not materially sustain a prolonged conflict[12] and later took comfort in what he found to be the impressive defense offered by the fortifications of the Maginot Line.[13] Like virtually all of his compatriots, Mauriac was thus totally unprepared for the shocking rout that France suffered so rapidly over the course of some six weeks of unmitigated catastrophe. On May 17, 1940, only seven days after the Germans had unleashed their offensive, Mauriac, as would millions of others over the course of those fateful weeks of May and June 1940, proceeded to evacuate his wife and two daughters out of Paris to seek shelter in his ancestral dwelling of Malagar near Bordeaux. Taking in some fifteen to twenty acquaintances who had also fled from the North, and seeing hundreds of other refugees in makeshift camps dotting the surrounding countryside, Mauriac found himself overwhelmed by the disaster dramatically unfolding all around, as the Germans streamed into Bordeaux and even into the little towns and villages nearby.

The spectacle of thousands of men, women, and children fleeing Hitler's troops over the open road, and thus exposed to the perils of inclement weather, acute shortages of food and water, movements of panic, and medical emergencies—ranging from women in childbirth to various sorts of wounds and injuries occasioned not only by the inevitable accidents but also by the Luftwaffe's aerial bombardments and strafings—did not fail to shake Mauriac and his compatriots to the core, as he readily avows in his editorial "Our Threatened Rural Areas": "I measure our nation's ordeal by

11. Barré, *Mauriac. Biographie intime, 1. 1885–1940*, 565–66.
12. Lacouture in *François Mauriac un journaliste engagé*, 60.
13. Lacouture, *Mauriac. 2. Un citoyen du siècle 1933–1970*, 106.

the immense stretch of territory that the horde [of civilian refugees] had to cross in order to reach this privileged corner of the world and interrupt this dream that was my refuge."[14] Mauriac ruefully found himself receiving a very concrete illustration of the moral lesson that he had served to those in cinema halls, who seemed unaware that the violence displayed by the newsreels could soon come to visit them as well. Observing families devastated by the deaths of loved ones and the destruction ravaging France's towns and villages, Mauriac expresses in the same passage his grief and disarray, bemoaning the pain felt even "in the stones and the gardens, of which we can say without blaspheming that they are also the flesh of our flesh."

Little wonder, then, that during the first two or three months of the Occupation, we see Mauriac hesitating and fluctuating. He respected and supported Pétain, who had not yet signed the infamous Jewish Statute nor officially committed Vichy to the policy of state collaboration with the Third Reich. For Mauriac as for the vast majority of the French populace amid the confusion and chaos of the May–June 1940 debacle, Marshal Philippe Pétain remained "the Victor of Verdun," a stalwart patriot not prone to partisan politics. Penned two days after Pétain announced over the radio that he had assumed leadership as France's premier and had contacted the Germans in view of putting an end to the war, "The Truth" expresses the shame and humiliation of defeat while offering gratitude and praise to the person of Pétain, still bathed in the aura of his World War I prestige and appearing as the one remaining beacon of hope and comfort amid the chaos and terror of war.

Although Mauriac would soon regain his composure and return to a more critical assessment, we would be remiss not to notice several prominent themes that, precisely because they were so widespread and deep-seated, proved crucial to Pétain's strong support and popularity in those beginning months of the German occupation in the summer of 1940. Most significant is Mauriac's adamant refusal to see France's downfall in purely military or logistical terms. This stridently moral interpretation of what

14. "Nos campagnes menacées," in *Mauriac sous l'Occupation,* ed. Jean Touzot (Paris: La Manufacture, 1990), 197–98.

Mauriac lucidly terms "the biggest defeat in our history" is all the more noteworthy in that it directly contradicts Charles de Gaulle's insistence on framing the defeat in terms of a military situation that could evolve and even reverse itself, thus leading to a victory over Nazi Germany. Mauriac, again like the majority of his fellow French citizens, apparently never heard de Gaulle issue his famed "call of June 18" over the BBC to his compatriots, exhorting them not to despair while he rallied the French military forces that had not yet fallen under enemy control. But even if Mauriac had heard the speech, it is highly unlikely that he would have been convinced.

At a time when Germany seemed invincible, and many expected Great Britain to fall to Hitler in a matter of months, any notion of future victory would for Mauriac have only impaired the process of self-examination that he, like Pétain and countless others in those fateful days of June and July 1940, saw as France's first priority: namely, for "all French people of every party and every social class [to] beat their chests," thus identifying the sources of the social, political, and moral "infirmity" to be "cauterized." Mauriac pursued the thematics of repentance and reform in another editorial from the same period, "La France en cellule" ("France Confined to Its Cell"), dating from July 3, 1940. Just as the intensely patriotic Mauriac sketches the war-torn French countryside in the form of a veteran wounded in the face, so he personifies his defeated country as a woman entering a religious order, donning a veil and confining herself to her cell so as to better meditate and expiate her failings with humility and devotion: her penitence focuses notably on recalling and regretting numerous manifestations of the fractious political rancor of the 1930s.

Mauriac's recourse to an architectural metaphor stating "that France was like these admirable old residential dwellings that appeared intact but were in fact being gnawed away everywhere within by termites" also bears citing. One of the most famous propaganda posters for Vichy's "National Revolution" that was to replace the Republic by the highly authoritarian rule of Pétain (which in later years proved permeable to Fascism) depicted the Third Republic as a house teetering on the brink of downfall: instead of having a solid foundation resting on bedrock, it had been placed over a motley collection of sandbags of various sizes bearing such labels as "selfishness," "disorder," and "greed," which in turn reposed on "laziness," "demagoguery," and "internationalism," rather than on "Work, Family, Country."[15]

The Truth

Le Figaro, June 19, 1940

On June 17, after Marshal Pétain had given a supreme proof of love to his country, the French heard a voice over the radio assuring them that France had never been so glorious.[16] Well, no! The only hope for saving our country is to never lie to ourselves again.

Let us acknowledge that we are at the bottom of a humiliating abyss. It is not an insult to our heroic soldiers nor to their commanders to gauge this abyss with lucid observation. We thank our foreign friends for the praises that they heap upon us. But we are prohibited from blinding our eyes in order not to see that the biggest defeat in our history did not happen by accident or misfortune.

Our chances of recovering depend on the extent to which we will realize the immediate and distant causes of this collapse. It also depends on the extent to which all French people of every party and every social class will beat their chests.

If there are still some among us who want to place the blame on their compatriots and declare before God and before France that they are in no way responsible, they are to be pitied and left to their illusions. The truth is that what appears in light of this disaster is that France was like these admirable old residential dwellings which appeared intact but were in fact being gnawed away everywhere within by termites.

The reforms must deal with everything, with both principles and methods. The official doctrine of our democracy has proven itself, and it has proven itself in every domain, for a war is a test of strength that informs us on how well a country is working. War judges our physi-

15. See http://jm3e5.blogspot.com/2011/03/la-maison-france-affiche-de-propagande.html.

16. In one of the most memorable lines of his speech on June 17, 1940, Pétain had stated that he was offering up his own person to alleviate the suffering of his country.

cal constitution but also our hearts and minds. The fall of France was terrible in its very rapidity, and leaves us without the slightest illusion.

The fall was not just due to the inferiority of our aviation and our armored mobile units. The disaster is not just due to material causes. It is too soon today to cauterize our open wound. But we must acknowledge without delay the weakness of our weapons, the absence of preparation, the lack of foresight among our leaders, the nation's somnolence facing our most dreadful adversary, the blind confidence, the arrogant conceit on display everywhere in the press, on the radio, and on the very walls of our cities: all of these things have their roots in a more deep-seated infirmity and this infirmity is of a spiritual order.

The French people must first of all come to terms with each other and reach an agreement over the underlying reasons for this immense catastrophe, and then only will there remain a chance for our sons to see the glimmer of the dawn of a resurrection; and if there will remain for us, their fathers, the hope of being forgiven.

Clearly, Mauriac was not immune to vacillations of thought and spirit that, as Philippe Burrin has masterfully shown, characterized so many writers at the time.[17] One must take care, however, to view them not only in the context of that particularly stressful and confusing moment, but also in the development of Mauriac's attitude over the course of the war, which would quickly lead him to throw in his lot decisively with the intellectual resistance.

We see the beginnings of this movement in "This Remnant of Pride," written shortly after the German occupation of French territory had officially begun on June 25, 1940. Mauriac admonishes his fellow citizens to maintain their dignity and act with discretion in their contacts with the German occupation forces, whose invasion had not only occasioned widespread chaos and mayhem among the civilian population but had also resulted in the highly visible and intrusive presence of German soldiers over wide expanses of French territory, before the most cherished Parisian monuments, at the center of small provincial towns such as those that

17. See "Un présent indécis," in Burrin, *La France à l'heure allemande*, 24–38.

Mauriac mentions, and even within private homes. Beginning in January 1941, such would be the case for Mauriac's ancestral dwelling of Malagar. Just as Mauriac winced at the violence inflicted on France's urban and rural landscapes, such encroachments were intimately felt in the French collective psyche as a violation of more or less sacred space.

While he understands the shock of those peering out of windows or even standing on sidewalks to watch German military convoys thunder through the center of their towns and villages, Mauriac decries such gawking not only as a failure to observe common sense discretion but as a lack of collective self-respect. Realizing that the defeat left ordinary French people momentarily powerless to repel or even contest the presence of these intruders, he nevertheless insists that it is possible to maintain a sense of composure and national dignity with two very simple gestures intended to maintain a proper distance from the Germans: turning away one's eyes and remaining silent.

Referencing Racine's rendition of Andromaqua as a standard of honor and decorum, Mauriac's exhortation for his compatriots to maintain their dignity and discretion in their contacts with the German occupation forces is part of a wider pattern of reaction to the defeat and Occupation. Several other writers and intellectuals gave similar watchwords to their defeated and despondent compatriots: ignoring the Germans' public military displays was necessary not only to refuse a servile voyeurism but even more importantly to help preserve hearts and minds from ideological contamination. Writing in Paris during that summer of 1940, Jean Texcier expressed similar concerns with his clandestinely circulated "Conseils à l'Occupé" ("Advice to the Occupied People"):

> Ever since you have been "occupied," they have paraded to your dishonor. Are you going to stand there watching them? Turn your interest to storefront windows instead.[18]
>
> Display a fine indifference; but secretly kindle your anger.[19]
>
> Monitor your barriers against their radio and their press. Monitor your shields against fear and facile resignation. Monitor *yourself.*[20]

18. Jean Texcier, *Écrit dans la nuit* (Paris: La Nouvelle Édition, 1945), 10–11.
19. Ibid., 15.
20. Ibid., 20.

Having lost control over the public spaces of their national territory, the French were thus—according to Mauriac, Texcier, and perhaps most famously Jean Bruller (see below)—nevertheless expected to protect the integrity of their inner space, the realm of thought and feeling, by holding up a wall of indifference and inattention not only to the Wehrmacht's concerts and parades, but also to more subtle attempts to win their favor with courteous gestures and casual conversation. The refusal of a gaze or a spoken reply is a posture that moreover corresponds to a collectively shared cultural tendency to conceive of liberty as the possibility of maintaining one's identity within a protected space created by setting up barriers to unwanted gazes and visitors.[21] We see just this strategy enacted in the difficult context of the Occupation: the impossibility of erecting physical walls to keep the Germans out is compensated by putting up virtual partitions that create an intellectual haven for clear, resolute thinking. Mauriac and Texcier's recoil from the groups of garrulous spectators that all too often rushed out to see the Germans illustrates a paradigmatic determination to preserve an island of independent thinking, national serenity, and self-respect.

Some two-and-one-half years later, Jean Bruller provided what was to become the most famous representation of such discreet yet determined assertion of dignity with his clandestinely composed, printed, and circulated book *The Silence of the Sea.* The narrative of a man and his niece forced to lodge a German officer in the upstairs bedroom of their modest provincial residence takes its title from their restrained, unspoken, yet adamant refusal to engage in verbal or social commerce with their uninvited guest, whom they pretend not to notice: "In tacit agreement, my niece and I had decided not to change anything in our way of living, not even the slightest detail: as if the officer did not exist, as if he were a ghost," explains the narrator.[22]

While modest in scope, such refusal of any sort of fraternization or chumminess was an indispensable first step in rejecting the complicity and collaboration immediately promoted by both Pétain and the Germans.

21. Laurence Wylie and Jean-François Brière, *Les Français*, 3rd ed. (Upper Saddle River, N.J.: Prentice-Hall, 2001), 30–32, 97–98.

22. Vercors [Jean Bruller], *Le Silence de la mer* (Paris: Albin Michel, 1951), 25.

The path to resistance was nevertheless neither clear nor straightforward for Mauriac during this first phase of the Occupation. Outraged by Churchill's naval bombardment of the French fleet at Mers-el-Kebir, happy to see the demise of the parliamentary Third Republic, yet highly suspicious of the Action française clan now prominent in Pétain's entourage, Mauriac defended France's intellectual and artistic tradition against accusations that it had weakened the nation, and finally abstained from writing any more editorials after the summer of 1940 because he did not feel free to express his opinions. For many friends and admirers anxious to see what position he would take,[23] Mauriac nevertheless constituted a role model in spite of himself.

This Remnant of Pride

Le Figaro, June 29, 1940

"Have eyes to see nothing." This is the watchword to give to the French people in the face of foreign occupation. Certainly, we must not be scandalized by the fact that all the people in our villages did not close their shutters right away, nor that the sound of the heavy German trucks might have drawn them out on their doorsteps for a minute. In the southwestern part of France, the sudden event is too unexpected for people to feel it yet. They were not prepared for this sort of tragedy. Their elders had not passed down to them, along with their bloodlines, the dread of being invaded, as in the provinces in the North and the East. They had never experienced it. The sight of German troops parading by was for them nothing more than a scene from a movie. It was a sort of sinister, picturesque sight that had nothing to do with anyone living between the Loire river and the Pyrenees.

But now all of a sudden we see the horde of invaders leave the screen, pass through the cinema hall, cross the little town square, and proceed in good order down the road to Bazas and on to Mont-de-Marsan, shaded by the plane and the cork oak trees, still wet from a big storm.

23. Barré, *Mauriac. Biographie intime, 2. 1940–1970,* 17–19.

> We can excuse this initial curiosity and these excited faces, as if they were watching the Tour de France. Alas, it is indeed a sort of Tour de France, an endless round that is not about to be over ... But you have understood now. The proper behavior that we must observe with respect to these uninvited visitors must be accompanied by our refusal to gawk at them and by the inattention of our entire being.
>
> May the occupation of France stop on the surface, on the cobblestones, on the pavement of our highways, and may it not penetrate into the core or into the secret of wellsprings and souls. And above all may it not arouse the interest of any heart. People of France who have lost everything, safeguard at least this dignity that tragedy confers on a nation that has gone down fighting! Imitate the princesses in Jean Racine's tragedies. Like Andromaque, stand up to the one who vanquished you with "This remnant of pride that fears being out of place...." Yes, let us show a quiet, humble pride ...

Occupation, Collaboration, and Resistance

With its manifold anxieties, trials, and tribulations, the ordeal of war posed for Mauriac as it did for everyone the question of humanity: what defines the human being as a person and as a species, what can one say about human destiny, and what are the ethical and political ramifications of this supreme trauma of human history. These interrogations thus concern the theological, for the answers matter not just provisionally or pragmatically, but for eternity, and ultimately, before God. "I am one of the people who have been haunted by the mystery of evil all their lives," avows Mauriac in "God Is Innocent." Far from evacuating spiritual preoccupations, the scandal of evil in the form of the violence and injustice of historical events only heightens his spiritual sensitivity and renders it more urgent, if more uncertain or even more hazardous than ever.

Writing at one of the darkest moments of the Occupation in late summer 1942, shortly after French police had conducted a shocking series of mass round-ups of Jews in Paris and in the unoccupied Southern Zone, but before the Allied landing in North Africa on November 8, 1942, and the Red Army's victory at Stalingrad on February 2, 1943, had founded new hopes for the defeat of Nazi Germany, Mauriac paints a veritable tableau of bucolic serenity and order that invites comparison with majestic, harmonious images of nature in Poussin's representation of biblical narratives. He invokes the "peace and light are our true destiny" emanating from "the countryside resting in the afternoon sun or guarded by moonlight" and giving "us a concrete sense of an infinite and proximate holiness." Mauriac also alludes to the story of Cain and Abel (to which he repeatedly returns when grappling with the problem of violence and responsibility), the Psalms, and the Sermon on the Mount.

At the same time, we find the basic paradigm that Mauriac articulates time and time again in response to particularly disturbing manifestations of violence. He refuses to solve the "mystery of evil" or "explain" the scandal by invoking some dialectical logic of events or teleological orientation of history unfolding to bring an outcome that might absolve or compensate the suffering and injustice of the moment. Instead, Mauriac depicts human beings as on the one hand belonging to a biological species obeying the implacable logic of "survival of the fittest," who soon learn to "eat or be eaten," while at the same time maintaining a divine filiation conferring an inestimable dignity and worth on each member of humankind.

God Is Innocent

La Gazette de Lausanne, August 9, 1942

The title of a play whose author remains unknown to me has been displayed on walls throughout the city of Paris and even in the subway halls these past few days: *God Is Innocent.* I haven't seen it on stage, but even if it were a masterpiece, the show could not have moved me any more than these three words written everywhere in this humiliated city: this is the answer peremptorily given to the question that so many hearts have secretly asked. For since the Redeemer has come, "the bloody instruments of destruction" have nevertheless dominated our world,[24] and the problem of evil still haunts our thought, and now more than ever, as everywhere the earth is drenched with blood.

24. The allusion is to Charles Baudelaire's poem "La Destruction" in *Les Fleurs du Mal* (*The Flowers of Evil*), in which the poet laments the relentless influence of Satan in the following terms:

Perhaps because I am one of the people who have been haunted by the mystery of evil all their lives, and who no longer expect the solution to the enigma to be given to them in this life, I lovingly accepted the affirmation inscribed on the subway walls. I subscribed to such boundless innocence with all my heart and all my mind. I kept on repeating to myself that since good comes only from God, evil comes only from human beings, who, to carry it out, in a way possess the power of a god.

And then came July, and as it was when we were happy children, the hall became encumbered with trunks: even though men are killing each other on land, in the sky, and beneath the oceans, we still keep to the humble ways that used to govern our peaceful days, and we leave for our country home during the long summer vacation.

Through the rail car windows, I thought that, passing through the delightful rural landscapes where our country's great suffering is not apparent, I could again read the three words written on the subway walls. At dusk, I opened the shutters of the old house still half asleep, whose silence was scarcely disturbed by our footsteps. We had not been there long enough to leave the furniture in life's disorder: the neatly stowed chairs had not yet been drawn together according to the random pattern of our games and conversations.

I stepped out. A cart full of hay coming up to the barn summoned up verses of poetry to my mind: " … heavy, groaning carts / That re-

---

Il me conduit ainsi, loin du regard de Dieu,
Haletant et brisé de fatigue, au milieu
Des plaines de l'Ennui, profondes et désertes,
Et jette dans mes yeux pleins de confusion
Des vêtements souillés, des blessures ouvertes,
Et l'appareil sanglant de la Destruction!
[He leads me thus, far from the sight of God,
Panting and broken with fatigue, into the midst
Of the plains of Ennui, endless and deserted,
And thrusts before my eyes full of bewilderment,
Dirty filthy garments and open, gaping wounds,
And all the bloody instruments of Destruction!]

Charles Baudelaire, *The Flowers of Evil*, trans. William Aggeler (Fresno, Calif.: Academy Library Guild, 1954); the full French text as well as Aggeler's translation cited here can be found at http://fleursdumal.org/poem/177.

turn in the evening when the road is dark,"[25] and also, " Far away a cart is faintly slipping through the shadows.... Listen!"[26] How calm it all was! A light breeze was slipping through the poplar trees; I could hear them shudder. In the valley, the smoke from grass fires was rising straight up as in this engraving in the Bible representing the sacrifice of Abel. And I once again recalled the title of the unknown play and believed in the innocence of God.

Now I know quite well what is hiding behind this apparent peace of the countryside! Over the animal and even the plant kingdoms, there seems to be only one commandment that thundered out: "Devour one other." We know that nature loves struggle and death, and we know that nature sacrifices the individual to the species. And even though the class of farmers who live in close contact with the earth may well possess their own specific virtues, it would nevertheless pro-

25. Mauriac first cites a verse from the fourteenth stanza of Victor Hugo's masterpiece of lyrical bucolic melancholy, "Tristesse d'Olympio" ("Olympio's Sadness"):

> La borne du chemin, qui vit des jours sans nombre,
> Où jadis pour m'attendre elle aimait à s'asseoir,
> S'est usée en heurtant, lorsque la route est sombre,
> Les grands chars gémissants qui reviennent le soir.
> [The milestone near the road, which had seen innumerable days
> And where she loved to sit down and wait for me,
> Has been worn down by colliding with the heavy, groaning carts
> That return in the evening when the road is dark.]

French text is found at http://poesie.webnet.fr/lesgrandsclassiques/poemes/victor_hugo/tristesse_d_olympio.htm. The translation is my own.

26. Mauriac now cites the first stanza of another of Victor Hugo's lyrical poems, "La prière pour tous" ("The Prayer for All"):

> Ma fille, va prier!—Vois, la nuit est venue.
> Une planète d'or là-bas perce la nue;
> La brume des coteaux fait trembler le contour;
> À peine un char lointain glisse dans l'ombre.... Écoute!
> Tout rentre et se repose; et l'arbre de la route
> Secoue au vent du soir la poussière du jour!
> [Go pray, my daughter! See, the night has come.
> Over there a golden planet is breaking through the clouds;
> The haze is making the contours of the hills tremble;
> Far away a cart is faintly slipping through the shadows.... Listen!
> All is coming back to rest; and the tree by the roadside
> Is shaking off the day's dust in the evening breeze!]

French text is found at http://poesie.webnet.fr/lesgrandsclassiques/poemes/victor_hugo/tristesse_d_olympio.html. The translation is my own.

vide some horrible examples for a history of human ferocity. That is all true, and yet . . .

And yet, when beholding the countryside resting in the afternoon sun or guarded by moonlight, it is not an illusion for us to feel at certain times that such peace and light are our true destiny that all people can attain if they rise above their selfish passions. Fields and trees do not teach us that humans are innocent, but they give us a concrete sense of an infinite and proximate holiness, from which we are separated only by the stain of our sins. Only those in the contemplative orders manage to do more than to sense this divine peace and light. Now people do not know that contemplation as practiced by a very small number is actually offered to all. It is a luxury that, among pastoral peoples, was doubtless available to the most humble. Shepherds have always more or less heard the angels' song, and still today, in certain rural areas, there are more people than we imagine who partake of this innocence of God. They draw so near to it sometimes that on a mountain, as in the case of Notre-Dame de la Salette in the Alps,[27] or in the hollow part of a rock formation, or beside a stream, this light beheld by the blind eyes of the elderly Tobias suddenly dazzles their childlike eyes.

All the blood spread over the earth since that of Abel was done so only by human passions: countless human envies joined together to create this great collective rage among peoples and to hurl one empire against another.

The observation of plants and animals and the evidence from a world of predators in which from the smallest to the largest, each individual is both hunter and prey, killer and killed, never convinced me that war was inevitable for creatures endowed with a loving heart and an immortal soul. For how could we establish a common denominator between war in the plant and animal kingdoms, where the goal is the selection of the species, and human war, this reverse process of selection that sacrifices the heroes and the strong and spares the sick, the clever, and the cowardly?

27. It was there that two young shepherds said they witnessed an apparition of the Virgin Mary in 1846.

> Above and beyond the iron law that governs plants and animals, the human species has long had the sense that a law of love was destined for humanity. It was this hope that trembled in the songs of David, and some of the great figures of classical antiquity were not unaware of it. And then, at one moment in history, on a mountain in Galilee, a few words were spoken, and we finally became acquainted with this law. Then the meek, the peacemakers, those who hunger and thirst for justice, and those who suffer persecution understood where their gentleness, their peace, their thirst, and their hunger came from. And they worshiped and blessed the source: the eternal innocence, the eternal infancy of God.

Far from immediate, Mauriac's condemnation of Pétain and Vichy developed progressively over the course of the first few months of the Occupation. His indictment of the marshal's collaborationist regime in his famous Resistance text, *The Black Notebook,* was nonetheless all the more devastating since, written under the pseudonym "Forez," it depended in no way on Mauriac's public or private identity. The path leading Mauriac to intellectual resistance, however, had been neither indicated by any moral compass, nor free of obstacles. In the waning moments of what was still the French Republic, just before the emergence of the Vichy regime following the scuttling of democratic institutions on July 10, 1940, Mauriac had penned two editorials (see above: "The Truth," published on June 19, 1940, and "La France en cellule," on July 3, 1940, both in *Le Figaro*) containing only the most laudatory references to "the Victor of Verdun." For the first few months of the Occupation, Mauriac seemed to consider Pétain's course of action as the only one viable. After that summer of 1940, however, he restricted his journalistic production to a handful of literary articles containing oblique praise of resistance and a series of articles published by the *Gazette de Lausanne.*[28] He similarly acquiesced to Drieu la Rochelle's editorship of *La Nouvelle Revue Française* and initially accepted an invitation to write a piece before ultimately refusing to publish there. He had seen the more than dubious articles published under Drieu's direc-

28. See Bracher, "Facing History: Mauriac and Lévinas on Nazism," 159.

tion. Keen on publishing his novel *La Pharisienne*, Mauriac indulged the German censors by visiting the German Institut to confer with two of its directors. Yet as the only member of the Académie française to participate in *Les Lettres françaises*, the flagship of intellectual resistance headed by prominent communists, Mauriac's contribution of what was to become one of its most prestigious writings, *The Black Notebook*, gave him unimpeachable credentials as a member of the intellectual resistance, along with such other notable writers and intellectuals as Jean-Paul Sartre, Albert Camus, and Maurice Merleau-Ponty. All, like Mauriac, also published books by the officially sanctioned French publishing houses during the Occupation.[29]

It is by no means coincidental that *The Black Notebook* devotes close attention to writing, including not only its own composition but also the "echoes in the press" and the shameful slurs on Paris published by what had been since the First World War France's most prestigious literary venue, the *Nouvelle Revue Française*. For centuries, France had staked a major portion of its prestige and even its identity on its literary prominence; support or opposition of prominent literati and artists was crucial. That is why the Germans devoted a considerable amount of attention and resources to winning the favor of France's most prominent cultural figures. That is also why notable writers who had promoted Nazism and collaboration paid dearly during the Purge (the punishment of collaborators and their removal from the public affairs of the nation; see chapter 3). Mauriac would not be the only one to voice indignation at the spectacle of French writers standing at attention before Goebbels at Weimar.

Intellectual resistance was serious business. Participants risked not only arrest and detainment but torture, deportation, and execution. In the context of the Occupation, paper, ink, typewriters, and duplicating machines were in short supply and tightly monitored. The mere material production of such clandestine texts thus proved highly problematic and their distribution dangerous, at times lethal. The production and dissemination of resistance literature was therefore just as significant as the specific content of the message; high quality writing such as that provided by Mauriac was

29. Cf. Burrin, *La France à l'heure Allemande*, 341–42.

prized. His participation in the literary resistance is even more notable when we observe that he found himself programmatically insulted and even threatened by collaborationist newspapers such as *Le Cri du peuple* and *Je suis partout*, as well as by Lucien Rebatet's virulently antisemitic and pro-Fascist book *Les Décombres*, all claiming to rid France of degenerative influences.[30]

Like virtually everyone in the late 1930s and early 1940s, Mauriac sensed that the turmoil, stress, and trauma of the time that he was experiencing in his private and public life was due to the intrusion of history. He insists, however, that history does not trump ethics. In a distinct shift of perspectives from the initial reaction that he penned at the moment of France's crushing defeat, Mauriac here stresses that the outcome on the battlefield proves nothing as to the validity of ideas and causes. He thus targets Vichy's relentless exploitation of the defeat to stigmatize the ideas and politicians of the Third Republic and of democracy in general. In this light, Mauriac cites Saint-Just, one of the most fervent exponents of the cause of democracy in its struggle to overcome the entrenched prejudice and injustice of the Ancien Régime, but also one of the most implacable theoreticians and advocates of the politics of Terror. This reference to a revolutionary hardliner marks a departure from his usual negative references to the Revolution. Here in *The Black Notebook* Mauriac refers most prominently to the Gospel as found in the words of Jesus and to the French Revolution in the proclamations of Saint-Just. The combination testifies to the political ecumenism that linked Mauriac to his fellow members of the *Lettres françaises,* which grouped Communists and centrists along with Catholics and outspoken atheists such as Jean-Paul Sartre, who had taken no little pleasure in skewering Mauriac's novels.

As attested by his many future references to Vichy's shameful and criminal acts, Mauriac harbors few illusions about the less than glorious behaviors of his compatriots under the extreme duress of the Occupation. Indeed, virtually everyone found themselves resorting to more or less desperate and often illicit means of securing food, fuel, and other basic necessities. Mauriac quotes from a post–French Revolution era writer Mallet du

30. Lacouture, *Mauriac. 2. Un citoyen du siècle 1933–1970*, 371–72.

Pan to maintain that such behaviors are sadly to be expected in times of extreme crisis. Decrying "the Jews crucified by your police," Mauriac gives notable attention to Vichy's antisemitic persecutions, the first specific offense that he mentions after pointing out that the French State's politics of collaboration served first and foremost to establish its own power and thus make it possible to impose reactionary policies.[31] While most other Resistance writings fail to mention the Jewish question, Mauriac points to what would come to be known as the most infamous of crimes committed during the Occupation, namely the cruel and degrading arrest, detention, and deportation of Jewish children: "In what other era were children torn away from their mothers, piled into cattle cars, such as I saw them one somber morning in the Austerlitz train station?" Equally if not more striking is his praise of the working class's dignity and courageous fidelity to democratic values, which Mauriac contrasts against not only the mediocrity of the property-holding well-to-do of the bourgeoisie, preoccupied first and foremost with preserving their own comfort, but also the cowardice of those who cowered behind the Germans in hopes of preserving their socioeconomic privilege.

Acknowledging such tawdry behavior as well as the most grievous complicity with the Nazis, Mauriac nevertheless refuses a totally negative view of humankind and instead affirms a human worth and dignity that can still prevail. Hence his exhortations: "We must overcome this temptation to despise humanity." "Let us not play their game: may our human depravity never blind us to our human grandeur." "But this very lucidity warns us against the facility of contempt." "Let us not give in to the facility of contempt." These repeated injunctions are not mere idealistic rhetoric: they seek to counter a propaganda campaign of disparagement and cynicism that was inundating newspapers and bookstores in occupied France. Mauriac explicitly rejects the (pseudo-)biological vision of humankind as a species engaged in ruthless struggle to eliminate the supposedly weak and inferior members.

At the same time, however, Mauriac is wary of getting carried away in

31. The "French State" was the formal name of Vichy France. Having denounced the essential tenets of republican democracy, Vichy naturally refused to designate France's political institutions as the "French Republic."

his own lofty idealism, which risks ignoring the frightful military conflict entailed by the resolve to resist the Nazi stranglehold. Mauriac has few illusions, admitting that extricating France from the grip of the Nazis condemns the Allies and the Resistance to their own ruthlessness, and muses: "Does he not condemn us to become like him in order to stand up to him?" Mauriac will return to the dilemma of avoiding the unscrupulous methods used by Vichy and the German occupying forces when he warns against the excesses of the Purge, visible in a number of cases of arbitrary arrest, brutal interrogations, and kangaroo court justice.

This incisive masterpiece of the underground literature published by the Resistance marked the French memory of the war years with a number of striking expressions. Considering the behavior of the various components of French society, Mauriac observes: "Only the working class has proved to be faithful *en masse* to a France that had been profaned." Physically repulsed by the conspicuous insignia of Nazi Germany, Mauriac shudders at the sight of "these flags whose swastikas look like a spider satiated and swollen with blood." How better to illustrate Vichy's shameful subservience to the Nazis than by pointing to "the French police relegated by Vichy to the task of watching over chain gangs"? How better to reject either a providential or a dialectical view of human events presumed either to carry out some divine plan or lead to some utopian classless society than to characterize history as "a tangled mess of errors and violence?"

The Black Notebook

Les Editions de Minuit, August 1943

In August 1943, in this early morning light, it is good to reread the notes I wrote three years ago, amid the deepest darkness. I reopen *The Black Notebook*: right away I find mutterings of rage written in the margins of Marshal Pétain's first homilies.

This ordeal is specific to our country: the triumph of traditional principles has been tragically tied to a military disaster and domination by the enemy. . .

You pretend to believe that the French people are demanding that those responsible be sought out and punished, and thus you aim to gloss over the horrible necessity of satisfying the victor's hatred.

And even if you were acting in good faith, History will accuse you of having served the vengeance of your masters, and of having sought to gain their favor by perpetrating a massacre … But do not think that the Jews crucified by your police might dispense you from paying your last dime in tribute to the victor.

You who calumniate France, you have never triumphed except by her shame and humiliation! You are doctors taking advantage of the fact that your patient has been bound and clubbed in order to ram your remedies down her throat!

Every day, I hear the echoes of the press, as one of my anonymous counterparts denounces me and points his trembling finger at me …

The hatred that arises out of Paris's pierced heart is silent, but its cry nonetheless drowns out the horrible whispering in its newsrooms …

One of the editors of the nazified *Nouvelle Revue française* compares Paris to "a slut that slowly drags herself out of bed every morning after a night of obscenity. …" Paris lies dispossessed, empty, pitch dark, as if quartered—more sublime than it ever had been!—and watched over by Orion the hunter during the nights of this ferocious winter …

And then peace of mind settles in at the same time that hope is reborn. *The Black Notebook*'s stammerings become interconnected sentences: my conscience returns to the past as it examines itself:

What a long time since I've been alone! The sort of incessant buzzing all around me, during which attacks even reinforced praises, has finally come to a stop! Today the worst affronts to my dignity have vanished in the great silence that follows the hurricane. Those insulting me are the very ones overjoyed that the Republic is dead (they think it is dead). Observe: each one seeks to take advantage of the disaster. The prophets of doom go up to the Capitoline Hill with the conqueror whose coming they had announced, or actually prepared. They gloat about having apparently been right, right for a short time …

But look, arms don't decide anything in a debate of ideas. Our victory of 1918 didn't prove that democracies were right, nor does our defeat in 1940 prove that they were guilty. The technology that defeated them will one day ensure their triumph.

And from the bottom of the abyss, we also cry that events show that we are right. The separation of politics and morality that we kept denouncing with all the meager might that we could muster has covered and continues to cover the entire world with blood. Machiavelli is the father of collective crime: he prepares and organizes it; he legitimizes, justifies, and glorifies it. It is true that we do not always find this perennial murderer on the same side: we are not so self-righteous as to claim as much! But we know on what side—and with what furious virulence—he has been raging in Europe for twelve years.

Let us not blush for having wanted the moral law governing relationships among individuals to also govern relations among nations. We were not so naive as to believe that Machiavelli could ever have been completely vanquished within and around us. We remembered the meditation on the battleground of Pharsale in the *Second Faust*: "How many times has this fight started up again," wonders Goethe. "It will always and forever start up again: no one wants to yield the empire to the other." We had to resign ourselves to this obvious fact. But it was enough for us that Europe should keep groping its way toward a world where Machiavelli could have to a certain extent been dominated, thanks to the organization of force in the service of justice. The patience of a few determined men going against the grain is enough to keep Machiavelli at bay.

Our grave misfortune was to be introduced to public affairs right after the Great War, when Europe seemed to have become disgusted with freedom. How outmoded this old country suddenly appeared in 1919, when it had shed so much of its blood for a cause in which the nations no longer believed! I remember having made young men laugh around that time when I cited the proud words with which Saint-Just concluded his plan for a constitution: The French people vote for the liberty of the world!

It took us a bit of time to realize that this faith in freedom had died out in the hearts of nations. One of our friends nevertheless discovered and proclaimed this fact at a time when the names of Mussolini and Hitler had not yet echoed all over Europe. On September 1, 1919, Jacques Rivière, who had just returned from a long period of captivity, wrote in *La Nouvelle Revue française*: "It is not at all certain that the world needs this freedom that we have won for it at the price of such monstrous sacrifices. It is not at all certain that freedom is today its most ardent desire and the nourishment for which it hungers the most. We can have doubt on the matter. We can legitimately worry that it might not just happen to have a very different appetite. For humanity as a whole, it does seem that the demand for liberty may well be lower than the supply that we are providing. It is to be feared that the market may not at all be what we had supposed it to be. We run a high risk of being stuck with an oversupply on our hands. . . ."

Jacques Rivière died too soon to learn that he was an amazing prophet. In order to revive the love of freedom within the hearts of nations, it has taken the ordeal of the gag and the straightjacket, the massacre of entire races, the deportation of Europe's working class, and the torture of children, a horror unknown since the time of the Assyrians. Once again, France has its word to say. That word is "Liberty."

Another grave misfortune is that never before this interwar period had the individual appeared more mediocre in our eyes. Nietzsche would have us believe that the individual is never stronger than under circumstances decidedly uncomfortable for our liberal civilization. What can we say to that? *Would we dare hold that Western democracy has safeguarded the human dignity that it now claims to champion*? The proletariat consists of millions of slaves whose eyes had been put out by the Free Masons, big business, and every one of us members of the moneyed propertied class: they powered the gristmill for us in our somber cities ... For his part, however, Samson lifted his blind eyes up to the heavens under the Philistine's whip. Drinking Pernod, watching indoor bicycle races in the Vél' d'Hiv', and going to the bordello: what great things to live for! There again, we had to reach the bottom of the abyss in order to find hope again. Those who gave their lives for their country testified to the mettle of the people. Only the working class has proved to be faithful *en masse* to a France that had been profaned.

At the moment when I am writing (in November 1941), so many other French people are driven by one basic passion: fear! They don't admit it while worshipping Marshal Pétain and invoking Jeanne d'Arc, but for them everything secretly boils down to one single necessity: that of saving their privileges and avoiding the settling of scores: "As long as the Germans will be there ..." That little reassuring phrase was what the likes of Renan and Taine were already muttering as they watched the Tuileries palace go up in flames. It was the same Renan who, on September 6, 1870, leaning out the window of Brébant's restaurant and surveying the carefree crowd walking in the streets, told Goncourt: "That is what will save us: the wishy-washy nature of these people...."

Well, no! We believe in humanity; we believe along with all of our famous essayists that human beings can be convinced and persuaded, even these bourgeois members of the propertied class who hide their money boxes amid their begonias. Yes, we believe that even these middlemen for the sale of every commodity close their eyes and perhaps clench their fists at the Place de Concorde, at the sight of these flags (I have never seen them without tears clouding my eyes), these flags whose swastikas look like a satiated spider swollen with blood.

We must overcome this temptation to despise humanity. To the extent that we would give in to the contempt that is the foundation of our enemies' doctrine, they would gain an advantage. In his preface to Machiavelli's *Prince*, Mussolini approves of such a pessimistic view of human nature and even takes it farther: "If I were allowed to judge my fellow human beings and my contemporaries," he admits, "I would in no way be able to mollify Machiavelli's judgment. Perhaps I would have to make it harsher...." That's because contempt for human beings is necessary for anyone who wants to use and abuse them. You cannot use an immortal and quasi-divine creature as an all-purpose instrument. That's why they first debase their victims.

Let us not play their game: may our human depravation never blind us to our human grandeur. Whatever shameful things we might find around us and in our own hearts, let us not be discouraged from giving credit to humanity: it is a matter of our reason for living, even for surviving.

Do not imagine, moreover, that the revolting spectacle that too many French people are giving us in the presence of the enemy is something new. This hideous humanity, with the French police relegated by Vichy to the function of chain gang guards, and with businessmen and men of letters getting rich from the occupying army, belongs to a type of human beings that have always existed. In January 1796 Mallet wrote: "Each seeks to escape at all costs from the distress affecting everyone else.... People think only of themselves, and then again of themselves, and always of themselves...."

We are not blinding our eyes, we are coolly taking stock of humankind. But this very lucidity warns us against the facility of contempt: it helps us to look beyond the phony elite and all that froths at the surface, and see those who have chosen to give their lives in sacrifice. After all, Monsieur de Montherlant, the prince of charades and pomposity, was almost alone in performing his number on an empty, abandoned stage. In the great silence that prevailed after the disaster, we could hardly hear anyone other than that braggart pretending to defy God.[32] How many men and women are risking their lives, suffering and dying under the bullets of firing squads for this shameful little herd composed of a few French writers who stood at attention before Dr. Goebbels in Weimar, along with a few painters and sculptors who had not understood that what they embodied went infinitely beyond their own mediocre selves and that in the face of the enemy they were about to humiliate centuries of the most illustrious art.

Let us not give in to the facility of contempt, let us above all not give in to the facility of despair. In June 1940, on the first page of this *Black Notebook,* I wrote one of Grimm's sayings: "The cause of humankind is hopeless...." Let us proclaim our faith in this lost cause. The elderly Goethe, on the threshold of eternity, no longer wanted to devote a glance or a thought to the politics of this world, to what he dubbed "a tangled mess of errors and

32. Written in the wake of France's disastrous defeat at the hands of the Germans in the summer of 1940, Henry de Montherlant's essay "Le solstice de juin" hailed the Nazi victory as the demise of Christianity and the return to what Montherlant, following Nietzsche, considered to be the virile order and sensuality of classical antiquity. See Montherlant, *Essais* (Paris: Gallimard, 1963), 953–63.

violence." This tangled mess is our own business: it concerns us and we will be cowards if we give in to that other facility called detachment.

Even for Christians, it is not that sort of detachment that is proposed. The God that they serve, the God who gave them a heart capable of knowing and loving Him did not turn away from the bloody history of humanity but instead plunged into the middle of it: "And the Word became flesh and dwelt among us." So far from having the right to flee humanity in God, they are enjoined to find God among human beings. May they first of all seek and find Him among those who suffer persecution for justice, whether they be Christian or pagan, Communists or Jews. To the degree that they have endured scorn and abuse, they directly resemble Christ, and the spit on their face authenticates that resemblance.

Are we to keep above the fray or look down on the tortured multitudes? From no higher than the cross, in any case. We must remain at the height of the scaffold, and we know that the scaffold on which Christ rendered his spirit was quite low since dogs often devoured the feet of crucified slaves.

Christians of all denominations should thus remain in the middle of the fray not in spite of their faith, but because of their faith. We will go forth hand in hand with them, and who could doubt that we will be going against the grain, counter to the desires and passions of the many. The progress of humankind is nothing but a myth: it does not exist outside of people of good will. It is not a historical given. It is only too true that we have drunk to the last drop the tremendous hope that inebriated our forebears in 1789.

"Happiness is a new idea in Europe," proclaimed the young Saint-Just. One-and-a-half centuries after these words were spoken, we know that happiness is a lost illusion. In order to accomplish Machiavelli's designs, peoples have been pushed together and deported, and entire races have been condemned to perish. At what other time in history have more innocent people been locked away in prison? In what other era were children torn away from their mothers, piled into cattle cars, such as I saw them one somber morning in the Austerlitz train station? Happiness has become an impossible dream in Europe, except for the low-minded. No, it is no longer a question of happiness: it's a question of standing up to Machiavelli, whose crimes will not be halted by any firing squad even after Germany's collapse, for the spirit of Machiavelli is tucked away and at work in millions of minds, even in France. *L'Action française, Gringoire*, and *Je suis partout* find countless readers here,[33] and they are the strongest, the richest, and the cleverest.

Machiavelli's offspring have no doubts about the unchanging laws of hu-

33. The titles cited are those of the most stridently antisemitic and antidemocratic Parisian daily newspapers.

man nature, and that is what constitutes their strength. To their eyes, we appear as so many pipe-dreamers and hypocrites. They have hold of reality. In the *Anthologie de la Nouvelle Europe*, Monsieur Alfred Fabre-Luce brought together the essential texts that are the foundation of totalitarian ideologies. Significantly, René Quinton's noted maxims hold an important place: "Nature loves struggle and death. War renders men to their natural born ends. War is the state of nature for males. The primary mission for males is not to reproduce but to kill each other. Nature creates species, it does not create beings. It is the natural tendency of individuals to fool themselves on the subject of their destiny and to believe that they are born for themselves ..."

What good would it do to deny that our hope has at times been disconcerted by the ferocity of creation? I am not frightened by the silence of this infinite space,[34] but by the implacability of this unending destruction.

But we have made our choice: we will wager against Machiavelli. We are of those who believe that humankind is an exception to the natural law that destines creatures to devour each other. We not only believe that humans are an exception, but that all their dignity consists of the Resistance with which humans oppose this natural tendency with all their hearts and minds. No, the human spirit is not fooling itself about its destiny. No, humans are not mistaken in protesting that the condition of termites and ants does not in any way shed light on that of humankind. Even if, over the course of centuries, there had only been one brief interval of time and space, or only one movement of charity, the endless chain of devouring and devoured creatures would have been forever broken.

Here I break off these excerpts from *The Black Notebook,* which is getting a bit too rosy for my taste. In such a murderous world, are not the adversaries of Machiavelli doomed to be targeted by predators? Is their vocation not that of the victim? As if I was forgetting the victor, and what a giant is covering us with his shadow and pressing little France between his palms ... Does he not condemn us to become like him in order to stand up to him? Even if he is defeated, will he not make us die to ourselves in order to recreate us in his own horrible likeness? Might in service of Right, Freedom protected by Might, imposed by Force ... We know how our forebears of 1793 worked their

34. Mauriac is alluding to one of the most famous of Pascal's *Pensées* (Lafuma 201, Brunschvicg 206): "Le silence eternel de ces espaces infinis m'effraie" (The eternal silence of this infinite space frightens me); http://www.penseesdepascal.fr. Mauriac's previous references to human grandeur and depravation, and the "wager" in the following paragraph, also echo Pascal's *Pensées.*

way out of that contradiction. I am fearful of proposing something insufferably dainty to my listeners. Our young scouts are beginning to suspect that the somber world of the Fall is a jungle in which one pays dearly for the pleasure of playing Robinson Crusoe and dancing carefree around a bonfire on the evening of the summer solstice. But we must first wrench ourselves out of the giant's grasp, remove his hands from our throats, and get his knee off our chest. Then it will be time to learn how a free nation can become a mighty nation, and how a mighty nation can still be a just nation.

"Written on January 1, 1944," was published clandestinely in the *Almanach des Lettres françaises* in March 1944 by the Comité National des Ecrivains, the group spearheading the literary resistance. Mauriac's article, unsigned, as were all the others for reasons of security, appeared with articles by a number of other notable literati and again took up the problem of history in human and ethical terms.[35] Mauriac's first priority here is to galvanize the spirit of resistance among his readers by affirming a humanist vision which rejects the notion that a combination of might, numbers, and implacably faceless forces determines the course of human events, as the Fascists would have it. Though dwarfed in numbers and military might by the Allies as well as by the Axis powers, France could still play an important role in defeating the Nazis, insists Mauriac, by demonstrating its courage and commitment to the cause of freedom.

Mauriac's adamant refusal to acquiesce to the determinist view of events also underscores the full responsibility not only of those who coldly calculated and carried out the Nazi crimes, but also of those French citizens who collaborated with them and who now sought to mitigate their guilt by denying the choices that were theirs. It was they who in effect celebrated France's defeat in 1940, claiming opportunistically that events had proved the inferiority of France's Third Republic and of its leaders and the ne-

35. Contributors included Georges Adam, Louis Aragon, Jean Blanzat, Jacques Debû-Bridel, Colette Duval, Paul Eluard, Jean Guéhenno, Joliot-Curie, Fernand Leriche, Jean Lescure, Claude Morgan, and Édith Thomas in March 1944. http://www.revues-litteraires.com/articles.php?lng=fr&pg=401), reprinted in facsimile as *Almanach des Lettres françaises* (1944) (Rambouillet: Société des Amis de Louis Aragon et Elsa Triolet, 2002), n.p.

cessity of obeying Pétain and collaborating with Nazi Germany. With renewed opportunism, they were now discouraging their compatriots from taking part in the fierce battles in which they claimed France had no stake. And indeed, many of them, beginning with Pierre Laval, had accepted and even volunteered to do the Germans' bidding. Later they claimed that they had only collaborated with Nazi Germany in order to protect the French people and better advance the interests of the nation. In the perpetration of historical crimes as well as in heroic attempts to oppose them, insists Mauriac, the exercise of human will is decisive.

Mauriac was also responding to comments on France delivered by Marshal Smuts. As prime minister of South Africa and a member of Britain's war cabinet, Smuts had on November 20, 1943, sketched out a map of geopolitical power of the world that would be newly fashioned by the outcome of the war. The old Europe was gone, asserted Smuts, and three of its former stalwarts, France, Italy, and Germany, had ceased to exist as major powers. While the British Empire would emerge more glorious than ever, it would nevertheless be dwarfed by the size, resources, and military strength of both the USSR and the United States. Under those circumstances, suggested Smuts, Britain should cultivate close relations with the smaller European powers who could not stand up to the Soviet Union on their own. Shocked by Smuts's blunt assessment, the French nevertheless strengthened their resolve to strive for a significant role in defeating Nazi Germany.[36]

Mauriac could never resign himself to such a bleak, fatalistic assessment for France. As if to further emphasize the fundamentally human and therefore non-predetermined character of historical events, Mauriac has recourse to personification. First he depicts France as one of those who, crucified by the German aggressor, will come down from that cross to sit in judgment and behold Germany on its own scaffold. Then a rapid succession of images toward the end of the article dramatizes an exhortation to resist. France appears first as a mother abandoned by her children, then as buried alive, and finally as the victim of a vicious aggressor: though pinned to the ground with a knee at her throat, she nevertheless struggles vigorously to escape.

36. See Yves Durand, *Histoire de la Deuxième Guerre mondiale* (Paris: Editions Complexe, 1988), 419–21.

Written on January 1, 1944

L'Almanach des Lettres françaises, March 1944

History is heroic and criminal because human beings create it in their own image. Never have I been less convinced that the course of history is ineluctably determined than in these first days of the year of grace, 1944. History is determined by the will of a small number of human beings. They themselves may be driven by various necessities. But for the immediate future, it is indeed human will—that is, the will of a few human beings—that renews the face of the earth. For the last twenty years, one Austrian and a few Germans have been driving their people down this terrible road with no return, and now we see the last turning point, where they have to restrain themselves from crying out as they continue to go forward.

Now these men knew what they were doing from the very outset: they measured the terrifying risk and agreed to take it. It is unimaginable and yet true that from the beginning they had envisaged the worst, namely that the Apocalypse would be unleashed on their old Germania according to their predictions. They always believed that, faced with either Europe's total domination or this ultimate horror, they did not have a choice. But they also believed, and perhaps they still strive to believe, that the abyss opening up under their feet would not engulf pell-mell both victor and vanquished. What they would consider tragic would be for them alone to collapse in the middle of a resuscitated Europe. That is the fate that the most intrepid among them do not dare to look squarely in the face. Having agreed to disrupt the entire planet, they had imagined Germany rising back up out of universal ashes. But now they shudder before this one single scaffold from which hangs a defeated Germany, surrounded by all the nations that it crucified and that have descended from their crosses to stand in judgment.

In order to protest against this nightmare, French journalists on the Occupying Forces' payroll pretend to believe that if ever Germany were to be crushed, France would in any case no longer exist. These are the same Frenchmen who in 1939 were openly wishing for France to be defeated, because France embodied all that they hate just as the enemy embodies all that they adore. Today, these same Frenchmen strive to persuade us that the great Nation has finished living and that she will no longer exist as anything more than a miserable satellite state of one of the great triumphant Empires.

Already in 1918, they had in their hearts judged that the strongest had been denied victory due to a coalition. Monsieur Drieu La Rochelle was already coming out with his *Mesure de la France*. They have never stopped conducting such measurements. They have incessantly recounted these poor forty million inhabitants, first with a legitimate anxiety, still penetrated with a remnant of love, then with spite and with an irritation that turned into rage and furor. For indeed this miserable little people had kept the habits they had when they were still a great Nation: they had the gall not to adore might and to refuse to submit to it. And as from one year to the next, the immense shadow of the Hitlerian colossus extended over them in their divisions and weakness, this pygmy nevertheless remained faithful to the liberty that it had taught the world to love. These poor forty million French people still clung with all their heart and all their mind to all the outmoded values that Maurras and his followers had criticized and derided for almost a half a century.

To the secret or proclaimed delight of the French Fascists, the incorrigible nation received the wages of its stubborn determination in 1940: it had to agree to be governed by the men that it had always viscerally rebuffed when it was free and sovereign. These men believed that one lost battle forever determined the fate of France and Europe. They were blinded by joy: they mistook this prologue to an immense drama for its outcome. They gloated and spoke of a divine surprise ...[37] But having started out so bad, the nation bounced back, as gigantic protagonistes joined in the fray. That's the weakness of might, so to speak: it always risks being outclassed. The great Nietzschean power gnashed its teeth and flexed its muscles ... But the fact is that the con-

37. "La divine surprise" was the title of an article published by Charles Maurras in February 1941, expressing delight in seeing Pétain at the helm in France. See Olivier Dard and Michel Grunewald, eds., *Charles Maurras et l'étranger—L'étranger et Charles Maurras. L'Action française—culture, politique, société II* (Bern: Peter Lang, 2009), 109.

queror of the little French nation is already tottering. Monsieur Drieu La Rochelle had not foreseen this reality, but one has to give him credit for overtly noting as much. What the author of *Mesure de la France* is now sizing up precisely in his articles for *Révolution nationale* is a vanquished Germany.[38] A lot of good it does for a nation to number eighty million souls! That is what Drieu ponders every Friday with a candor that testifies to the fact that his masters have better things to do than to correct his paper these days.

He pretends like he is putting Germany on the same level as France along with the little countries whose fate has been sealed and who will have no choice other than to obey one of the masters of the planet and so get worked to death. But at the bottom of his heart, Monsieur Drieu recognizes the fact that these two nations have a different destiny, because, thanks to the heroism of her children who have not betrayed her, France will occupy a place—alas, a modest place!—at the victor's table.

The last hope for the Frenchmen serving Germany is for that place to be so small and for France to be reduced to such a degree that their collaboration with the enemy might lose all importance. They do not want to hear about anything other than great empires. This is a proverbial smokescreen. Wherever nations no longer exist, the word betrayal no longer means anything to anyone: you cannot betray a dead nation. Just look at these phony orphans pretending to believe that they no longer have a mother! If they have kissed the victor's knees, it is because they no longer have anyone to turn to: "Look," they say, "your best friends like Marshal Smuts agree that France is dead. Who could blame us for having devoted our affection to Europe since the love for our mother country now has no object?"

The dead do not hear the speeches that their friends give at their grave. France must indeed be alive in order for her to hear every word from the bottom of her tomb: friends are mourning her and believe her to be dead, but the adversary who has a stranglehold on her and who

38. Published in 1922, Drieu la Rochelle's book *Mesure de la France* bemoans the fact that the Great War had weakened France. *Révolution nationale* was a collaborationist review, as indicated by its name, taken from the label officially given to Pétain's political agenda.

> for three years has been shoving his knee into her chest, perhaps better than France's friends, this adversary hears her heart beating and feels her immense body tensing up. He knows that his victim is resisting, suffering, waiting, and hoping, and that she is being fortified by all the tears and blood shed by her sons and daughters.

Liberation and the Discovery of Genocide

Upon his triumphant arrival in Paris on August 25, 1944, de Gaulle was acclaimed at the city hall, where he punctuated the liberation of the French capital with a rousing, oft-cited speech celebrating the long-awaited restoration of national sovereignty. Pierre Brisson, editor in chief of *Le Figaro*, requested Mauriac to compose "The Very First among Our Own" in anticipation of a special occasion.[39] As if swept up in the same patriotic euphoria after having endured more than four years of humiliation, sorrow, and anxiety, Mauriac rivals de Gaulle in eloquence. On the one hand, he expresses the widely shared spirit of patriotic unity rallying Catholics and Communists, cosmopolitan intellectuals and aristocratic nationalists, in common resistance to the Nazi oppressor. Declaring at the outset that "France's hope reposed on the shoulders of one man" and reemphasizing national unity at the very end in wishing that "no force in the world may ever again pit against each other these French citizens that de Gaulle has united in the Resistance," Mauriac was heralding one of de Gaulle's most important achievements, that of bringing together under his authority as the head of the Provisional Government of the French Republic the many resistance groups that had at first sprung up independently, organized according to a wide variety of professional and political orientations. The divisions running through France's legendarily fractious population had indeed been particularly deep and rancorous throughout the crisis-ridden 1930s and would soon prove highly problematic in the aftermath of the war and German occupation, for violent conflicts pitting the Resistance against Vichy and pro-Nazi collaborators had brought the country to the brink of civil war.

39. Lacouture, *Mauriac. 2. Un citoyen du siècle 1933–1970*, 169–70.

In order to underscore all that made de Gaulle the rallying point for the various resistance organizations and for the French nation as a whole, Mauriac recalls his dramatic beginnings as a relatively unknown general, issuing from London over the BBC a call to continue the war. He then proceeds to celebrate de Gaulle as the salutary leader whose unrelenting efforts in the most dire of circumstances had enabled France to return to its proud heritage as a beacon of liberty and enlightenment. For Mauriac, de Gaulle appears as the very embodiment of France. From the very first lines, de Gaulle embodies and voices the hopes of the nation. He even appears as a savior figure, offering up his very person to his humiliated mother country, which Mauriac personifies first as a prisoner gagged, bound, and destined to be executed. Then, in terms alluding to the humiliation of Christ, Mauriac specifically cites Victor Hugo's memorable personification of France as a white-robed maiden. The rhetoric of personification also takes on religious overtones when Mauriac describes de Gaulle's present vocation as maintaining a deep communion among the various groups having sacrificed their lives in resistance. Mauriac goes so far as to present de Gaulle as the "living Symbol" of all those baptized in the blood of martyrdom.

While unequivocally celebrating the Resistance and the restoration of the Republic, with its concomitant values of representative democracy and civil liberties, Mauriac nevertheless displays his attachment to a traditional conception of a nation whose citizens are bound by blood and history. He moreover vaunts a leader whose legitimacy has been conferred not only by elections, but also by an innate capacity to embody France in his very person. Ironically, Pétain had used similar language when on June 16, 1940, he announced that as the new premier, he was offering up his very person to ease France's suffering. We shall see that during the marshal's trial in the summer of 1945, Mauriac remained troubled by the person of Pétain, and that during the 1960s, he would repeatedly hail de Gaulle as the very embodiment of France's restored grandeur.

The Very First among Our Own

Le Figaro, August 25, 1944

In the saddest hour of our destiny, France's hope reposed on the shoulders of one man, and was expressed by the voice of that man and that man alone. How many did they number, those French citizens who then came to share in his solitude, those who had in their own manner understood what it meant to "make a gift of one's person to France"?

Be they now living or dead, these yeomen of the first hour will remain embodied for us in the leader who had called them. After having left everything behind, they followed him, while so many others held their fingers to the wind seeking out their own advantage and betraying their country.

It is to him and to them that, unbound and freed from its gag, France cries out; it is to him and to them that, freed from the executioner's stake, she stretches out her poor hands.

France remembers: Vichy had condemned this man to death in absentia. The young French military commander who had been the first in Europe to discern and define the new conditions of waging war was thus condemned and cursed by an old marshal who had been blind to them for twenty years. The lackeys of the French press working for the oppressor covered him with sneers and insults. But throughout all these evenings of the ferocious winter, we remained there with our ears glued to the radio, while the footsteps of the German officer shook the ceiling over our heads. We kept on listening with our fists clenched, without holding back our tears. We would run to alert those in the family who were not yet listening: "General de Gaulle is going to speak … he's speaking!" At the height of the Nazi triumph, everything that is being accomplished today under our eyes was being announced by this prophetic voice.

Because of him, and because of those who were the first to take part in his solitude, we did not lose heart. In those days, our eyes dared not measure the interminable road of the cross that remained for us to travel and we did not imagine that this Frenchman would garner our infinite gratitude with other accomplishments. But when we saw him defending year after year the sovereignty of a France that had been vanquished and humiliated, we loved him even more for such patient and unfailing dignity! We were wholeheartedly with him throughout these talks that we surmised were exhausting, just as at certain times we sensed and shared his suffering!

Let us be perfectly clear on this point so as to dispel any misgivings from the very outset. In 1830 and 1850, when the ruling classes rushed to kneel down before Louis-Philippe and Napoleon III, they were giving themselves over to feelings that were doubtless excusable, but they appear abject to us today. Do we really need to declare that none of us, not one member of the Resistance held de Gaulle to be an iron-fisted soldier who would use force to keep the nation obedient or who would with sword in hand defend the privileges of a few?

In my view, he represents on the contrary the figure he was from the very outset: he who suddenly rose up to defend the cause of liberty that had been betrayed. In those days, Vichy's disciples of Maurras were trembling with joy as they were finally trying out their system on a France that had been beaten down. It was then that this Frenchman, who had by some mysterious predestination inherited the very name of ancient Gaul, wiped the spit off the face of the defiled Republic. As for me, who, I must confess, had no longer believed in the Republic since my teenage years, I finally recognized the Republic of our forebears and believed in its resurrection.

Today de Gaulle is bringing back to us this trust that France, betrayed and delivered into the hands of its enemies, had placed in him. He is rendering it not only to us who belong to the French bourgeoisie, but to the entire nation, of which each part and each class have provided their contingent of hostages and martyrs. In a France thus restored to itself, his mission is to maintain a deep communion with the image of the France that, in mass graves, mingles the bodies of murdered Communists with those of murdered priests.

De Gaulle did not charge himself with this mission. As soon as the prisoners and the deported have emerged from their hell, France will be summoned to ratify the vote of the millions among the living and the dead who have given all in order that the light of this day of all days should at last shine forth.

The Fourth Republic is the daughter of these martyrs. She has been born in blood, but in the blood of martyrs. This blood of Communists, nationalists, Christians, and Jews has baptized us all with the same baptism, of which General de Gaulle stands among us as the living Symbol. What a number of inherited or acquired inclinations he had to vanquish in order to become this man who has expressed the entire, indivisible soul of this poor French nation divided against itself! What a number of mental habits he had to surmount! It behooves each of us to achieve such a victory over ourselves.

We have no illusions about humankind; we know very well that most seek their own interest. The goal that we must reach is that the Fourth Republic should enter into History in the way dreamed of by those who were not seeking their own interest, since they gave their life. Our goal is to carve out this Republic lovingly, in likeness to the invisible face that beheld the last gaze of Gabriel Péri, Abbé Tiat, Decour, Politzer, Father Guilhaire, Roger Pironneau, Estienne d'Orves, and Abbé Gilbert ...

This evening, I am thinking back to the verses of Victor Hugo with which I often soothed my suffering during these past four years:

> O Free France arisen at last!
> O white robe washed clean of the stain![40]

May God grant that this white robe, like the seamless garment of Christ, stay indivisible, and that no force in the world may ever again pit against each other these French citizens that de Gaulle has united in the Resistance.

40. Victor Hugo's original text reads:

> O libre France enfin surgie!
> O robe blanche après l'orgie!
> O triomphe après les douleurs!
> Le travail bruit dans les forges,
> Le ciel rit, et les rouges-gorges
> Chantent dans l'aubépine en fleurs!
> [... O triumph after the suffering!
> Work rustles in the forges,
> The sky laughs, and the robin redbreasts
> Sing in the flowering hawthorn bushes!]

See http://www.poesie.webnet.fr/lesgrandsclassiques/poemes/victor_hugo/lux.html. The translation is my own.

As announced by the title of this article published by the vanguard of French intellectual resistance, "The French Nation Has a Soul" focuses on the image of a woman humiliated, martyred, yet finally resurrected and holding her children to her bosom. While using animal imagery to foreground the particularly violent ways in which the Nazis, aided by Vichy, lashed out against the Resistance while oppressing the French population in general, this iteration of Mauriac's repeated personification of France emphasizes first and foremost the special character which confers a specific vocation to the French people. In portraying France as a person, Mauriac borrows from the nineteenth-century historian Jules Michelet. Championing the common people, the French Revolution, and the Republic, Michelet insisted that the French people collectively remember the experience of trials and tribulations over the course of their centuries-long quest for justice and freedom not only from one event to another but even from one era to the next and indefinitely.[41]

Having for centuries enjoyed the prestige of constituting one of Europe's preeminent powers, France had indeed come close to being not only dominated but absorbed by the so-called new European order that the Nazis were claiming to establish for the next millennium. While doing little to discourage Vichy from pursuing its illusory goal of becoming a privileged partner of Nazi Germany, Hitler had in fact planned to relegate France to the very caricature that Mauriac so indignantly rejects: that of a quaint, picturesque land with wines, cheeses, and luxury goods appreciated by tourists.[42] Having endured so much and paid such a heavy cost in terms of lives lost and destruction occasioned by the ongoing combat to liberate France, Mauriac like the vast majority of his compatriots was keen on winning proper respect from the "noble and powerful allies" (and in particular, Franklin D. Roosevelt) who had not yet given due recognition to de Gaulle, the Resistance, and the French nation in general. Hence the references to the "triumphant behemoths" and "dominant empires," who in pursuing world affairs seem only to follow calculations of economic

41. Paule Petitier, "Introduction," in *Histoire de France: choix de textes présentés par Paule Petitier* by Jules Michelet (Paris: Flammarion, 2008), 10.

42. Burrin, *La France à l'heure allemande*, 54–55, 92–103.

and military power. Tacitly acknowledging the impossibility of competing with the United States or the Soviet Union on that material level, Mauriac identifies the soul of France as stemming not from bloodlines or the land, but from its humanist vocation of inspiring young hearts and minds to pursue the ideals of freedom and civilization. Here again, Mauriac echoes Michelet, who portrayed the French nation as the champion of the democratic ideals it had largely invented and as the rightful leader of the world.[43]

The French Nation Has a Soul

Lettres françaises, September 9, 1944

It is not possible for us to pride ourselves on anything but our faith, which throughout the nightmare of these four years has in the end not died out. Even in June 1940, when it was easy for the Third Reich to shout its joy to all the microphones of the Western world, just as it was easy for the Maurrassians at Vichy to tremble with joy as they finally tried out their ideology in a France that had been emptied by all of the octopus's tentacles and suction cups, yes, even then we remained wildly hopeful.

It is not that we had always remained unaware of the temptation to despair, especially during these last months, as the beast's paws tightened its grip to the point of cutting off our breath. As the beast's blood was flowing from a thousand wounds, we felt caught in the stranglehold of its last convulsion. It may seem strange that we should at times have had to struggle against a mortal anguish when we were so close to deliverance.

Yes, I am well aware of the monotonous rumbling of death under the sun or the stars, and the old home shuddering with all its windowpanes, and France's young people hunted down by Vichy's cops serving the Minotaur, and our friends suddenly disappeared, and these torture chambers where we knew they had refused to talk, and the firing squads greeting each dawn of those radiant springs and of those

43. Tzvetan Todorov, *Nous et les autres: la réflexion française sur la diversité humaine* (Paris: Éditions du Seuil, 1989), 284–85.

summers when it never rained, and, resounding twice a day to our never ending shame, Philippe Henriot giving Vichy's call to commit all sorts of cowardly acts ... And yet, no, all those horrors were not in the end sufficient to keep us down: under the blows of outrageous fortune, what old bruised nag would not have picked itself up off its trembling feet with one last burst of energy?

And we did indeed keep picking ourselves up. Thank God we never doubted that France was to live once again. But did we give any thought to what her place would be once the great storm was over, or to what rank she risked finding herself reduced? Would she still have enough strength to maintain herself there? Among the traitors, the cleverest clearly sensed our anxiety: all their speeches and writings aimed to stir it up. If they had managed to persuade us that the great nation of yesteryear would no longer be anything more than a stooge in the conflict of empires, they would have with one fell stroke also been absolved of guilt in their view and ours: wherever nations no longer exist, the word treason no longer has any meaning. How happy they would have been if they had been able to pass off France as being dead! For one could not betray a dead nation! To hear it the way they tell it, they had kissed the victor's knees because they no longer had a homeland to turn to. From a distance, we observed these phony orphans who pretended to believe that they no longer had a mother country.

Are we going to keep on questioning ourselves with a heart devoured by worry and doubt? We weren't so demanding in the first days of our slavery. It was hardly a matter of what place France would later hold among the nations of the world or of the hegemony that she had lost! In those instants, there was for her no other dilemma than to be or not to be. The one and only anxiety clutching our throats was that she should not die before being delivered, that she might survive, that she might make it through. Covered with wounds and bleeding yet, but alive among all the living nations, she rises up before Europe, holding tightly against her bosom her sons and daughters that have delivered her.

Are we going to turn our backs on the joy of this resurrection and, along with the likes of Drieu La Rochelle, incessantly go back over the number of each empire's inhabitants and square kilometers and, with these statistics in hand, doom France to be no more than a miserable satellite country of one of these triumphant behemoths?

When those who expect to gain everything from our despair tirelessly shove our noses into these figures that register the economic power of each nation, I'll grant you that it does no good to cover our eyes. Yes, even a restored France will find itself relegated to a modest rank, and on that score, there remains no chance for us to regain the first place. We could doubtless try to act like Machiavellians and argue that none of the dominant empires has received promises that it will be there forever, that each of them bears within it elements of disintegration and deadly germs, that their respective interests pit them against each other, and that a France having once again become the first of the second tier nations would find in such antagonism the basis of a grand political strategy. Actually, no: Machiavelli's point of view is not ours, for we ardently desire that a grateful France look her noble and powerful allies in the eye without the slightest hint of any ulterior motive. With their aid, we will not abandon the hope of lightening the burden weighing the heaviest on human destiny. Amid the killing fields, we proclaim our faith in a world where all the power of our minds and all the goodness of young hearts will no longer be used for committing collective murder and destroying the cathedrals inhabited by God and the outskirts of our cities inhabited by the poor.

We believe that a resurrected France must lay claim to a grandeur of that order. Those who are betting on our humiliation and our infinite fatigue will in vain add another negative trait to the self-image that they are trying to impose on us every day: it is a caricature of an old, backward, decrepit, agrarian nation from which the magnates of two worlds expect nothing but cheeses, wines, and fashion models. We shall tirelessly remind them of what they are pretending to forget and which is in their interest to forget: the French nation has a soul.

Yes, a soul. I am not unaware of the fact that certain words irritate the French people of 1944.

"The Eyes of the Dead" provides us a glimpse of the Occupation that Mauriac experienced in the most direct and concrete manner both in his ancestral estate of Malagar in the Bordeaux region and at Vémars, just north of Paris, where German soldiers leaving the area would pass through and camp in his yard. The proximity of the occupying forces and the repulsive odor of urine that they leave in Mauriac's yard only heighten the joy of deliverance. It is from his own experience at Malagar that Mauriac draws the depiction of friends huddled over the radio listening to de Gaulle's broadcasts from London (both forbidden and scrambled by the Germans) while the German officer having requisitioned lodging paces back and forth in his upstairs room. That this scenario of an isolated group of individuals stubbornly clinging to their sense of integrity and hope even in the presence of a German officer is reminiscent of one of the most celebrated works of Resistance literature, Jean Bruller's *The Silence of the Sea* is most probably not merely coincidental. As one of the most prestigious writers contributing to the *Lettres françaises*, Mauriac would have surely received a copy of the work that had been of necessity and at great risk clandestinely printed (using highly coveted and difficult to obtain ink and paper) and distributed to select members of the underground movement.[44]

Once again we find France personified in the form of the feminine effigy of its capital city, more crucially emblematic of national identity than any other capital: "to look at Paris is to look France in the face," notes Mauriac. Like de Gaulle in his oft-cited speech given at the city hall on August 25, 1944, Mauriac proudly underscores that Paris has liberated itself from the Nazi stranglehold. In order to emphasize France's grandeur in spite of its humiliating failures and painful ordeals, Mauriac hails the Liberation celebrated with church bells and also recalls the feast day of Saint Louis and the nation's royal heritage. At the same time, he gravely ponders the legacy of the Resistance, of martyred towns such as Oradour-sur-Glane, and of the Jews, whose unspeakable suffering and death were hidden from public view, but whose gaze, he suggests, solemnly follows him and his compatriots.

44. See Lawrence D. Stokes, "Historical Introduction," in Vercors [Jean Bruller], *The Silence of the Sea / Le Silence de la mer*, ed. James W. Brown and Lawrence D. Stokes, trans. Cyril Connelly (New York: Berg Publishers, 1991).

The Eyes of the Dead

Le Figaro, September 1, 1944

My torment recalls that of Tantalus, as thirty kilometers separate me from Paris now liberated. I, listening to the crowd noises and strains of "La Marseillaise" over the radio, but the enemy's trucks are still passing by the front of the house. There, where as late as yesterday they were camping in the yard, the awful stench of latrines that they always leave is still lingering under the trees.

So I close my eyes and seek euphoria by envisioning the sky above the Place de la Concorde now free of the hideous flags that used to wave there. The swastika no longer profanes the view. Our clear blue sky is no longer darkened by this spider swollen with blood. This day must be dedicated to you, tortured hostages, French youth shot dead and left on the roadsides, women and newborn children of the village of Oradour, farmers of the community of Ascq, Jewish children torn out of their mothers' arms and piled into boxcars like lambs: in one fell stroke, this day redeems so many unprincipled deeds, complicities, and crimes.

We dedicate this day to you, whom the collaborators never spoke of in their newspaper articles. It was never about you in those papers. We can go back over this entire set of writings: in vain would we seek a single allusion to what you have suffered. These gentlemen were approaching things on a higher level. They were holding forth on nations fading away and empires dominating the world. Drieu la Rochelle, as dogmatic as Bossuet, wrote his own sort of sequel to the latter's *Histoire universelle*.

These fine minds kept gliding high above the earth, but the common people, and especially the people of Paris were not: they were staying right next to the ground, hugging this earth that kept on indefinitely drinking the blood of Abel, this earth that was constantly being opened to receive the bodies riddled with bullets, whose eyes could not be shut by any friendly hand.

These eyes of the dead are still gazing down on Paris in these days of glory. To look at Paris is to look France in the face. With this dried blood on her face, this little France whose tight dimensions you never tired of recalling now stands before the world. Acknowledge now with us that she appears taller and more majestic than she ever was.

Paris: I remember an evening in the dark winter of 1940. We were in the living room of a home way out in the country, huddled around a little fire. Over our heads, the German officer's boots were tapping in the hall. In a hush, we were listening to a radio report from London about street singers in Paris. Suddenly there arose this poor old refrain, accompanied by an accordion: "Paris, queen of the world...."[45] Do you remember? This tune from the live music of a café, more sublime than any other music, tore our hearts apart. The enemy's heavy steps were still shaking the ceiling ... "Paris, queen of the world...." Even those of us who up until then had shown a stiff upper lip in the face of our destiny no longer attempted to hide their tears. We wept shamelessly in the presence of each other over Paris, this Paris that today has not been delivered but has delivered itself. No, this is not a dream: the City once profaned has sprung back up from its dung heap and has torn the green vermin off of her body. All the things that she had lost have been returned to her. And she is listening, holding her head high on this feast day of Saint Louis, king of France, to countless church bells ringing the most ecstatic *Te Deum* in history that ever resounded under its sky.

Only two weeks after the unconditional surrender of Nazi Germany had marked the triumphant resolution of the war for the Allies, "The Sages' Dream" shows Mauriac stepping back from the immediate situation to contemplate the deeper, long-term implications of the unprecedented violence that had characterized the conflict. It is in just such a piece as this that Mauriac so masterfully deploys his talents, not only as a political commentator but as a man of letters steeped in history and literature, and as a man of faith intent on approaching the sound and fury of history from the perspective of the Sermon on the Mount. The ultimate stakes of his reflec-

45. The words of this music hall song, whose lyrics were written by Lucien Boyer with music by José Padilla, can be found at http://www.franceinter.fr/evenement-paris-en-chansons.

tions here are of the highest order. Beyond the crucially important question of France's role in the new world order just emerging at the conclusion of the conflict are somber questions about the very character of humanity and the destiny of the human race, as posed by the dreadful use of military might by both the Allies and the Axis. In Stuttgart, Mauriac saw concrete evidence of the methodical dehumanization of prisoners in concentration camps and the industrial annihilation of peoples undertaken in the death camps.

Over seven decades later, one would be hard-pressed to dispute the major assessments that Mauriac delivers on the eve of the Cold War and the atomic age. Contrary to the fervent hopes of the Enlightenment and the smug pronouncements of late nineteenth-century positivists such as Anatole France, the advancement of science has not only failed to usher in an era of human harmony and understanding, but has all too often been exploited by the will to power of the newly dominant nations, namely, the United States and the Soviet Union. Their arms race confirmed the grim observation that an "Empire" would "not shy away from any of the various means of destruction with which researchers have equipped it." Equally perspicacious is the grim observation that humankind's massive and willing indulgence in the most degrading and destructive forms of violence had irremediably impacted the terms and concepts traditionally employed in speaking of the human condition and that as a result, "There are some pretty words that enchanted our forebears and that we no longer dare to pronounce." Though more stridently corrosive and subsequently qualified with a number of nuances, Theodor Adorno's assertion that it would be barbaric to indulge in poetry after Auschwitz points to the same dilemma facing those who pursue art, literature, and the humanities in general. It is only fitting that, instead of advancing some momentous conclusion or attempting to provide some intellectual resolution to the predicaments that he points out, Mauriac closes this piece simply by echoing the invitation of the disciples of Emmaus as a prayer.

The Sages' Dream

Le Figaro, May 22, 1945

In the rubble of Stuttgart, I remember the words that Anatole France, standing in front of the statue of Ernest Renan, had spoken in Tréguier in 1903: "Slowly but surely, humanity makes the sages' dreams a reality." One of the dreams entertained by the sage Renan was that one day a small number of scientists would hold the secret of destroying the planet and for that reason humans would have to obey. Today we can clearly see that if humanity has made the sages' dreams a reality, it is not without having given them some sinister modifications.

It is true that the laboratories of the United States have perfected their methods to the point where the last city leveled was done so in twenty-three minutes. An optimist might conclude that Renan proved to be a good prophet and that scientists will indeed have the last word—and that they will have the last say all the more since there will be no one else left. But Renan and his disciple Anatole France were quite naive to believe (after all, maybe they were just pretending) that the secrets of matter would be held by those who are virtuous. Why would the people who are mean not be good at experiments too? If, in the race to annihilation, the Third Reich's laboratories were defeated by those of the United States, they didn't do such a bad job, either: the furious madmen turned out to be skillful chemists, and they alone dared to carry out experiments on human guinea pigs. One of our friends' boy who was deported to Buchenwald bore the initials that meant "*Nacht und Nebel,*" night and fog: that mark pointed him out to the German researchers who were given license to use and abuse his young body. But the laboratory where he was supposed to end his life amid utter torment had been blown up the day before his arrival thanks to a bomb that had been perfected in New York. Thus the mad dream of the German was, thankfully for our friend, disturbed by that of the Anglo-Saxon sage.

But here's the worst part: it is not only the criminally insane fanatics and the virtuous sages who are arming themselves to face each other with terrifying inventions. This is not just about a duel unto death between the bad guys and the good guys. Was it possible for Renan and Anatole France to believe that sages never devour each other? Because it is the anonymous, impersonal result of laws over which individuals have no power, the Empires' will to power is an irrepressible instinct that does not shy away from any of the various means of destruction with which researchers have equipped it. Those are doubtless bitter thoughts, but they are salutary. In 1903, Anatole France's contemporaries resembled the sleepwalker singing as he ran near the edge of the roof. We, however, are terribly awake. At Buchenwald, Auschwitz, Ravensbrück, and Dachau, we have seen just how far humanity can go in its ferocity, and, alas, to what extent humans are capable of degrading their fellow human beings by depriving them of bread. Humanity has been forever awakened, but it has also been unmasked. It has stopped trying to fool people. There are some pretty words that enchanted our forebears and that we no longer dare to pronounce, and the victorious nations scarcely ever resort anymore to the old diplomatic language in order to cover up what opposes them.

We know what remains: what word, what hope that are still the same, and for almost two thousand years have been the only things that have withstood all of destiny's denials. Here we see that the least Christian among us are tempted to repeat the prayer of the two men who were pilgrims on the road to Emmaus, spoken to that Stranger on the threshold of the dark inn: "Stay with us, for the day is declining...."[46]

Taken from the German, as Mauriac explains, "Night and Fog" was also used by Alain Resnais as the title for the haunting, if somewhat flawed, documentary about German atrocities, whose script was written by Jean Cayrol, a friend of Mauriac's from Bordeaux deported for Resistance activity. What is remarkable is that, not content to take stock of the unspeakable cruelty that the Germans perpetrated with industrial efficiency, Mauriac insists that these crimes are in no way restricted to the Germans:

46. Luke 24.29.

they point to unsettling truths about the human condition and thus summon humanity to search its soul. In the immediate aftermath of the war, it would have been tempting to attribute the capacity for unfathomable evil to an enemy regime and its followers, particularly for a French citizen having endured the German occupation marked by severe shortages of basic necessities, suppression of civil liberties, and harsh reprisals for any and all forms of resistance. Mauriac instead identifies the potential for the most destructive and degrading forms of violence as part and parcel of humanity, found in every person and within every culture. Hence his ironic variation on one of the most well-known lines from Descartes's *Discourse on the Method*: "cruelty [and not common sense] is the most commonly shared thing in the world." Less than a decade later, the widespread use of torture and extrajudicial executions by French police and armed forces in Morocco and Algeria would prompt Mauriac to develop this point more fully, and to charge that the French were in fact using the same methods as the Nazis.

Nacht und Nebel [Night and Fog]

Le Figaro, June 15, 1945

A few weeks ago, I made reference to the initials of *Nacht und Nebel*, "night and fog," that in the punitive concentration camps doomed a category of young men to be used as guinea pigs for scientific research. Under this label, these unfortunate individuals were subject to unlimited exploitation. An anonymous correspondent has informed me (was I perhaps the only one to be unaware of the fact?) that in Wagner's *Das Rheingold*, "*Nacht und Nebel*" are the first of the magic words which enabled Alberich with his helmet to disappear, replaced by a cloud of fog: "In Buchenwald," my kind correspondent adds, "they saw to it that these magic words actually took effect."

These Germans will never cease to amaze us. What is stunning is not so much their cruelty, even though it surpasses all measure. Actually, cruelty is the most commonly shared thing in the world, since all peoples have their manner of ferocity: in one case, they're more skilled at burning, and in another, they lynch better than anybody. There are specializations of torture, with each nation having a particular style. But, with their research into the most profitable tortures, their rationalization of crime, and their special way of combining sadistic desire with scientific research, the Germans are champions over us all with their method of applying mass murder, and particularly in destroying an entire people. Yes, nobody in the world can remain ignorant of that fact any longer, and the Germans' preeminence can no more be challenged. The fact remains that, at least for me, the Wagnerian origin of *Nacht und Nebel* opens a new perspective on the German abyss, and therefore on the human abyss, for in the end the Germans are human beings.

I had always thought that artists, especially poets, and musicians as well as any person worthy of understanding them, carried within an intact purity and a secret, unscathed childhood, even as guilty as they might have been, even beneath the heap of sins accumulated over the course of a lifetime, despite their most lamentable deeds. The foul transgressions of the likes of Baudelaire, Verlaine, or Rimbaud are covered by this night of inspiration, by the fog of this dream: *Nacht und Nebel* ... And one would almost say that this deep darkness and this fog purify them.

I know someone particularly fond of Mozart and who, throughout these four years of abomination, was not able to listen to a single one of the records that formerly helped him to live, for the abyss that had opened up between celestial music and this era doomed to be murderous was too wide and deep. In his view, the divine art no longer had anything in common with the criminal reality of life. But now we see that, on the contrary, music and poetry inspired crime for the Germans during these years. Wagner came out of his grave to collaborate with the executioner and the cry from the victim's slit throat became a kind of note in the symphony.

This is one more sign among a thousand others of the total subversion of the German mind. And I wonder: how should we treat this strange, monstrous patient? What will our reaction to him be? Abel, what are you going to do with your brother Cain? I'm specifically wondering about our personal attitude, about the manner in which each of us will envisage the Germanic problem for ourselves. Now as far

> as the great victorious empires and their political strategy toward the vanquished ... Let's hope that they will not hole up in their respective zones, motivated by the sole desire of using them and fortifying them with God knows what ulterior motives! If that is the way it should turn out to be, a sad burst of laughter would arise out of the deep darkness and fog—*Nacht und Nebel*—that shrouds a destroyed Germany, and a voice, perhaps the voice of Hitler or the voice of mankind's eternal Enemy, would cry out to us: "I succeeded after all!"

"The Rest Is Silence" confronts the fact that, instead of immunizing against such collectively planned, organized, and executed acts of prolonged atrocity, or serving as antidotes, close knowledge of art and science have been exploited in the conception and realization of collective crimes. That is why Mauriac ponders the implications of the war for writers whose vocation it is "to understand, interpret, and transpose the world." Largely indifferent to history and politics during the 1930s in spite of many momentous developments, Jean-Paul Sartre famously pointed to his personal experience of the war—first as a meteorological observer stationed on the border with Germany and subsequently as a prisoner of war in a *Stalag*—as providing the shock of discovering history and thus the necessity of taking sides politically. Sartre avows that this is the case even or especially in works of literature, as he maintains at length in his famous essay "Qu'est-ce que la littérature?" ("What Is Literature?"), which not coincidentally also dated from the postwar period.[47]

By contrast, Mauriac was embroiled in the polemics of partisan politics throughout the decade preceding the war, just as he had been from his earliest involvement in journalism in the World War I era.[48] As the legendary figurehead of the team of intellectuals of *Les Temps modernes*, Sartre, as is often noted, served as a master thinker for the postwar generation and beyond. Insisting that artists must "situate" themselves decisively in politics and society "by situating" their productions with respect to the events

47. Jean-Paul Sartre, *Situations II* (Paris: Gallimard, 1948).

48. See John Flower, *François Mauriac, journaliste. Les vingt premières années, 1905–1925* (Bern: Peter Lang, 2011).

and issues of their time, Sartre championed the historical awareness and ideological commitment that became the hallmark of intellectuals in postwar France. The war and the Occupation had indeed occasioned a seismic shift not only in international affairs and domestic politics, but also in the realm of the arts and sciences. Not only here in "The Rest Is Silence," but throughout the articles penned in this twilight of the Second World War, Mauriac proves himself to be fully attuned to the unsettling realities of history. Pondering unprecedented violence visible in the camps and the widespread bombing of civilian populations, he points to the long-term repercussions not only in the domain of public affairs but equally in the world of letters. Here again he raises the question of humanity in general. As is repeatedly the case in Mauriac's editorials, the biblical narrative of Cain and Abel points to the criminal violence that has been part and parcel of human society from the very beginning. At the same time, Mauriac insists on each individual human's responsibility for the well-being of fellow humans.

The Rest Is Silence

Le Figaro, October 19, 1946

Throughout the entire day, I kept on seeing these gallows from another era.

In my mind, I had seen Goering's body carried into the torture chamber on a stretcher. The last words of certain condemned criminals unsettled me as does everything that bears out the following law: in order to reach his ends, the power of darkness uses even the sinner's virtues. If evil is a mystery even for the Christian who believes in redemption, here we have the most disturbing aspect of this mystery: the best part of us collaborates in our crimes.

And yet I managed to go to the theater that evening and sit down amid a noisy, happy crowd, without leaving the train of thought that had been sweeping me along: this was Hamlet played by Jean-Louis Barrault. Can one say that he was playing the part? He was Hamlet. He is Hamlet even when he is out on the town, and even when he is interpreting another role: he is always the Prince of Denmark who emerges out of a foreign text, and his burning gaze interrogates the ghost.

Shakespeare is for all times, but he corresponds closely to our own time, laying over it this style that it is still lacking and that we are incapable of providing. He brings to us this conscience, this power of "reflection" (in every sense of the word), that, faced with so much horror, one would say we have lost. The writers alive today are not up to the level of our everyday history, and it is doubtless not possible for them to be. We rush with avid admiration to get hold of books such as Hemingway's *For Whom the Bell Tolls*, but he only managed to write it by stepping back a bit from the Spanish Civil War that was fading away into the distance. As for the rest of us, how could we depict this horror in which we are still immersed?

The novel is dying of this contrast between the psychology of peaceful eras, which is its traditional subject matter, and, after a formidable seismic shift, this sudden appearance of the cavemen that we have remained. An entire superstructure of Christian feelings and knightly passions has been destroyed. In these outdated books in which we are buried, dilemmas of conscience have a miserable time outliving consciences that are dead. Fiction has lost its purpose. Other feelings are born, perhaps, out of this society that is decomposing (or perhaps in gestation?), in which we are surprised to be still breathing, but no great work has begun to express them. I discount these gloomy, monotonous obsessions of American eroticism that the young critics praise to the heavens.

The Marxist influence comes into play here. From their viewpoint, the Communists are right to teach that the important thing is not to interpret the world but to change it, which is moreover what Christians could say. In that way, however, they create an atmosphere unfavorable to artists whose vocation is precisely to understand, interpret, and transpose the world. And yet these monsters hanged by those who vanquished them were not hanged with an apparatus big enough to scare monsters of the same species, who are perhaps still prowling in the human jungle. We would only be able to incorporate both them and their judges in a new civilization through the work of art: only a work of art would justify that.

While waiting for the artist who will at last lend form and style to this epitome of abomination, we still have Shakespeare, whose genius is at the level of our ordeal perhaps more than he had been for the ordeal of his own time. He took what he needed in History, pillaging civilizations and centuries. If he had been able to rule over the eras that had not yet come into being, our own time would have held some prize game animals for him! What fauna for his use would he have found in the creatures that devour each other on a planet for which one imagines that a God is already concerned with numbering the atoms.

But if this Shakespeare were alive, he perhaps would not have been capable of uttering a word if he had witnessed what our eyes have seen. I kept reflecting on that yesterday evening, while listening to Hamlet sigh before our ephemeral crowd. Through the mask of Jean-Louis Barrault, the Danish prince seemed to be gazing out at us from the very end of the centuries: "The rest is silence."

3 ∽ POSTWAR TRIALS AND TRIBULATIONS

The Ordeal of the Purge

The widespread exultation that punctuated the Liberation of Paris quickly gave way to a host of sobering realities facing France in the fall of 1944. The military campaign to definitively defeat Nazi Germany was still far from over, many French cities and much of the country's infrastructure were in shambles, and a number of vexing political and judicial issues needed to be resolved. One of the most urgent was how to handle those who as Vichy officials or direct collaborators with the Nazis had perpetrated crimes. The head of France's Provisional Government, General Charles de Gaulle, was eager to reestablish the rule of law and thus put an end to the extrajudicial executions and settling of scores that the fierce battles of the previous summer had occasioned. As could have been expected given the huge number of trials hastily organized in difficult circumstances in an effort to settle the fate of thousands of prisoners, the process proved problematic and quickly gave rise to heated polemics. As perhaps the most prominent of

Parisian editorialists intervening in this matter, Mauriac penned a series of articles—indeed, no less than fifty from August 25, 1944, until the end of the year[1]—that illustrate the salient realities of French society and politics in the immediate postwar period.

We can once again clearly see that the role of writers and intellectuals was very serious business, particularly when they intervened in public debates by way of their newspaper editorials. It has often been observed that writers and intellectuals were much more harshly punished for collaboration than were businessmen and industrialists. Just as Mauriac and his counterparts risked everything merely by contributing pieces published clandestinely under the Occupation, so those writers and intellectuals who had placed themselves in the service of collaboration and Nazism faced capital punishment when, as in the cases of Georges Suarez, Paul Chack, Charles Maurras, and Robert Brasillach, their writings were considered to have directly contributed to the recruitment of French citizens into the German armed forces or to the arrest, deportation, or execution of Jews and members of the Resistance. It was doubtless thanks to one of Mauriac's editorials that Henri Béraud, pardoned by de Gaulle at the eleventh hour, escaped a similar fate.[2]

It was in this context that Mauriac, having begun his outspoken opposition to Fascism in the mid-1930s, and having now acquired a new legitimacy as a widely recognized member of the intellectual resistance, enjoyed even greater stature and prestige as an intellectual whose distinct voice counted in the public arena.[3] The singular position that Mauriac occupied on the Parisian political landscape stemmed from his equally singular personal and professional situation in the liberated capital. On the one hand, Mauriac maintained particularly strong ties with the Left. Within the ranks of the Communist-dominated *Lettres françaises*, recognized as the vanguard of the intellectual resistance, he placed himself in the curious, if not contradictory, position of an upper-class Catholic member of the Académie française (indeed, the only member to lend his voice to the Resistance) and fervent Gaullist who nevertheless remained intent on

1. Lacouture, *Mauriac. 2. Un citoyen du siècle 1933–1970*, 177.

2. Ibid., 196–99.

3. Barré, *Mauriac. Biographie intime, 2. 1940–1970*, 83.

pursuing his alliance with the Communists, just as they were equally keen on keeping him on board: the alliance thus modeled various components of French society and politics that had united in the Resistance under de Gaulle and were now determined to forge a vibrant future together.

Yet on the other hand, personal and family ties were pulling Mauriac toward the center right. His own considerable admiration for de Gaulle was evidenced in his vibrant editorial "The First of Our Own," while the head of the Provisional Government of France demonstrated his esteem for the writer by sending a car to bring him in for a personal meeting on September 1. In addition, Mauriac's eldest son, Claude, was serving as secretary to de Gaulle, who clearly told the young man, by necessity remaining at all times by his side, that his father would do him and the country a great service by conspicuously parting company from the Communists.[4] The fact that François Mauriac's own brother, Pierre Mauriac, a prominent doctor who presided over a professional organization, served as the dean of the medical school in Bordeaux, and had distinguished himself as a Pétainist, was accused of helping designate a Communist doctor for execution was doubtless weighing heavily on his mind.[5]

As has always been the case in France, advocating a just mean from a centrist perspective proved to be a difficult task. Vaunting their merits as "the party of those executed by firing squads," in other words, as the group who had paid the most dearly for their participation in the Resistance, the Communists were pushing for more severe punishments, while Mauriac argued for the presumption of innocence, the use of impartial jurors (instead of jurors selected on the basis of their participation in the Resistance), the recognition of certain extenuating circumstances for those having done little more than serve as officials for Vichy (since it had until November 8, 1942, been formally recognized by both the United States and the Soviet Union as the legal government of France), and a degree of clemency in the interest of national reconciliation.[6]

Such was the context for Mauriac's famous exchange of polemics with another prestigious writer acclaimed for his participation in the intellectu-

4. Lacouture, *Mauriac. 2. Un citoyen du siècle 1933–1970*, 172, 178–79.

5. Barré, *Mauriac. Biographie intime, 2. 1940–1970*, 126–31.

6. Lacouture, *Mauriac. 2. Un citoyen du siècle 1933–1970*, 183, 194.

al resistance, Albert Camus, then the star editorialist for the paper *Combat*. In view of the mistreatment and torture inflicted on the accused, Camus would grow disenchanted with the Purge in 1945 and concede in a letter sent to Mauriac in 1948 that his former adversary had been right to plead against the execution of those accused of collaboration. In the fall of 1944, however, Camus adamantly insisted on an implacable application of "human justice," satisfying the legitimate demands from the Resistance that collaborators pay for their offenses. He had no patience for what he disdainfully termed the "divine justice" defended by Mauriac, even though, as Lacouture points out, the latter was in fact basing his position not on theology but on well-established principles of justice in liberal democracies.[7] In any case, the selection of Mauriac's editorials reproduced here clearly articulate a nuanced, moderate position sensitive to the many conflicting aspects of events that were creating a vexingly complex situation.

Written only a couple of weeks after the momentous Liberation of Paris, "The Unyielding" proves that even amid the euphoria of the Liberation and while serving as one of the most prominent heralds of both Charles de Gaulle and the mainland Resistance within the Communist-dominated *Lettres françaises*, Mauriac neither forgot nor swept under the rug the widespread, ongoing support for Pétain and the sympathy for the latter's collaborationist policies. He thus recalls two hallmarks of French submission to the Nazis. First, he refers to Pétain's meeting with Hitler on October 24 at the little town of Montoire, from which the widely published photo of a handshake between the head of the French State (Vichy) and the Führer had left a lasting impression as the very emblem of the former's decision to engage in collaboration with Nazi Germany. Second, he points to the infamous declaration by Pétain's prime minister, Pierre Laval, who, on the day of Germany's invasion of the Soviet Union, June 22, 1941, had openly stated his support for the Nazis' Russian campaign. If Mauriac found it necessary to devote an entire editorial to denouncing the unrepentant intransigence of Vichy diehards, he gave tacit recognition to the reality that neither the partisans of Pétain nor the supporters of collaboration had been definitively marginalized at the time of Liberation.

7. Ibid., 193–95.

Nor does Mauriac refrain from citing some of the most unsavory and inglorious aspects of French collaboration, such as the fact that a significant portion of the propertied bourgeoisie was not displeased to do business with the Third Reich while seeing the working class held in check. He once again deploys a forceful battery of rhetorical artillery, likening de Gaulle to a prophet, the once again high-flying French flag to the wing of an archangel, and the Germans to pimps wallowing in the pleasure of their occupation of France.

The Unyielding

Le Figaro, September 6, 1944

During these days when everything, freedom, honor, and the joy of being able to look at people of another race in the face, has been given back to us, it is unimaginable and yet it is true that a few French people are secretly raging and turning their eyes away from this tremendous happiness. I'm not thinking of fifth column traitors or disguised members of Vichy's Militia here,[8] but of good people such as we have all known, who kept saying that Marshal Pétain was Joan of Arc, who had hung his picture over their bed, and who, today, behind their closed windows, dream gloomily of the fine evenings when Henriot was speaking on the radio.

There are still some such people, not many, of course, but more than one might think. Even a writer or a novelist whose profession it is to put himself in other people's shoes stands facing French people of this sort as if facing inscrutable monsters.

And just what were these wretched folks hoping and waiting for in the end? If the politics of Montoire had borne their fruit,[9] if in the

8. "La Milice," as it was called in French, was designated in January 1943 as the vanguard of Vichy's effort to repress the Resistance and track down Jews in hiding. Formed out of Vichy's official war veterans organization, a number of its members followed their leader, Joseph Darnand, in joining the Waffen SS. As the Occupation turned more and more violent in 1943 and 1944, the Militia became notorious for its brutality and use of torture. See "Milice française" in Bertram M. Gordon, ed., *Historical Dictionary of World War II France* (Westport, Conn.: Greenwood Press, 1998), 243–44.

9. It was at the train station in the little town of Montoire in the Loire valley that Pétain shook

unlikely case the French people had not reacted against the poison with which Henriot was massively injecting them every day,[10] do they dare contemplate the fate that would have been ours today? From London on June 22, 1940, General de Gaulle asked them the question: "No one can predict," the prophetic voice cried out to them, "whether the nations that are neutral today will remain neutral tomorrow and whether Germany's allies will always remain its allies. If the forces of liberty finally triumph over the forces of servitude, what would be the destiny of a France that would have submitted itself to the enemy?"

The ship of the French nation would find itself tied to the Nazis' vessel, which is already listing and from which rats are escaping. All would be lost, and honor first of all. My good people, it could not be such an abomination that you are regretting, could it? What, then? A German victory? "I hope that Germany will be victorious ..." Such a wish was indeed expressed by a government minister whose clever, sly dealings you kept vaunting: "It's the time for a horse trader, you were saying, France needs somebody slick to manage its business and snooker its trading partners ..."

In this breezy air that we now breathe, under the skies of Paris, under this light blue azure, where the French flag resembles the living wing of a great archangel that one cannot see, close your eyes and strive to imagine what that might have meant: the Alsace-Lorraine region, the North of France, and the Briey bassin would be lost forever, along with Corsica, the Savoy region, Nice, and Tunisia ... Actually, that's not going far enough: all would have been lost, since the Germans would have never finished with their occupation of our country. Oh, they really loved France, these Germans! They really loved it here! They settled in and wallowed in it. They would have never had their fill, because wolves are always hungry.

---

hands with Hitler, as recorded in a famous photo that became a detested emblem of Vichy's politics of collaboration.

10. Beginning in January 1944, Philippe Henriot served as Vichy's minister of information and propaganda, and used his considerable talents as an orator in radio talks that encouraged the French public to reject the Resistance and support the Germans. His assassination by the Resistance in June 1944 prompted fierce reprisals on the part of the Militia, which targeted Jews in particular in its numerous acts of murder. See "Henriot, Philippe," in Gordon, *Historical Dictionary of World War II France*, 177–78.

If that is not what you long for, then what is it? Perhaps that state of servitude in which, protected by Nazi tanks, one could after all go about one's little business in complete safety, provided that one was serving Germany. It was quite convenient, quite comfortable to work in a world where workers, as it were, could no longer be distinguished from the machines they were operating. And then, there was this unmentionable, but delectable secret satisfaction of seeing the Communists hunted down and the Jews hounded. In politics, there are some thirsts for revenge that one never tires of slaking.

These few French people gloated over the Occupation: "busy and contented," was regrettably their motto. They kept their eyes closed and did not notice that the Nazi pimp was losing blood and turning pale. These blind people did not see that what de Gaulle had prophesied on June 22, 1940, was actually happening: "The same conditions of war that caused us to be defeated by five thousand planes and six thousand tanks can in the future bring us victory by twenty thousand tanks and twenty thousand planes."

Will these last supporters of Vichy finally open their eyes to the light that bathes the mutilated palaces of the Place de la Concorde and that in our joyful streets shines in splendor on so many young faces delivered from bondage?

"True Justice" once again points to the sober reality that support for Vichy's politics of collaboration and repression and for Pétain had not magically vanished at the Liberation. That is why Mauriac underscores Pétain's fundamental hypocrisy: having claimed to be above and beyond politics in repeating that he "hate[d] these lies that [had] hurt [the French people] so much,"[11] Pétain was in fact "the person who exemplifie[d] them all." Far from any binary, Manichean view that would conveniently place perpetrators of atrocities into one national category, Mauriac suggests that the Occupation had occasioned a return to the sorts of repression and torture that had at times been implemented by "the inquisitors and magistrates of

11. See "La fin de la IIIe République," http://www.lexpress.fr/culture/livre/poches/la-fin-de-la-iiie-republique-l-effondrement-d-une-nation_1239102.html#cs7D5mrCPFVI9zGf.99.

the France of yesteryear." But Mauriac goes even further to warn against the dangers of seeing the Resistance indulge in victors' justice: that would risk mirroring the cruelty and injustice that they had so courageously opposed. During the 1950s, the widespread use of torture by French authorities seeking to quell anticolonial revolts in North Africa would sadly provide Mauriac the occasion to once again cite Montaigne's condemnation of cruelty and lament that some of his compatriots should resort to the methods of the Gestapo.

Mauriac does allude to the Sermon on the Mount in this piece, yet in pleading for the presumption of innocence and due process, he does not invoke theological dogma as Camus would charge, but, as Jean Lacouture points out, simply recalls the fundamental precepts of the rule of law in a liberal democracy.[12] It behooves France to be rigorous in practicing democratic ideals all the more since Hitler took pleasure in openly and cruelly flouting them and since France was keen on proving its stature among the Allies. Mauriac moreover takes care to invoke the humanism that, outside of all religious creeds, should beckon his Communist colleagues to respect the basic humanity even of those charged with the most egregious crimes.

True Justice

Le Figaro, September 8, 1944

Is it the rainy weather that is dampening our joy, or rather these telephone calls and letters of supplication? Some men and women who were still laughing just a short time ago are now finding that it is their turn to cry.[13] We would be entitled to say to them: "You managed to live happily during these years when so many of your fellow citizens were suffering and dying ..." But people are pointing out to me that there have been unverifiable errors and misunderstandings: it is reported that several people have been arrested by mistake. And then there are those who look for an excuse in the detestable ambiguity that Vichy imposed on our nation ... (Hah! I bet that today they do indeed

12. Lacouture, *Mauriac. 2. Un citoyen du siècle 1933–1970,* 194–95.

13. Cf. Mauriac is alluding to Luke 6.25: "Woe to you that are full now, for you shall hunger. / Woe to you that laugh now, for you shall mourn and weep."

"hate these lies that hurt them so much," along with the person who exemplifies them all!)

I am not concerned here with pleading for the guilty, but only with recalling that these men and these women are the accused, the defendants that no court has yet convicted of the offense or the crime of which they are being charged.

Yes, I know: the Gestapo and the Vichy police did not have such delicacy. But that's just the point! We aspire to something better than simply having victims and executioners trade places. The Fourth Republic must at all costs avoid wearing the boots of the Gestapo.

It may be that I am wrongly alarmed, but in any case I can be sure of not getting alarmed too soon. But let me say what I really think here. A nation cannot emerge unscathed after living for four years in the degrading atmosphere of a police state. Throughout these four years, professional executioners, passionately devoted to their craft, perfected methods that must have shocked the inquisitors and magistrates of the France of yesteryear and made them turn over in their graves. All these fine, upstanding dignitaries of the good old days knew perfectly well that we would return to torturing people again! As if there were any other way of forcing one brother to hand over another or one friend to betray another.

And thus, thanks to Adolf Hitler, we saw the ancient cruelty that had prompted Montaigne to state, "I cruelly hate cruelty," and which had been partially repressed, spring back up again in forms that were as inventive and joyful as in the times when humans were the most ferocious of wild beasts. We have become closely acquainted with these ghastly refinements: as much as we may have suffered, let us take care that we do not unwittingly become insensitive to the way in which some treat their fellow human beings.

I am not at all writing this to invoke any pretexts nor to deprive those among us who hunger and thirst for justice of the satisfaction to which they are entitled.[14] How could someone who has seen Jewish

14. Mauriac is alluding to Matthew 5.6: "Blessed are those who hunger and thirst for righteousness, for they shall be satisfied."

children jammed together in boxcars like some poor lambs recoil before demands for a strict justice? I am still haunted by the frightful gaze of a woman whose young husband had just been slain with other hostages. And then there is this letter that I dare not reread and in which one of our daughters relates how, before enshrouding the young men who had been shot by firing squad, she would close their eyes. But it is this necessary rigor that must make us more scrupulous. We have to be sure that we are striking justly when we have resolved to strike hard.

And then, let us never forget: this Allied victory, our victory, shall be a victory for humankind. The democratic nations remain united in a certain idea of human dignity that Hitler's executioners have flouted and degraded throughout Europe. In the Marxists' view, humans are the supreme being. We Christians have faith in mankind's divine filiation and in the infinite value of every creature who comes from God and returns to God. Thus by different paths we all end up at this respect for the human being who, even guilty, even laden with crimes, must be punished without being debased.

While Mauriac continues to allude to the Gospel in "Revolution and Revolution," he refers more heavily to the French Revolution in order to warn against the abuses of justice that were marring efforts to rid French public life from the influence of collaborators and to bring to justice the perpetrators of collaborationist crimes. Again, he bluntly points to the "Fascism, Nazism, and the ideology of Maurras" that continue to "subsist murkily in a few segments of public opinion in France, even though they have been thoroughly defeated."

Up until then, Mauriac had never demonstrated much affection or admiration for the Revolution and its leaders, most often invoking them as dangerous precedents to be avoided. Visiting the Conciergerie, which during the French Revolution had housed one of the most infamous prisons, particularly for those condemned to be guillotined, his son Claude was shocked by the sad spectacle of prisoners, including pregnant women and octogenarians, crowded in squalid conditions.[15] Such realities were

15. Lacouture, *Mauriac. 2. Un citoyen du siècle 1933–1970*, 186–87.

hardly of a nature to make Mauriac more favorably disposed to Robespierre, Danton, and their counterparts on the Public Safety Committee. The occurrences of antonomasia, such as in the references to "the Marats of our time" and "our Jacobins," are emblematic of Mauriac's rhetorical strategy in the entire article as he juxtaposes the personalities and practices of the French Revolution with those of the immediate postwar period. At the same time, Mauriac's handling of these references proves to be much more delicate due to his close alliance with the Communist members of the intellectual resistance, for whom the Revolution remained a powerful reference. Indeed, the Communists likened their activity to that of an insurrection, particularly during the intense period following the Allied landing in Normandy, which occasioned, among other things, pitched battles between a number of Resistance groups and the armed forces of both Nazi Germany and Vichy.

While suggesting that Robespierre had indeed turned into a monster, Mauriac nevertheless paints a highly nuanced, even somewhat laudatory picture of the man now synonymous with the Reign of Terror and its most notorious piece of legislation, the "Law of Suspects" passed on August 12, 1793, and providing for the arrest of those who had not sufficiently demonstrated or put into concrete action their support of the Revolution. When speaking of "the same soldiers … as in the Year II of liberty," Mauriac is alluding to the legendarily heroic revolutionary troops hastily recruited, trained, and thrust against the more seasoned armies marshaled by the reactionary European forces seeking to crush the French Revolution. These soldiers of the Revolution had moreover been immortalized in Victor Hugo's poem "Ô soldats de l'an deux!" published in the famous collection of 1853 titled *Les Châtiments*. In juxtaposing them with the scarcely trained, largely inexperienced forces of the Resistance that he nevertheless hails as their equals, Mauriac is saluting their courage, resolve, and resourcefulness, while at the same time offering a tip of his Catholic, bourgeois, academician's famous hat to his Communist counterparts in the intellectual resistance. The "visits and letters from the provinces" mentioned here indicate that, against the injustices they felt they were suffering under the Purge, many were turning to Mauriac as a recourse, for his widely recognized integrity, eloquence, and deep sense of fairness.

Revolution and Revolution

Le Figaro, October 13, 1944

Revolutionary times have in common certain types of grandeur: Year I of deliverance saw the same soldiers rise up as in Year II of liberty. Faded during a century of renditions by various choral groups and official bands, the Marseillaise has once more become the impassioned, youthful song that had just been invented by the Volunteers.

But revolutionary times can be recognized by other signs. Today as during the French Revolution, the French people hungering most for justice are the ones who risk being suspected of injustice.[16] Already in 1792, the frightful accusation of "moderatism" preselected for execution André Chénier, who refused the notion that the long arm of the law should strike out at random.

That is really the issue. We want and we demand punishment for the guilty, but not for suspects. And we do not take lightly either the life or the liberty of the innocent.

There are crimes that are defined, over which no disagreement is imaginable. But the vague and virtually amorphous accusations hanging over the heads of citizens and feeding the rhetoric of the Marats of our time constitute one of the worst calamities that could hit a nation as overburdened with suffering as ours already is.

Today we can better understand that slightly stiff lawyer from Arras whom Camille and Lucile Desmoulins had chosen to witness their happiness together,[17] which would later be threatened. At the time, Monsieur de Robespierre did not at all have the appearance of a monster. People admired the exacting purity and his wary patriotism. But he had the wrong idea of the Purge: his entire tragedy, and that of many good people whose heads he made roll, stemmed from that.

No execution of any one individual could ward off the dangers of such vague, amorphous crimes as federalism, "aristocratism," "moderatism," and aid provided to "Pitt and Cobourg."[18] The Reign of Terror

16. Mauriac is alluding to Matthew 5.6: "Blessed are those who hunger and thirst for righteousness, for they shall be satisfied."

17. The lawyer was Robespierre.

18. Robespierre, Saint-Just, and the Public Safety Committee tended to present their adver-

could have lasted many months after 9 Thermidor without the public mindset being changed by it, or else it would have changed more and more, but in a way dreaded by Robespierre.[19]

That was the Incorruptible's tragedy: he had no valid reason for stopping, for his terrifying logic had led him down a road with no return. Since there was no correspondence between the disorder, which was a state of mind, and the remedy, which was the guillotine, he waited for his enemies themselves to provide him with a solution, which they gave by taking him out.

But in a similar fashion, Fascism, Nazism, and the ideology of Maurras, which all contributed to collaboration with the enemy, subsist murkily in a few segments of public opinion in France, even though they have been thoroughly defeated. Such a state of mind will not only persist after the settling of scores, it will be strengthened by certain abuses of power and by the injustices that are inevitable in a purge.

I am beginning to receive visits and letters from the provinces. For my part, I pay close attention to them. They always enable us to grasp an essential difference between the great Revolution and the one of our time. The Jacobins in Paris found their support in the provinces with the buyers of nationalized possessions and with all who had personal reasons to be fearful of a backlash.[20] Today, the small landowning farmers in my area seem on the contrary to be worried and confused: even though they are fervently patriotic, it is not sure that they approve of everything that is taking place.

It would be interesting to know their innermost thought. From that standpoint, we should regret that each party is not going to run its candidates under their respective banners in the municipal elections. This exclusive list of candidates from the Resistance that the Front National

saries as agents of William Pitt the Younger, prime minister of the United Kingdom through the period of the French Revolution, and of Prince Frederick Josias of Saxe-Coburg-Saalfeld, military leader of the Austrian forces invading France in 1793, who were seen as emblematic of the foreign reactionary powers wishing to crush the Revolution and thus maintain the existing royal and aristocratic European powers. See Charles Lacretelle, *Histoire de la Convention Nationale,* vol. 2 (Paris: Treutel & Wurtz, 1825), 336.

19. The followers of Robespierre were overthrown on 9 Thermidor, the equivalent of July 27, 1794, in the revolutionary calendar, bringing the Reign of Terror to an end.

20. The Jacobins were partisans of strong, aggressive policies by the Public Safety Committee.

is putting forward will doubtless prove to be an edifying consolation from a patriotic standpoint. But the election results will not tell us anything about the various mindsets in France: all the indications will be distorted, whereas I find it indispensable for us to have a clear idea of the matter.

Only one thing is certain: nothing will prevail against the will of the nation. If then our country wants things to be appeased, and if it demands as much, the government will have to stop carrying out the purge. It will have to stop not for lack of citizens to be purged, for there will still and always be more: we could never expect to see the end of the matter any more than Robespierre.

No, if amnesty is to be granted, it shall be for no reason other than the demand and the interest of the country. In that case, some guilty parties will perhaps escape punishment, but innocent people will be freed: justice will thus gain on the one hand what it loses on the other. The Jacobins among us should therefore find consolation in recalling that many of those who gave their lives uttered words of pardon when they died, words which, through their executioners, reached their misguided compatriots.

The following piece, "When Honor Leads Astray," underscores the national unity needed in order to face the daunting tasks of reconstructing France after the war and Occupation that had left it economically, materially, and psychologically devastated. Mauriac pleads more openly for clemency in favor of those who had supported Pétain and Vichy. The fact that his own brother Pierre, an eminent doctor who had openly supported Pétain, was being investigated for his actions as dean of the medical school in Bordeaux doubtless weighed on Mauriac's views of the Purge.

When Honor Leads Astray

Le Figaro, October 17, 1944

When torn between conflicting passions and overwhelmed by our feeling of powerlessness, we must keep on telling ourselves that at least one thing is up to us: the effort to understand our adversaries, to use our minds to put ourselves in their place, and, among all the reasons for their opposition, to look for those which are not vile.

Our first inclination is to attribute tawdry motives to those who oppose us. These motives doubtless exist and too often prevail against all others. Posterity will perhaps forget the book that Georges Bernanos has called *La grande peur des bien-pensants*, but its title is most surely immortal: in six words, it expresses the reactions of a social class that ever since the French Revolution has never had a clear conscience and has always fretted over losing what it possesses.[21]

The Germans and their French collaborators were not mistaken when they played on those fears in their propaganda: it worked then and it still works now. All in all, however, this fear cannot explain everything. The truth is that our virtues contribute to our downfall. I expect more than one reader to get angry with me on this score. I must nevertheless dare to write it because it is true: today, certain French citizens are expiating their crime of fidelity, a misguided, corrupted fidelity.

Nevertheless, we are still dealing with fidelity, fidelity to a man to whom people had entrusted themselves. This is one of our instincts that goes all the way back to the age of vassals: throughout the entire history of France, we see it leading astray and ruining countless little faithful vassals in the service of some treacherous lord.

I understand quite well that France did not exist as a nation in those times, and that the excuse is no longer valid today, when it would be monstrous for a French citizen to hesitate a single second between what he might imagine to be his duty to some misguided old leader and what he owes to his country. But everything, even the sense of honor, teams up against one who is noble in such times. I know some people (and I have observed some close up) who, seeing the old man

21. *The Great Fear of the Smug and Self-Righteous*, published in 1931. Known for the uncompromising Catholic traditionalism of his novels and political pamphlets, Bernanos repeatedly lashed out against what he considered to be the hypocrisy of political leaders and parties left and right, as well as against the increasing dehumanization of daily life in the wake of money and machines in modern capitalist society. See Arnaud Guyot-Jeannin, "Georges Bernanos contre les bien-pensants," http://www.lespectacledumonde.fr/index.php?option=com_content&view=article&id=54:bernanos-547&catid=48:portrait&Itemid=72.

they loved about to plunge into the abyss, kept saying: "It is not now that I will abandon him …"

That is doubtless the wrong sense of honor in which there is a large part of arrogance. Again, their honor was to serve France whatever the price they might have had to pay. But do you prefer the little journalist who, having skipped along breezily from one article to the next, hesitates a bit, holds his finger to the wind for a long moment, decides just in time to contribute to the last issues of an underground newspaper, and finally gains a lock on his security by signing up with the leading party where he thinks he'll have it made? Sure, it is possible that my imagined young jack-of-all-trades might have actually been touched by grace. Let's say that he probably belongs to that lucky type of person whose convictions, as sincere as they may be, always happen to coincide with their interests of the moment. When all is said and done, however, my heart favors the one who has been led astray, deceived, and duped by his virtues.

Who could dare to deny that these virtues were not all pure? The passions of partisan politics, bitter rancor, and all sorts of obscure, unseemly inclinations that brood within the most noble of characters were mixed up with them. But I refuse to confuse such French people with the traitors who handed over their brothers or with the lackeys paid by executioners.

When General de Gaulle testified before the world in his admirable speech the other evening that "France is made up of all the French people, and in order not to perish, France needs the hearts, the minds, and the arms of all its sons and daughters," it was, through this great voice, France itself that was bringing the promise of serenity to the tortured conscience of our brothers.

"War and Justice" acknowledges the impossibility of the sort of "sacred union" that had bound together the various social and ideological components of the famously fractious French nation during the First World War. Mauriac nevertheless pleads for "national reconciliation" in the face of the daunting prospects of what he quite accurately sees as a grueling military campaign necessary to bring Nazi Germany to its knees. Once again, Mauriac alludes to an episode from the French Revolution as a cautionary tale. Recalling "a number of prisons overflowing with detainees" that the revolutionary armies left behind in Paris while on their way to their surprising victory over the Prussians at Valmy on September 20, 1792, Mauriac rather uncharacteristically (particularly when it is a matter of the Revolution) soft-pedals his history lesson. He refrains from recalling that over one thousand suspects, comprised largely of priests refusing to swear loyalty to the Revolution, aristocrats, and common-law criminals, were brutally massacred by strident partisans of the Revolution during the first week of that same month in 1792.[22] Without forgetting that Vichy Prime Minister Pierre Laval had publicly expressed his hope for a Nazi victory nor that a considerable number of people in France secretly regretted Germany's demise, Mauriac pleads for composure and serenity in the application of justice and for clemency when it proves to be in the national interest.

War and Justice

Le Figaro, October, 19, 1944

One by one, the flags are disappearing from windows. Those still there seem to have been forgotten. The glowing haze that was floating over the Paris of the insurgency has been dissipated by the autumn rains. And now we have life as it is, and this face of the world as fashioned by the passion of human beings.

Far from giving in to sentiment, as some people have charged, I feel I am keeping cool and lucid. The war goes on. A pessimist could even say the war is beginning. Yes, the war against Germany is beginning.

It is not just beginning for our Allies, but for us as well, and in a certain sense, especially for us. Following the disaster of 1940 and except for the magnificent Italian campaign that is just coming to an end, this is indeed the first time that French armed forces are heading into a classic battle. The romanticism of the desert, the Maquis, and

22. See "2 septembre 1792, Les massacres de septembre," http://www.herodote.net/almanach-ID-1638.php.

the barricades[23] is going to dissolve into this learned destruction and this well-organized horror.

This war against Germany interests us for other reasons. This fiercely untamed country whose Nazi masters are destined to hell is full of French workers and prisoners of war. This is hardly a matter for grandstanding. Each one of us knows what it means.

On the verge of such an ordeal, and following so many other trials that have worn us down, it was not possible to form some sacred union as was the custom in other eras. It is indeed the case that circumstances hardly lent themselves to such strategy. And it is also the case that there exists in our nation another tradition besides sacred union in the face of the enemy. In 1792, the armed forces of the Republic rushing to defend its borders left behind a number of prisons overflowing with detainees. It makes one wonder, at least it does for those whose imagination is vividly stimulated by History.

Is this one benefit of the war, perhaps the only one, which was to create one unanimous country, also to be denied us? Let's not forget the fact that there were some French people who proclaimed their desire to see Germany victorious, and that there are others who still today regret in their sad hearts that such was not to be. But let us believe the head of our government on this subject: there are only a handful of such people.

The fact of the matter is that our suffering country longs for harmony and national reconciliation. From one day to the next, it is tensing up, bracing itself not against the demands of justice but against a system (if this excess of disorderly, confused, and arbitrary actions can be called a system).

It is not too late to acknowledge that the work of carrying out a purge on the scale of a large country cannot be improvised. Regardless

23. Mauriac is alluding first to the battles waged by the British and by de Gaulle's Free French forces against the Germans in the deserts of North Africa, where they repeatedly stymied the Wehrmacht's attempts to gain total strategic control of the region, its ports, and its resources. With "the Maquis," Mauriac is referring to the many groups of young men who, refusing to be sent to do forced labor in German farms, mines, and factories, instead took refuge in "the brush" of rural areas and formed groups of armed resistance. The barricades are those erected by the French Resistance in Paris during the August 1944 insurrection that led to the liberation of the French capital.

of what you say, the level of confusion and anxiety in people's minds is huge. It is growing from one day to the next, from hour to hour. You don't see it: the press is blocking public opinion from your view. And that is the disadvantage of having just one newspaper: yes, just one, for though we may have a number of papers, there is in effect only one, that of the Resistance.

Sure, other are discontented and are complaining: they are those who think the authorities in Paris should be ashamed for being so slow to strike out at the guilty. It may be that their complaint is justified in part. But do they prefer the hasty justice of certain areas in the provinces? Is it in times when arbitrary arrests are the rule that we should take away the last chance for the convicted to receive a reprieve? Again, don't accuse me of giving in to sentiment. With respect to such reprieves, I am saying with a cool head that this matter is a prerogative of the state, and that national interest is at stake with certain verdicts.

We must first and always think of France: there is no justice contrary to France.

Mauriac's "Response to *Combat*'s Editorial" is his answer to Albert Camus's contestation of the call for reconciliation and clemency. The editorial stands out by virtue of the strikingly courteous, collegial, and even friendly tone that Mauriac, more commonly prone to deploy his devastating wit, irony, and sarcasm, studiously maintains throughout. He gently teases his younger counterpart, turning the accusation of misplaced theological imperative back against Camus. The author of *The Myth of Sisyphus* thus finds himself charged with in effect harboring, if unwittingly, rather inquisitorial notions of cutting off an offending member or immolating the body to save the soul. Mauriac was clearly eager for acceptance and approval from Camus, who, while courteous and respectful, would always remain reticent in the face of the bourgeois Catholic member of the Académie française.

Response to *Combat's* Editorial

Le Figaro, October 22, 1944

I could not swear to the fact that *Combat*'s editorialist, who has written a long refutation of my last article on "War and Justice," really understood my thinking. I am even less sure that I understand his. I run up against his last paragraph, walk around it, sniff around, and back away a bit to better grasp the whole thing. Either I do not understand, or else what I understand is horrifying. And since I have reason to believe that the author of the article is one of my junior colleagues for whom I have the greatest admiration and liking, and whose flawless style I usually very much enjoy, I find myself in an awkward position, which I admit with my usual naive simplicity.

"My conviction," writes the editorialist for *Combat*, "is that there are times when one must be able to speak against one's own inclination and so give up one's peace of mind. This is one of those times and its dreadful law, which it is useless to dispute, requires us to destroy a still-living part of this country in order to save its very soul. . . ."

I am hurt by every single one of these words. I would be a liar if I said that in all my life I had preferred my peace of mind over all else. But have I ever lost this peace of mind by "speaking against myself"? Here we have the first point on which I fear I might be misinterpreting my younger colleague. Did he mean that today it is important to speak against one's own thought? Impossible! I'll set aside that interpretation. Is he suggesting that one must sacrifice one's personal preferences, overcome one's natural inclinations, and that, if one tends to be faint of heart, for example, one must strive to harden one's heart and forget that from early childhood on, one was nourished with the milk of human tenderness?

Well, then, I say no! May the meek not deprive this somber world of their tenderness! May the merciful be not ashamed of the promise that was delivered to them one day on the Mountain of the Beatitudes![24]

24. Mauriac is alluding to Matthew 5.5–7: "Blessed are the meek, for they shall inherit the earth. Blessed are those who hunger and thirst for righteousness, for they shall be satisfied. Blessed are the merciful, for they shall obtain mercy."

There will always be enough cruelty on earth. There will always be enough cruelty in people like us who believe ourselves to be meek and who are merciless.

I had not thought of taking the defense of certain big interests that had been damaged, as my contradictor insinuates. It is not for them that my heart is concerned. But would it not be possible for the legal revolution to be carried out if there were no longer any innocent people in France's prisons? Does my naiveté perhaps make you smile? What do you expect? The folks in my generation grew up in a Europe trembling and divided because a Jewish officer was in a penal colony paying for someone else's crime.

But I am well aware that a man determined "to destroy a still-living part of this country in order to save its very soul" could not possible be shocked by the judicial system that has been raging in France for two months. And on that score I am quite astonished! My younger colleague is more of a spiritualist than I had imagined, more so than I am, in any case. The Inquisitors also burned bodies to save souls.

But again, I fear I am misrepresenting his thinking. What does "the soul of a country" mean for him? Just how does the salvation of this soul depend on sacrificing "a still-living part of this country"? Indeed, there remain a few bits of Christianity that have not been completely removed from the young intellectuals at *Combat*. It's better than nothing to have retained the vocabulary, and it would be ungracious on my part to reproach them for it.

What I have trouble discerning, however, is what exactly this theological language, with which I have been familiar since my teenage years, stands for. What is this law that we are forbidden to discuss and that requires us to destroy a living part of France? Would my contradictor be so kind as to enlighten us by clarifying this point?

Smiling at the nickname "Saint Francis of the Assizes Court,"[25] formulated by adversaries in an attempt to portray him as a sanctimonious sentimentalist ignorant of political reality, Mauriac refutes such charges in "The

25. See Lacouture, *Mauriac. 2. Un citoyen du siècle 1933–1970*, 172–83.

Political Consequences of the Purge" by engaging in the very hard-nosed realism he attributes to such saints. Pointing to the practical difficulties posed by the sheer volume of cases (over 50,000) to be processed by the judicial system, Mauriac warns of the political cost to be paid by a purge casting its net too far and wide and dragging on for years. Yet he concedes that the Purge is a "necessary evil" that the very existence of Vichy and the politics of collaboration made unavoidable.

The Political Consequences of the Purge

Le Figaro, January 12, 1945

Apparently, the courts are going to be very busy. There are 18,700 cases in progress, and that's just a beginning. This year, more than 50,000 dossiers will keep 623 magistrates working through their evenings. We can well see how this matter is beginning, but it is the outcome that we have difficulty imagining. Where will this journey to the end of the Purge lead us? Will we ever even get there? I am thinking not only of the time that it will take to get done with these 50,000 cases. Others will continue to pile up: there is no lack of such matters. Unless it is decided one fine day in all police stations to throw the denunciations in the wastebasket, 623 judges will find themselves every morning like Sisyphus facing his boulder.

It is important to move quickly. You cannot operate on a dead body and we are not talking about a dissection here. How will our nation react to this bloody operation that has been dragging on for months? The patient is exhausted and has not been anesthetized. After one year, what do you think France's temperature will be? From a Machiavellian point of view, that would not make much of a difference if we were so many Jacobins having firmly resolved to withstand public opinion and impose political reality on the country. But we remain advocates of democracy who respect legality. We will let the people speak. Their response will decide everything: doesn't that make you afraid?

The political minds of the National Assembly and the press never look at the issue from that angle. I am not acting on sentiment here, and we are no longer in the realm of charity. I was not the last to chuckle at being designated "Saint Francis of the Assizes Court." Nevertheless, you should be aware that saints often prove to be great realists, and that Cardinal Richelieu's agent and adviser, Father Joseph, was very advanced in the ways of mysticism. But this is not the time to joke. I would like for my friends and my counterparts in the press to agree to look at the Purge in terms of domestic politics.

There have been discontented ones under every regime. But no regime could bear such an organization of discontent. Up until now, the immense prestige of General de Gaulle, along with all that France owes him on both the domestic and international scenes, the euphoria of the Liberation, and the exhilaration of recovering France's grandeur have thankfully limited the damage. It would nevertheless be foolish to ignore certain threats.

It is not for me to criticize the measure, doubtless inevitable, that eliminated from the Consultative Assembly the representatives and senators that Monsieur Laval had swindled into voting for Pétain, and who more or less all became resisters. The fact remains that voters in their respective districts listen to many of these congressmen infuriated by the injustice of which they feel victim, and that they along with their voters risk forming numerous pockets of opposition. The fact also remains that among the innocent or the suspects who have been arrested and released, there were a number of influential men who will never pardon this affront. I have glimpsed a sea of rancor in certain gazes. Some of their speech trembles with a hatred strong enough to guide them for a lifetime. Even among the most humble, each person arrested creates an ever-widening circle of irritation and deep anxiety.

All that would not matter if it were not for these formidable personalities, who find that the financial interests and secret influence they recently enjoyed are now threatened, and who are preparing to orchestrate bitterness and terror throughout the country. Not everything can be said and not everything can be written ... Most of my readers are not aware of the power that one single man still possesses if he is a billionaire, though some know.

I desire only to prompt useful thinking. These wretches must at all costs be prevented from using against us the ghastly words that Chateaubriand used in speaking of Decazes after the Duke of Berry had been assassinated: "His feet slipped in the blood."[26] On the evening of an electoral defeat, we do not want our enemies to dare use this disgusting argument against the party of martyrs and those sent before firing squads. Granted, the Purge is a necessary evil. Those who express the most indignation pretend to forget that the politics of collaboration sowed the seeds of this Purge, and that the Purge is the price we must pay for Vichy. But I believe that it is not too early to seek a way out of this bloody, monotonous labyrinth.

Nowhere does Mauriac better demonstrate his refusal of Manichean distribution of heroism and crime than in "The Trial of One Man Who Is Paying the Price for Us All." While celebrating de Gaulle and the Resistance, he clearly shows that he had neither forgotten nor whitewashed the extent to which Pétain, Vichy, and his compatriots had compromised their own honor and that of France over the course of the Occupation. Just as de Gaulle had insisted from the outset in June 1940, Mauriac observes that the acceptance of an armistice led directly to the politics of state collaboration, and thus implicated Vichy in the crimes perpetrated by the Third Reich, regardless of how much Pétain had or had not attempted to bargain for a better deal or play a double game.

Mauriac's observation that the trial of Pétain was that of the French nation will be repeatedly confirmed for decades to come. Such was the case even after the shock of Marcel Ophüls's documentary *The Sorrow and the Pity* and the Paxtonian Revolution. It would be particularly evident in the trial of Maurice Papon, which extended from October 1997 to April 1998, when those who insisted on the symbolic importance and necessity of the procedure ironically took up the refrain, "*car Pétain, c'est la France, et la France, c'est Pétain*" (for Pétain is France, and France is Pétain), originally pronounced by Cardinal Gerlier in November of 1940. It was moreover for

26. The assassination of the Duc de Berry on the steps of the Opera Garnier in Paris on February 13, 1820, represents, not coincidentally, an eminently political act of extremism, since the assassin was a fanatical advocate of republican democracy, while the victim was the only person who could have fathered a successor to King Charles X. See http://www.herodote.net/13_fevrier_1820-evenement-18200213.php.

just that reason that de Gaulle commuted Pétain's death sentence to one of life imprisonment: he did not wish to make a martyr out of someone to whom so many French people remained attached.

Unlike de Gaulle, however, Mauriac refuses to suggest that these faults were committed by only a handful of Vichy officials and venal collaborationists. As indicated by the second part of this editorial's title, he argues that all those who had failed to prevent Hitler from building his war machine, had hailed the Munich accords as a godsend, or had clamored for an end to hostilities as quickly as possible at all costs should now engage in some very serious soul-searching instead of heaping guilt on the back of the elderly Marshal Pétain. Such exacting assessments apply to Mauriac himself, who, as we have seen, rejoiced on the occasion of the Munich accords and saluted Pétain's speech announcing both his assumption of power and of an armistice initiative, positions which he later explicitly regretted.

The Trial of One Man Who Is Paying the Price for Us All

Le Figaro, July 26, 1945

Whether or not the armistice was inevitable, it was bound to give birth to the politics of Montoire.[27] Could Marshal Pétain have doubted that reality for one instant? Armistice with Germany implied collaboration with Germany. But to collaborate with the Third Reich, whose ghastly methods, though they were not as well known as they are today, had been evident for several years already, was to enter into partnership with crime and to follow in the steps of a madman who was both sly and ferocious: to collaborate was to commit France to the politics of agreeing with a monster. The double-dealing excuses nothing, since there is no bargaining without complicity.

But just how many in Europe were more or less accomplices to Germany? I am not trying to find excuses for the old Marshal Pétain, it's just that we must have the courage to testify to the fact that he did

27. That is, the politics of state collaboration with Nazi Germany officially announced by Marshal Pétain after his meeting with Hitler in the little town of Montoire on October 24, 1940.

not inaugurate a policy, but was the result of it. He had had precursors at Munich, and that was not even the beginning: at Munich, Europe harvested the fruit of an uninterrupted series of betrayals and acts of cowardice. Before and after that fateful abdication of responsibility by democratic countries, Hitler kept on stockpiling the raw materials that they were the only ones to supply. Right up until the last minute, on the eve of his most egregious crime, he benefited from the world's overt and covert aid.

Before God and man, Marshal Pétain assumed responsibilities from which no one has the power to relieve him. But we would be hypocrites if, before chiming in with all those who are accusing him, we did not each ask ourselves: what did I do, what did I write or think at the time of the Munich accords? The day after the Munich accords, a huge crowd had gathered to acclaim Daladier (who was himself stupefied not to find them spitting in his face) right after he had stepped off his plane. That crowd was providing the Führer's secret and avowed accomplices the assurance that they could go forward carried by an entire nation's weakness and abdication of responsibility. The French citizens who were there sharing in this ecstatic crowd's feeling should therefore keep quiet today, for is this trial in fact not also somewhat their own?

It is they, but also nations and political parties, who are on trial. The politics of horse-trading and double-dealing that, to our shame, Vichy carried out were the politics of those who remained neutral, when they had not openly bought in with the Germans. Why belabor the point? The example came from the top. We know who supported, counseled, and approved Marshal Pétain.

And our nation was doubtless already regaining its composure and standing up to the invaders. If we deserved to have Pétain, we also deserved, thank God, to have de Gaulle: the spirit of surrender and the spirit of resistance were both exemplified among the French people and squared off in a duel unto death. But each one of these men represented infinitely more than himself, and since the least among us shares in the glory of France's premier resistant, let us not recoil from the thought that a part of ourself was perhaps, at certain times, an accomplice to this thunderstruck old man.

Mauriac's courageous lucidity seems to falter in "Lorenzaccio" as he attempts to portray Pétain as a well-intentioned old man who, not realizing he had outlived his time, offered himself in sacrifice to his country by betting on the definitive victory of Nazi Germany. Doubtless overdetermined by his own original attachment to Pétain, Mauriac's defense of the marshal is all the more curious in that he clearly acknowledges Pétain's responsibility for the "deeds to which French citizens can no longer dare to mention without lowering their heads." Surely he would not have claimed that those deeds somehow would have been acceptable if Germany had managed to maintain its stranglehold over continental Europe? Yet Mauriac persists in presenting the head of the French State at Vichy as a sort of tragic hero manipulated and exploited by others. As firmly established by archival research, however, Pétain was an outspoken proponent of collaboration with Nazi Germany, beginning with his highly publicized handshake with Hitler at Montoire on October 24, 1940. He was also one of the leading architects of the infamous Jewish Statutes providing the "legal" basis for a whole series of persecutions and exclusions initiated and carried out by Vichy.[28]

Lorenzaccio

Le Figaro, August 5–6, 1945

For journalists, it is both an advantage and a liability to be situated a long distance from the event on which they are commenting. Being in this peaceful place amid the valleys whose thirst has just been slaked by a storm, and seeing in the background snow-covered mountain peaks bathed in a light that is no longer of this world, how might I imagine that hot, stuffy room crowded with reporters, witnesses, lawyers, and judges, where there seems to be only one person absent:

28. See "L'original du statut des juifs accable le Maréchal Pétain," http://www.lefigaro.fr/actualite-france/2010/10/03/01016-20101003ARTFIG00082-l-original-du-statut-des-juifs-accable-le-marechal-petain.php Par lefigaro.fr 03/10/2010; and "STATUT DES JUIFS EN 1940—Découverte du texte original, durci par le maréchal Pétain," Publié le 03/10/2010 Le Point Source AFP, http://www.lepoint.fr/societestatut-des-juifs-en-1940-decouverte-du-texte-original-durci-par-le-marechal-petain-03-10-2010-1244322_23.php.

namely, this old man estranged from his own destiny, this stone-faced statue having already entered into an everlasting indifference?

He listens as a page of history concerning him is read, but it has been inscribed in indelible ink, and the insults, accusations, and jumbled murmurings of love and hate stand no chance of changing one iota. We see this grand, glorious, and ornamental soldier promoted to the level of a sinister character or one of the great tragic figures of legends. What does it all matter to him in the end? He is no longer here.

Yes, I am too far away from these arguments to recreate their atmosphere. My idea of the man, however, is no longer charged with emotion or confused: I wonder about him, and I try to take stock of the situation in order to understand. I do not recall having succumbed to the charm that seems to have taken in the toughest of our politicians. Having had the curiosity to reread the articles that I published here in this very column at the time of the armistice, I have been satisfied to discover only two or three sentences politely devoted to "the Victor of Verdun." In fact, the two first pages of *The Black Notebook* written in July 1940 already reveal my repugnance, not for the person Marshal Petain, but for the spirit of Vichy, the elated, preachy euphoria of those figures that the French people had vomited out at each election and who finally had their revenge, and the deadly emotions that drove them to compromise the most sacred and holy causes through their dealings with the Nazis.

But today, I ask the essential question for every Christian: did Marshal Pétain want to betray France? Did he have the intention to betray? But what about the foreign refugees who were handed over to their executioners, the hostages who were turned in, those who were sent to Germany as forced laborers, along with the government bureaucrats, magistrates, and police who became accomplices to deeds which French citizens can no longer dare mention without lowering their heads? Should we consider all that as a lesser evil or an abomination that the head of the Vichy government believed he had to accept in order to avoid the worst? It seems to me that the accused would be wrong to refuse that responsibility, as frightful as it is. From the bottom of that abyss of old age and solitude which have almost completely engulfed him, why doesn't he declare to his judges: "Immediately after France's disaster, when the British Empire was alone struggling against an all-powerful conqueror, the fate of the world was with three cards: a German victory; a compromise peace deal reached after a hard, exhausting fight; or an English victory. Only one would win out, but one would have had to be God to turn that card face up. I tried to save face in case Hitler carried the day or in case he only won a partial victory. Since another Frenchman remained faithful to our English Allies, France's survival instinct was functioning in a way that preserved the country from total loss whatever the outcome. But the Frenchman who gambled on a German victory knew from the beginning that if he lost his bet, he would become a traitor in the eyes of his contemporaries, and perhaps in the judgment of History a criminal guilty of having tried to tie the fate of his country to the destiny of a defeated and dishonored nation. I accepted this risk. Like a ninety-year-old Lorenzaccio, I dishonored myself: I sacrificed my honor so that whatever may come to be, France would be saved."

Thus I strive to give an overly subtle interpretation to the conduct of a very old man who was actually led on and used by others. (We know the authors of some of his messages . . .) Does he understand today that death had forgotten him, that his story was over twenty-five years ago, that he was the protagonist in another play, and that he was shoved into this role by treacherous hands?

The Dawn of the Atomic Age and the Onset of the Cold War

If one sought to assess offhand in August 1945 the wider implications of the two atomic bombs having just ended the war in the Pacific by annihilating Hiroshima and Nagasaki along with tens of thousands of their inhabitants, one would be hard-pressed to find a commentary more appropriately grim and eloquent than that penned by Mauriac in "The Bloody Dawn of Peace." While naturally glad to see an end to the conflict, he finds little to celebrate in a world now divided up between the two competing superpowers, especially since France will find its heretofore preeminent role greatly diminished. Mauriac's sober assessment of the postwar international scene proved prescient: in his final paragraph devoted to this "bloody dawn" of a "peace having intervened before the end of the world," he suggests that in the aftermath of the worldwide conflagration, the bloodshed is hardly over.

The Bloody Dawn of Peace

Le Figaro, August 11, 1945

The women and children of Hiroshima and Nagasaki shall not have been annihilated for nothing. Through the thick black smoke that has been suffocating us all for three days, we can glimpse something rather similar to a little olive tree. In order for a power so well known for its preaching and moralizing as the United States to have decided to take on before God and before History a responsibility whose gravity could escape only those totally devoid of imagination, the stakes must have been worth the risk.

For his part, the Muscovite bear has once again slammed his huge paw down at just the right moment. He barely made it in time for the divvying up of a carcass that is not paltry. For it really concerns a prey other than this slender flattened criminal Japan: the ebbing of the Nipponese tide has uncovered the vast territory of China. But what empire could measure up to the two ravenous appetites that are facing off? Specialists of this region can contemplate that subject and describe for us beforehand all the vicissitudes of this battle over the peace that the atomic bomb has kicked off.

For our part, we French, who are the greatest among the smaller nations and, after Poland and Holland, the victims who have been hit the hardest by war and occupation, should be mindful of what our mission consists of from now on. As expressed in the poetry of our own Alfred de Vigny, it is up to us "to harken to the heavy moans of suffering / That humanity softly exhales with each tired breath," and to provide a rhythm and a clearly defined meaning to that desperate supplication.[29]

29. Alfred de Vigny, "La Maison du Verger," III.26: "C'est à toi qu'il convient d'Ouïr les grandes plaintes / Que l'humanité triste exhale sourdement." http://poesie.webnet.fr/lesgrandsclassiques/poemes/alfred_de_ vigny/la_maison_du_berger_iii.html. Mauriac cited the same verses during the Spanish Civil War, in his article "Open City."

> The dawn of peace is too bloody for us to celebrate with hymns and apotheosis. May this peace having intervened before the end of the world stir up within us the determination to observe attentively and with a critical mind the rivalries between what are called the "great" powers, for there exists but one greatness to which we should consent to bow, the grandeur of empires that will not only give a precarious peace to humankind overburdened with suffering, but will also once again give us hope. It will revive a hope covered by a thick layer of burning ashes, buried under so much rubble. It will give us, then, reasons to believe that all that was only a nightmare, that we have emerged from an abominable ordeal, that the ghost of Hitler no longer lurks among men, and that the reign of murderers has ended.

Having parted company with his Communist colleagues of the *Lettres françaises* at the end of 1945,[30] Mauriac often sparred with them in his editorials during the Cold War years of the late 1940s. As is the case in the following editorial, "The Complicity of Silence," he repeatedly denounces the widespread occurrence of the most serious violations of human rights evident in the show trials and camps throughout the Soviet bloc. The refusal of many Communists and Socialists to denounce the systematic oppression characteristic of life behind the Iron Curtain was an emblematic reality of French intellectual and political life of the period.[31] The motives for such a political orientation were several. To begin with, the shameful legacy of Pétain, Vichy, and Parisian collaborationists such as Drieu la Rochelle and Robert Brasillach had discredited the Right. Moreover, Stalin's Red Army had played a crucial role in defeating Nazi Germany in Europe, while in France, the well-organized Communists had mounted the most dramatically visible military resistance. In the eyes of such central figures as Jean-Paul Sartre and his team of writers for *Les Temps modernes*, these historical realities validated the Marxist doctrine of history as a dialectical series of events leading to a classless society.[32] For French intellectuals and writers, the nascent Cold War

30. Lacouture, *Mauriac. 2. Un citoyen du siècle 1933–1970*, 224.

31. See Tony Judt, *Past Imperfect: French Intellectuals, 1944–1956* (Berkeley: University of California Press, 1992), and Tzvetan Todorov, "Originaire de Bulgarie," in *L'homme dépaysé* (Paris: Éditions du Seuil, 1996), 29–71.

32. See "D'André Gide à Jean-Paul Sartre," in Winock, *Le Siècle des intellectuels*, 391–401.

years were thus marked by Marxist perspectives on domestic politics and international affairs, by the preoccupation with history understood as an ongoing succession of events whose logic imposed political imperatives on nations and individuals, and by the imperative of commitment. The previous focus on literary aesthetics thus gave way to the imperative of political commitment.

In devoting himself less to his novels and more to his editorials, Mauriac not only set out in a decisive direction for his own career, he also participated in the general trend that was shifting intellectual energies away from literature and focusing greater attention on philosophy and politics.[33] But even though the most serious violations of basic human rights were widespread and amply attested in the Soviet Block, Sartre, his cohorts, and other "fellow travelers" with the Communists among the French intelligentsia refused to condemn these abuses for fear that it might validate the American position. Mauriac thus distinguished himself from the dominant trend in protesting vociferously against the Stalinization of Eastern Europe. He accordingly chided *L'Humanité* and *Le Populaire* (France's Communist and Socialist newspapers, respectively), for failing to ask the chilling questions raised by the series of political crackdowns, trials, and executions in Soviet-dominated Eastern Europe.

Coming from a bourgeois Catholic member of the Académie française writing for the staid bastion of the center-right press, *Le Figaro*, Mauriac's attacks on the Stalinism so conspicuously asserting itself both behind the Iron Curtain and within the elite circles of French writers, artists, and intellectuals are perhaps not surprising. Yet Mauriac refused to toe any systematically predictable ideological line. However omnipresent the political choices may have been, he managed to see beyond immediate events and controversies and delve into the specific ethos of those times, as the world pondered the ominous implications of Hiroshima and the Soviet stranglehold on Eastern Europe.

33. Ibid.

The Complicity of Silence

Le Figaro, August 1, 1947

What I admire most among the Socialists is their emotional modesty, which is the refinement of well-heeled souls that deters them from overtly displaying their feelings. They cannot be unaware of the fact that the politicians arrested and imprisoned in Romania belonged to a specific political party. They know that in most cases these were their own brothers. But in order not to hurt the feelings of their Communist comrades, they refrain from making the slightest reference to that fact. It's amazing to see *Le Populaire* and *L'Humanité* trading acid comments over their squabbles every day, as irascible members of the same political leaning who get upset over trifles. What really separates them, however, is the huge invisible army of deported or executed Mensheviks, which has been continually increasing for thirty years and constantly making new victims.

Certainly, we admire such excess of refined scruples that turns Socialists away from condemning the violence to which their own are falling victim wherever their brother party rules. But we deplore that attitude even more, for it is from such refined scruples that we are going to perish.

The longer I live, the more I hate the silence of human beings in the face of the violent attacks suffered by other human beings, especially the silence of those whose voices would carry because they are the leaders of a proletarian party and the heirs of Jean Jaurès and the entire legacy of French Socialism.[34] How strange it is that they have not found among them a single person to play this sublime role! Have you thus forgotten of what mindset you are? And doubtless they would return the compliment and ask me, "And how about you?" Of course, we Christians can lower our heads as well. But for the moment, it is hardly important for us to demand mutual accountability. What both of our groups can do is to refuse to let certain violent attacks receive

34. Renowned and revered to this day for his intellectual honesty, political courage, rousing oratory, and devotion to peace and justice, the Socialist Jean Jaurès was born on September 3, 1859, and assassinated on the eve of World War I, on July 31, 1914.

the approval of silence. Silence is consent: in the present context, the commonplace saying suddenly has an unexpectedly tragic ring.

Of course, our protest must not be one-sided. We admit that one day liberty can be assassinated elsewhere besides behind the iron curtain. We are not seeking pretexts for giving ammunition to militant anti-Communism. We are only striving to bring to light the scandal that the silence of the Socialists represents. For so many generous souls who have rallied to the Marxist cause and who believe they are fighting for the liberation of humanity, that's what it's all about in the end. That should be your vocation for you SFIO Marxists to recall each day,[35] whether timely or untimely, what a certain conception Marxism has made of human beings (and especially of those who are Socialist) and what has become of the human condition wherever this conception has triumphed: opponents have been silenced and in countless cases eternally silenced.

And yet you say nothing. You waste your time and energy raging over outdated problems and give yourselves over to mediocre partisan politics on domestic issues. You do not understand, for example, that the approval of one single injustice here and now, under the pretext of the Purge, legitimates all the crimes committed elsewhere against your fellow Socialists. You should be fearful of being reminded of that some day by the very ones that you think it is clever to deal with today, when they will have become your judges and your executioners.

But maybe you no longer deserve these reproaches: for ten days I have been wandering over the highways and byways where neither *L'Humanité* nor *Le Populaire* have ever penetrated, and perhaps you have already expressed this protest of the human conscience, this cry of brotherly love that we expect of you: "Cain, what have you done with your brother?" It is not just the murderer of Abel that our Father thus questions, but also this other trembling brother who turns his eyes away from the bloodshed, because he has the same fear as Cain.

35. Founded by Jean Jaurès in 1905, the Section Française de l'Internationale Ouvrière is the ancestor of the present-day Socialist Party in France. See http://www.larousse.fr/encyclopedie/divers/SFIO/144647.

In "Making It through the Holidays," Mauriac turns away from the political polemics that he relishes to offer us the distinctly elegiac strains of a memorialist keenly attuned to the passing of time and to the presence of the past that he strives to resuscitate through his melancholic descriptions. He thus conjures up childhood memories to ponder not only his own mortality but that of entire civilizations, all of which are threatened by the possibility of nuclear warfare.

Making It through the Holidays

Le Figaro, January 1, 1948

As a child, I was amazed that our mother was so anxious, as she put it, to "make it through the holidays," as if Christmas and New Year's were a painful ordeal for her. We have long since discovered and now ourselves experience the secret reason for her impatience: it is not All Saints' Day that brings back the dead on November 2, but the last days of the year. That is when they reemerge out of the back of these rooms where, half a century ago, we would tremble with joy at the sight of a golden horn or a goat's foot sticking out of the gift wrapping. As if their eyes had never closed in death, they are still looking upon us affectionately, as if we were still at the age when all those we knew loved us.

Our parents had fewer reasons then than we do now for wishing that the holidays would go by quickly so as to be done with these days when ghosts appear before us and when we no longer dare to exchange our holiday greetings. For I imagine that it was the thought of their own death that haunted them in those days. At least they thought that after them the world would continue on its same course, or on a course scarcely different from the one they had known. These old folks from the years before World War I knew nothing of this anxiety that is ours every time we pass the milestone of a new year: that of seeing signs foretelling the tremendous disaster in which what will perish will be not only that which by nature was supposed to perish anyway, in other words ourselves, but also the monuments, books, beliefs, mores, and language by which we expected to live on after our death.

It is hard to envisage that all of that—this solid, rich substance of the world in which we were schoolchildren and adolescents, this bench at the end of the path, this smell of country cooking, this reflection of the fire on mahogany furniture, and this rustling of rosary beads in venerable old hands—is part of our own nothingness and that, if not the whole world, at any rate our own world will end with us, and that nothing of us will remain in any human brain after the Caesar of the East and the Caesar of the West have settled their dispute and are dividing up the rubble and the boneyards.

And that perhaps is the emptiest regret: as if we had not always known that the world would pass away! As if we Christians had not received the words of eternal life! But this heart of human flesh which soon will have stopped beating is attuned to this ephemeral life, and it would have been nice to think that, after we were gone, this life would last a bit longer, perhaps keeping in someone's memory the trace of our steps on the sand path, or of a strophe or a verse, and of our strides when in our games of August and September we ran about among the ferns, crushing them.

It is true that we have loved this life, but we have also known and judged it. We know well that this little world of yesteryear, this nest of comfort and quietude, only subsisted thanks to a lot of injustice. If it were to make room for a better humanity, we would heartily agree that it should perish! If we thought we were witnessing the painful birth of such a new era, our hearts would be as filled with joy as were the French people who were euphoric in 1789. But in the face of what is preparing to happen, who would dare listen to anyone speak of progress without shrugging their shoulders? And yet there remains a reason not to lose heart: it is the fact that we are still hopeful. If the Caesar of the East and the Caesar of the West have not yet succeeded in killing human hope, it is doubtless because hope springs eternal. And the fact that hope subsists in the hearts of our miserable species remains the last sign, the last testimony that we are right to wait for salvation and to believe that we are loved by Someone.

Mauriac penned "My Answer to Albert Camus" in response to Camus's article "L'artiste est le témoin de la liberté" ("The Artist Is Liberty's Witness") published December 20, 1948, by *La Gauche*,[36] the official paper of Sartre, Rousset, and Altman's RDR (Rassemblement Démocratique Révolutionnaire) party. The entire piece forms one extended apostrophe, responding to Camus as interlocutor. Instead of expounding his theses directly, Mauriac presents a monologue, as if Camus were present. It is important to remember that Mauriac is a seasoned writer of fiction, quite prone to deploy the tools of his literary craft in the composition of his editorials. A number of his most poignant articles, and in particular, the eloquent denunciation of torture published in January 1955, were indeed written in the form of a dialogue, perhaps all the better to dramatize the human dimensions of the issues at stake and thus more effectively win his readers over to his point of view.

We also observe a classic case of praeteritio, the rhetorical strategy which focuses attention on a particular point all the while claiming to put it aside. Thus, claiming to leave Christianity out of the discussion in order to address matters on a purely political ground, Mauriac in fact focuses intensely on the components of his religious faith that crucially inform his values and perceptions of events. First and foremost among these is his notion of the place of human beings within history, a history paradoxically characterized not by the intervention of Providence or by the imposition of some Divine plan or even by some immanent presence of the Deity in human events, but on the contrary by the absence of God in events, which are instead shaped and driven by human beings. Agreeing that history is not endowed with any inherent or predetermined meaning, Mauriac situates himself close to Camus in conceding that a world characterized by the wanton, chaotic, and meaningless destruction of life occasioned by war and genocide must indeed be considered "absurd," even if Mauriac does not put it in such explicit terms. Camus similarly eloquently portrays all human experience as irremediably fragile, ephemeral, and unfulfilled in a world dominated by injustice and violence: that makes him appear as an *anima naturaliter christiana* (a naturally Christian soul) in Mauriac's eyes.

The Camus that Mauriac addresses here in the nascent Cold War era

36. See Granger in Mauriac, *Journal. Memoires politiques*, 903n2.

continued to dream of an international organization of pacifists and Socialists; he was interested in and supportive of Sartre, Rousset, and Altman's RDR, but did not join. In May 1948 Garry Davis renounced his American citizenship in order to better promote his international peace movement as a self-designated "citizen of the world." There, gathered around him in Paris, was a "Council of Solidarity" composed of writers, artists, intellectuals, and journalists, including Altman, Breton, Camus, l'Abbé Pierre, Emmanuel Mounier, Raymond Queneau, Vercors (Jean Bruller), and Richard Wright. Davis got himself arrested on November 19, 1948, when he tried to interrupt a UN session to voice his demands. Camus's remarks at a spontaneously organized press conference immediately afterward were published in the November 20–21 edition of *Combat*. Camus stressed that since the UN purported to support world peace, it had placed itself in an untenable position by having had Davis arrested. Then in December *Combat* published a petition for peace signed by some five hundred writers and intellectuals, including Camus, Maurice Nadeau, and many others.[37]

Davis had served in the military in World War II, flying combat missions as a pilot, and was also an actor. His renunciation of U.S. citizenship and his foray into the ongoing session of the UN were widely covered in the world press and newsreels. Emphasizing the importance of individual action, Davis also established a World Citizenship registry in Paris in January 1949. In the fall of 1949, Davis went on to demonstrate in front of the Cherche-Midi prison in favor of amnesty for conscientious objectors.[38] He acquired quite a following and received significant recognition, filling the Vélodrome d'Hiver with his rallies and even gaining a visit to French President Gustave Laniel. He had clearly touched a chord in many countries, from which there was an outpouring of support. Learning of Communist efforts to infiltrate his movement, he took that as proof that the cause of peace was a serious threat to the Soviet bloc. In early 1949, he proposed a world constitution.[39]

37. Jacqueline Lévi-Valensi, ed., *Camus at Combat: Writing, 1944–1947*, trans. Arthur Goldhammer (Princeton, N.J.: Princeton University Press, 2007), 295–97.

38. Scott H. Bennett, *Radical Pacifism: The War Resisters League and Gandhian Nonviolence in America, 1915–1963* (Syracuse, N.Y.: Syracuse University Press, 2003), 182–83.

39. Joseph P. Baratta, *The Politics of World Federation*, vol. 2: *From World Federalism to Global Governance* (Westport, Conn.: Praeger Press, 2004), 410–12.

My Answer to Albert Camus

La Table Ronde, February 1949

"Answers for the Skeptic": that's the title of the article that you wrote in *Combat* in order to convince me that I was wrong not to follow in the path of Garry Davis. I pondered for a long while the fact that, strangely, I am the one who seems skeptical in your view, and you are thus the believer. Would the movement that leads you to join the following of this little man be of a religious nature? Would I have, in this particular case, given in to the bitterness that I have often felt at the sight of these souls who so easily follow the first one to come their way when they have said no to the Son of Man?

But that meditation would lead me too far afield, and in particular onto a dangerous terrain where I would run the risk of once more making you wary. How difficult it is to come to a common understanding—and that's putting it mildly—how difficult it is for one generation to speak to another! Each time that we've met and have broken bread together, I have, after a few awkward moments, become a friend for you just like all the others: we would then speak freely and I was quite capable of making you laugh. But right the next day, you once again kept your distance, that irreducible distance that separates the one who's coming from the one who's going away.

I've had the time to think about that, since I have reached what I call "the age of the coconut tree." Do you know what I mean? It's when the old man holds on tight to the palm branches and from up high he looks down on the young cannibals: his position is all the more precarious in that he's wearing the cocked hat of the Académie française and his legs are tangled around his Academician's sword. I would add that he has to fight against the formidable temptation to make coconuts rain down on these young heads spiked with the hair-do made popular by Cocteau back in 1917 (for many of your friends have taken almost all their cues from that distant era, even their hair!).

You can relax, I've finished joking now. I am not unaware that this controversy goes beyond our own individual destinies and that what is at stake is the destiny of humankind. But you said as much in the fine article published in *La Gauche*. Every word of that piece finds an echo in my soul: "There is no life without dialogue." A dialogue, not a controversy: that's what we should establish between us from now on. I would like for you to understand how close we are to each other, or if you prefer, how close I feel to you. Do not at all fear that, as a Christian, I'm trying to pull you over to my side. Certainly, you are the very type of person to whom Saint Augustine's term *anima naturaliter christiana* applies. I am not making this observation to compromise you, but rather to justify, if need be, the trust that inclines me to admit to you my doubts and difficulties on the subject that appears to divide us. If I were seeking at all costs to be brilliant and to win out over you in the public's view, I would doubtless strive to find the soft point in your armor. But that is not what this is about. It is a matter of taking stock of where we are on this issue, and seeing very clearly with you and with your help, where I stand with respect to this problem that none of us can elude any longer.

Since you sensed right away the strength of my position and since you cannot deny the fact that Garry Davis's movement will spread on one side of the planet only, upgrading Stalin's hand with an unexpected card, you avoided that obstacle and proceeded to attack, listing the consequences of the position I was defending: according to you, I would find myself bound hand and foot, given over to the United States on foreign policy and to de Gaulle for domestic matters; I was going to have to buy into the Cold War, lead a bloody fight against Communists, approve of the politics of repression in Greece, and be reconciled with Franco; and, since time is admittedly on Russia's side, I would even have to accept the idea of preventive warfare.

Well, no, my dear Camus! There is not one of these prospects that horrifies me any less than it horrifies you. I reject the alternative in which you would lock me up. Here is what I really think: in politics, I no longer believe that there are solutions based on feelings. I observe that such notions always end up playing into the adversary's hands. But neither does that does mean that I believe in might. Jacqueline Pascal entered into the religious order at Port-Royal because, she said, you could in a reasonable manner find your way to salvation there.

I believe that a reasonable political strategy based only on the facts might still save our generation from the nuclear threat.

Does it surprise and perhaps scandalize you that a Catholic would use such language? It is nevertheless the Christian in me who can no longer escape the obvious fact that all human politics are by nature criminal, or rather (since the idea of crime implies the idea of responsibility) that politics are foreign to moral law as much as are the instincts of tigers and leopards! If you push me onto this terrain and ask me what place I leave for Providence in History, I respond that our God is the God of human hearts. I can say that I know, I touch, I adore his presence in human hearts. May he be blessed for this grace that I have so often misused. But History is written by human beings and the dark desires and forces that drive human beings. I consider History to be the frightful sum total of our greed and envies ever since the murder of Abel. *Libido sciendi, libido sentiendi, libido dominandi* are the three rivers fueling this History that rolls on, throwing civilizations one after another, one on top of the other into the same nothingness.[40] And yet humanity remains. If this "inextricable depth of History" that you spoke of in the Pleyel auditorium destroys all flesh, it is powerless against "what is unique in humanity," to use your words again: the soul in other words, why not name it? The human soul is governed, dominated, submissive, or rebellious, but it always depends on uncreated Love. It is, it shall ever be: heaven and earth will pass away, you and I shall never pass away.

Having sketched out my position as a Christian, I shall now, with my feet sunk into the clay, settle back down to earth. If God does not make himself manifest in politics except by his absence—God's justice toward the Nations is always negative, it seems to me—then we must act on the basis of that absence, but without being of the school of Machiavelli, and taking care to avoid his traps. That's the problem for us to solve in

40. Mauriac is alluding to Pascal, *Pensées* (Brunschvicg 458): "'All that is in the world is the lust of the flesh, or the lust of the eyes, or the pride of life; *libido sentiendi, libido sciendi, libido dominandi*.' Wretched is the cursed land which these three rivers of fire enflame rather than water!"; thus citing 1 John 2.16: "For all that is in the world, the lust of the flesh and the lust of the eyes and the pride of life, is not of the Father but of the world." Pascal is also remembering St. Augustine, who lashed out against these three vices in *The City of God*, decrying not only their deleterious effect on individuals but their role in shaping the events of history. In 1923 Mauriac also published a novel with the title *The River of Fire*.

fighting against war. We must indeed give in to the gravity that Simone Weil puts in opposition with grace, since gravity is the law of politics. But we have to guide it if possible, and choose our landing place by relying on the enlightenment of natural reason. We shall fight against war, not with the language of feeling, which is unintelligible for the Empires and those that embody them, but by using an idiom that they understand. We can win this peace game by opposing the politics currently used with a more effective political strategy. What is this strategy?

It is of course not the set of policies implemented by the United States up until this month of December 1948. I have no reason to hide from you my feelings on these policies. I would not want to write anything that would hurt our American allies' feelings. In the end, however, one must agree that they have pushed the lack of political imagination to the edge of crime. In China, Korea, Greece, and everywhere they intervene, they have managed to achieve the incredible result of having Stalin benefit from hurt national pride and from the hatred that privileged people stir up in every country in the world when they resort to outside aid in order to ensure their domination. No rectification of these policies could come from an England subjected to the old imperatives of the Commonwealth, and more incapable than ever of having the disinterested gaze that France, in spite of its poverty and its shameful shortcomings, nevertheless casts on the world.

For a France that could finally extricate itself from the swamp in which its members of parliament condemn it to vegetate, there would be a politics of peace to put in place, not in the clouds, nor oriented toward unattainable goals, nor suspended on the hopes for a United States of the World and other cock-and-bull ideas, but founded on what is, on what cannot not be: on facts. And first of all, on the following fact: at present, Soviet Russia has no interest in starting a war. It dreads war. It would risk a war only if an interior crisis (always expected, always hoped for) put the adversary at its mercy: a crisis, my dear Camus, that might have as one of its causes an uncontrolled movement stirred up by one little man. There is the solid rock on which we could begin to build. But here we run into the first obstacle, which is the impossibility of dialogue between Soviet Russia and the West. That is certainly not an intellectual impossibility: the Iron Curtain is of the most physical nature. The Soviets have no worry greater than that of preserving their people from any and all liberal contamination. Since for them this is a matter of life and death and since we must observe that from their point of view they are right (the outside contacts that the war occasioned for the Red Army proved very costly), we should take account of that necessity and make the Kremlin admit that peace between the East and the West could only be founded through the intermediary of one to one contacts. France should be first, but not all alone. For the Russians as well, it would be necessary to find spokespersons and intermediaries: Czechoslovakia already appears to be prepared to play this role, at least if the Soviets agree. In the exchange of words that I imagine between Stalin and Truman, the first sign of good will that would have to be obtained from the Soviets would therefore be the easing of the Iron Curtain and the designation of some of the satellite nations, certainly not as arbiters, but, to borrow an old expression from the language of love and preciosity, go-betweens.

From such a standpoint, I have no reason to rally around de Gaulle's RPF [Rassemblement du Peuple Français] party, as you can imagine. There is not one of the unavoidable outcomes that you are trying to pile up against me that I cannot overcome. I believe that, whatever may happen, the RPF has no real hold over the segment of the French proletariat won over to Communism. It's because I have been a Gaullist from the very beginning that I remain strongly attached to the General, and because I take nothing away from the admiration and affection that André Malraux has always inspired in me, I considered the idea of this political party to be a disaster. Furthermore, its apparent success is a dreadful outcome for the careers of both of these men for whom I care deeply. As someone who has stood out in demonstrating his independence from the United States and Great Britain, General de Gaulle could have been exactly the man to create new inroads toward the goal of peace. I would grant you that he would have had to overcome other tendencies in his character. But that's not the question.

These views on peace that I am giving you are just examples. On those issues or others, I will leave it to the specialists to decide. But I hold that it is possible to defend the cause of peace effectively on the basis of reason, given the fact that the irrepressible will to power that drives even the most liberal democracies (such as the Netherlands in Indonesia or, as I write, England in Palestine) to stop at nothing, to run every risk, and to gamble the fate of humankind if need be in order not to relinquish one desert needed to assure the defense of their Empire. Why try to blind ourselves to reality? You will not do away with the forces that are in conflict with each other, but for a little while, you will perhaps succeed in balancing them against each other, as has happened in history. You can be reassured: I am not going to give you a course in diplomatic history and I am not a former student of political science. This science nevertheless exists. It has produced results. Monsieur de Norpois gave the world a reprieve that would have been longer if he had been less a creature of habit.[41] As dumb as he may have been, the clever people seem more to be feared, since in order to save world peace they trust in these visceral impulses that they are incapable of controlling and whose results they do not foresee. I understand that you deny you are old-school pacifists, that you have constructive views about a world parliament, and that Garry Davis, judging by the audience that he has obtained right after having appeared on the scene, attests that the time has come to run the risk. For a long time we saw the Ferris wheel, a vestige of the 1900 World's Fair, mill the clouds in the sky over the Champs-de-Mars. It is impossible for me to get interested in wheels that do not move anything, and especially the one that you dream of constructing, and which even before being finished, will be subjected to countless pressures from conflicting interests and will face these countries' implacable opposition to anything that claims to limit their sovereign rights.

Is that to say that I do not like anything about your effort? On the contrary, I like something that I myself would like to stir up and maintain in other areas: you have created a new meeting ground with possibilities for dialogue and agreement among people who do not know each other. Those are steps in the direction of my own goals, for you

41. In Marcel Proust's *Remembrance of Things Past*, the Marquis de Norpois is a well-to-do, staid diplomat who advises the narrator's father on matters pertaining to investments and careers. See http://proust-personnages.fr/?page_id=242.

must not think that I have given up on using weapons of the spirit in the defense of Peace. In my narrow sphere of a Christian layman, I strive to sound this "cry repeated by a thousand sentinels," "this call of hunters lost in the great woods."[42]

As sojourners on this earth, we are separated from each other by generation gaps, social milieu, and social class. And I who am making my way along have the certainty of belonging to the small number of those who hold a lamp in the heart of darkness. In their unworthy hands, they have safeguarded the light that they received from childhood and whose reflection I feel on my face and my heart, as on the faces set aflame in the paintings of Georges de la Tour.[43] And it is here that I reach the main obstacle that keeps me from attaching much importance to Garry Davis: it's the disproportion between what is at stake and these publicity campaigns in the press and in speeches. The smoke from the crematoria at Auschwitz has cleared away to reveal *humanity that now knows who it is*. The hideous politics in which the surviving nations have engaged even before the killing fields were covered over has provided the ultimate proof that the cause of humankind would be without hope if there had not been the Incarnation, if the Son of Man were not to return. The frightful simplification of History that we are witnessing no longer leaves any place for illusions about our species, nor about the fruits of death that it will continue to harvest right down to the last one: that of total annihilation. We no longer have the right to pretend to believe that a human action that doesn't lead to death is still possible. Saint-Cyran speaks somewhere about that which stains

42. Mauriac is citing lines from the penultimate strophe of Baudelaire's poem "Les Phares" ("The Beacons"), which lauds art's testimony to the human condition:

> C'est un cri répété par mille sentinelles,
> Un ordre renvoyé par mille porte-voix;
> C'est un phare allumé sur mille citadelles,
> Un appel de chasseurs perdus dans les grands bois
> [They are a cry passed on by a thousand sentinels,
> An order re-echoed through a thousand megaphones;
> They are a beacon lighted on a thousand citadels,
> A call from hunters lost deep in the woods!]

Baudelaire, *The Flowers of Evil*, trans. Aggeler, http://fleursdumal.org/poem/105.

43. A seventeenth-century French painter known for his portrayal of biblical scenes in intimate interior settings warmed by candlelight.

every soul "and defames it before God."[44] What defames humanity before God after Auschwitz and Buchenwald (without mentioning other names, for what nation has not been stained with crimes?) has surpassed every measure. We no longer have the right to hope for the power to save the cause of world peace by ourselves alone.

Do not at all believe that I should claim to prohibit Christians from becoming involved in human undertakings. What I am confiding to you only holds for me: I heed but one word, trust in one promise: not even for a second would I want to let go of this hem of the robe that I am clutching in the deep darkness. But that only concerns me. I give you the thoughts of decline: I speak to you as a man whose eyelids are growing heavy and who knows on whose shoulder he hopes to have the grace to fall asleep.

"We Do Not Like Justice" was the third editorial in a series inspired by the sensational trial of an adolescent and his two teenage accomplices accused of killing another adolescent boy, Alain Guyader, out of jealousy.[45] Mauriac again displays enduring interest for those who find themselves facing institutional justice for having committed various crimes of passion. Far from anything happenstance, quirky, or simply anomalous (as the French "fait divers" might suggest), manifestations of violence are for the novelist and the editorialist emblematic of deeply human tendencies and social pathologies too often conveniently overlooked or whitewashed in public life.

In two preceding editorials, Mauriac had focused on the futility of commonly cited psychological typologies of the day and on the particularities of the adolescent age that should encourage clemency for rash acts of violence.[46] Now, frankly portraying the harsh living conditions that engender violence among the impoverished, Mauriac issues a withering condemnation of the judicial regime and penal system that offer the young in urban

44. Mauriac is doubtless recalling a passage from Charles-Augustin Sainte-Beuve's *Histoire de Port-Royal* (Paris: Eugène Renduel, 1840), 354, which quotes Saint Cyran as saying: "Laver, purger ce qui souille toute âme et la diffame devant Dieu!" (Wash, purge what fouls every soul and defames it before God!)

45. Touzot in Mauriac, *La Paix des cimes*, 260n1.

46. François Mauriac, "Le Mystère des J3" and "L'Adolescence et la folie," in *La paix des cimes*, 260–64.

shantytowns little possibility of escaping from a life of despair and crime. Such is hardly the type of discourse that one would expect from a newspaper such as *Le Figaro*, known as a bulwark of orthodox perspectives on politics, society, and culture, a paper most commonly read by a staid, well-educated, well-to-do bourgeoisie much more fond of hearing about the evils of Communism. Mauriac's conclusion, a denunciation of the diffuse violence endemic to the established order of things and of our habitual apathy in the face of the "human ferocity" unfolding before our eyes, should prove to be just as unsettling for us today as it surely must have been for the readers of *Le Figaro* in 1951.

It is in just such an editorial, of which there are numerous examples, that Mauriac defies standard categorizations of "left wing" or "right wing" by vigorously denouncing the structural injustices of the socioeconomic order and the widespread indifference to the human suffering caused by that order. Mauriac's preoccupation with justice and compassion for the condemned indeed are recurrent features of both his novels and his editorials throughout his long career.

We Do Not Like Justice

Le Figaro, May 22, 1951

The play is over, and people are leaving. Tomorrow, in order to save another culprit, the plaintiff's lawyer will apply the same fierce determination as he did today in order to condemn these young men that the gendarmes are leading away. They disappear off the stage, already out of our memories. They leave the newsreels and sink down into an anonymous stench of misery, in order to be subjected to the treatment that has always produced the normal contingent of human failures to which society resigns itself. The play is over. Professional psychologists are going to apply the precious meanings that they have received from heaven to untangle the knot of motives and causes: "How fine it is, a fine crime!" is what a certain Jean-Jacques Weiss would cry many years ago already.[47]

We make believe that the play is over, and yet we know well that

47. Jean-Jacques Weiss, 1827–91, wrote on literature, history, the theater, and morals. See http://data.bnf.fr/12434025/jean-jacques_weiss/.

this was only a prologue and that the real tragedy is just beginning: it consists entirely of the slow destruction of a young person by a penitentiary regimen from which few escape. We play our role in this drama, every one of us: it is the role of destiny, a destiny that is neither blind nor deaf, and which could speak out, but does not get involved. Not that there is nobody today who will defend such a regimen, especially since the Resistance and the Purge have made the bourgeoisie familiar with its horror. Nor can we say that we have not been at every instant alerted to this situation, often by the very ones whose job it is to apply this abominable ruling. Concerning what I have already written in this column about a young man who does not recognize the deed that he committed as an adolescent because he has in fact become another person, one of these professionals assured me that it is the same for all prisoners regardless of their age: most no longer have anything in common with the criminal that they were at the time of their arrest. Many of the specialists who have thought about this problem believe that this process of degradation could become a process of restoration. But outside of these specialists, who indeed takes interest in the people in prisons? The public authorities object that reforms would be expensive, and it is true that it is a budgetary matter. But when special interests are involved, there is no budgetary matter that does not wind up being solved. The truth is that captives do not scare anyone and have no available means of exerting pressure. What candidate would have the idea of placing penitentiary reforms on his agenda? Since they do not vote, prisoners do not count any more than the dead. They are people who have been abandoned because they have no voice.

From now on, the death penalty can be given to child killers. But we shall continue to live in a world where shacks produce the highly abundant species of unworthy parents and abused children. Yes, highly abundant: thousands of children are only partially abused and their parents are only partially abusive. They cry out all night, in an overcrowded room, they soil their mats, they are dirty and ugly. The father has to get up at dawn: his exasperation stems from overwhelming depression. The conditions of their lives create brutes. We will kill the brutes, but we won't change these living conditions.

> It is not true that we love justice if we only rise up to protest against the injustices that we have an interest (almost always a political interest) in denouncing. It is not true that we are merciful if we are only moved by the spectacular execution of a black man or by a massacre of hostages, nor are we merciful if human ferocity leaves us cold when it has become customary and when it is expressed at our doorstep in regulations, age-old texts, and an established routine.

As does "Making It through the Holidays," "The End of All" links the concrete, personal experience of the everyday and the mundane to the historical drama of an entire generation. Noting the unprecedented human and material destruction perpetrated during the course of the two world wars that had marked the first half of the twentieth century and that had brutally dashed the optimistic hope for universal progress in the wake of scientific discoveries, Mauriac contemplates the twin specters of the atomic bomb and Stalinist oppression that now loomed over postwar Europe and ponders the resulting anxiety that permeated some of the most mundane aspects of everyday life. Here again, Mauriac's literary talents prove invaluable to his vocation as an editorialist, for his depiction of Parisian commuters does not simply provide a sketch of modern-day *tedium vitae* in the métro: the somber faces also betray the diffuse anxiety stemming from the fundamental tensions of the Cold War and the grave dangers that it posed to all people everywhere.[48]

While Mauriac was no existentialist, he was nonetheless keenly attuned to all that was indeed unsettling for a generation having experienced a world war. In spite of its extreme human and material ravages, the war seemed to have ushered in not an era of peace, but rather the threat of a new and potentially even more catastrophic conflict. That is why, in response to certain right-wing Catholics who accused the existentialists of undermining the morals of young people and thus sharing responsibility for the murder of Alain Guyader, Mauriac defends Camus and Sartre. While affirming that Christianity could offer direction to humans anguished by the

48. Cf. Nathan Bracher, "The Cold War Christian Humanism of François Mauriac," *Christianity and Literature* 52, no. 3 (Spring 2003): 394–95.

hostility, violence, and injustice of a world seemingly devoid of hope and meaning, he vigorously rejects the notion that their writings were sources of decadence and disorder. Mauriac insists that it was on the contrary essential to see the Existentialists as the voice of a troubled time.

It is almost a tautology to observe that literature is a reflection of its time. There is an obvious link between philosophies of the absurd and the historical circumstances between 1919 and 1949: the Russian Revolution, the exhaustion of French vitality, the disastrous foreign policy of the democratic nations and its direct effects, Fascism and Nazism, and in addition, the Spanish Civil War, Munich, World War II, the humiliating rout stands out clearly. And it goes without saying that the philosophy born from those events is in turn influencing minds. The fact remains that in France, Sartre and Camus have provided to a generation without God the metaphysical commentary on the History that it had just endured, the History that we, their elders, condemned it to endure, and of which Shakespeare, through the voice of Macbeth, had previously given the definition: "It is a tale told by an idiot, full of sound and fury, signifying nothing." Signifying nothing unless we apply to it the Christian "frame of interpretation."[49]

Beyond the important domestic and international issues of the Cold War that occasion his rhetorical jousting with counterparts writing for *Les Temps modernes* or for *L'Humanité* (the official paper of the Communist Party), Mauriac grapples with the fundamental question of humanity and the human condition, and thus with questions of religious faith. By all accounts, the unprecedented violence of the twentieth century had stripped away many dreams and illusions, and left humankind squarely facing troubling questions about human identity and destiny. For Mauriac, these questions of humanity are ultimately and ineluctably questions of Christianity, a Christianity not understood as providing an escape from the pressing issues of history, society, and politics, but on the contrary as providing the basic meaning of human existence that must motivate and direct his approach to the urgent issues of the day.

49. François Mauriac, "It's Voltaire's Fault," in *La Paix des cimes*, 78–79, cited and translated in Bracher, "The Cold War Christian Humanism of François Mauriac," 391.

The End of All

Le Figaro, January 29, 1952

The other day a lady from the provinces told me she was amazed that people in the Paris Métro appear sad. Everyone carries with them their own ordeal, I responded. And then, for most, how tedious is the task that each new morning serves up again! But there is something more: the newspaper they read as soon as they get up, with this "tournament of errors" in which all the governments of the world are competing and which they all deserve to win.

On the first page of *Babel,* a somewhat Manichean poem in the manner of Victor Hugo that Pierre Emmanuel has just published with Desclée de Brouwer (the worthiest tribute that this generation could pay to Hugo for his one hundred fiftieth birthday), I read the following: "A news vendor lying flat on his stomach was yelling out the headline: 'The End of All!' was written across the top, spanning eight columns. Somewhere under the rubble, typewriters were tapping away. The world was losing its ink out of all its wounds." It is losing not only its ink, or even its blood: it is losing faith in what it believed. The atomic bomb and Stalin's concentration camp empire are two outcomes that were not announced in Anatole France's speech before the statue of Renan in Tréguier, when he glorified science, reason, and the secular state. But we Christians have nothing to gloat about. What disquietude, what irritation, what confusion reigns among us. Among the priests and the faithful, there are doubtless a great many of the meek that Romano Guardini talks about, "who have become calm within and who stand before God in simplicity and peace."[50] But they are not the ones that we meet the most often, nor those that make a lot of visible commotion. Moreover, the mainstream press is beginning to loudly publicize certain defections.

Shall I say what I really think about this matter? I prefer the deep anxiety of today over the smug self-righteousness of the circles in which I lived as a child and an adolescent a half century ago. "The end of all" announced by Pierre Emmanuel's poem could be the beginning

50. Guardini was a German Catholic theologian who lived from 1885 until 1968.

of everything, if there were enough of us to want it. Every ordeal that afflicts us offers an answer if we question it. Never has History given harder or clearer lessons to those of us who hear no other voice but its own, and to others who have the faith, never has God spoken in a more visible way than by the events that are masters that he gives us by his hand. As painful as they may be, the small number of defections I was referring to among the clergy and the lay people deliver quite a lesson to the attentive mind. For it is not up to us to judge those who stray away: rather it is incumbent upon us to ask ourselves what drove them away. And how will you bring back these lost sheep who must be dearer to you than all those others who have remained faithful?

The fact of the matter is that people today have to be accountable in all domains, and must revise their methods. They get an idea of what they should not have done, but also what there is still time to do in order not to perish. For it is possible for us to perish, even in matters of faith: the promises of eternity do not do away with the deeply troubling question that I often have occasion to cite. It is the question that Christ put to his own without himself giving the answer, because it is up to each generation to answer for its own sake: "When the Son of Man comes, will he find faith on earth?" Today this question is addressed to us with such pressing insistence that none of us can dodge it. And that is why there are all these plays in the theater in which metaphysics occupies a prominent place.

These are trying times, yet to my mind, they are finer than the so-called "*Belle époque*" whose stale clichés still nourish our nostalgia for a facile life. Doubtless human history has constantly been caught up in the trials we are experiencing. But peaceful eras covered them with a facade and an order satisfying our reason and pleasing our taste. Now the facade has been stripped away, the illusion has been shattered, and nowhere can form take the place of substance. To be or not to be: whether we be philosophers, politicians, or religious leaders, shepherds of the flock or sheep, we are caught up in this dilemma, and I fear that there remains little time for us to solve it.

4 ∽ DECOLONIZATION AND THE WAR IN ALGERIA

The Defeat at Dien Bien Phu and the Road to Decolonization

For France as for other nations, the process of decolonization proved to be long and painful, marked by violent protests, fierce repression, massacres in Madagascar and Morocco, and ultimately insurrections and bitter wars in Vietnam and Algeria. The colonies of the French empire had furnished a large contingent of troops (some 350,000 in all) to the French army that participated in the liberation of French territory and in the defeat of Nazi Germany. Fighting against "Nazi barbarity" and for the sake of liberty, human dignity, and civilization, these indigenous troops had heavily contributed to the war effort that enabled France to regain a measure of respect within the Allied forces and to have a seat at the victors' table and on the Security Council of the United Nations. Following the war, they demanded the right to enjoy the same rights for which they had fought. Although de Gaulle had recognized that colonial troops had given renewed energy and legitimacy to these demands and had hinted that the colonies would be emancipated after the war, even the modest efforts at reform attempted during the postwar period were met with fierce opposition and sabotage by the Europeans defending their entrenched interests.

The situation was becoming increasingly tense when Mauriac was awarded the Nobel Prize in Literature in December 1952. In retrospect, the attribution of this supreme distinction was not without a certain irony, since the announcement made not the slightest reference to his career as an editorialist in the Parisian press, where he had played a highly prominent role since the mid-1930s.[1] Instead of using his newly acquired literary prestige to launch a new set of novels, however, Mauriac devoted himself ever more intensely to his editorials, demanding justice for the oppressed, the excluded, and the abused, particularly when they were victims of France's colonial order. As had been the case in the Spanish Civil War, Mauriac's protests against the brutal methods used by French police and military forces represented a major evolution of his perspectives, since even in the postwar period he continued to view French presence in the colonies as the vocation or even prerogative of a preeminent civilization and world power. Within the context of the Cold War he often sparred with the French Communists writing for *L'Humanité* and exchanged polemics with Sartre and the team of *Les Temps modernes*, who were more or less systematically pro-Soviet. Mauriac was all the more reticent to espouse the cause of colonial liberation in that he saw it all too often coopted by the enemies of the free world, who had little real interest in the rights and welfare of the colonized.

The insensitivity and ethnocentric presumptions marking Mauriac's defense of the war in Indochina, however, rapidly gave way to a pursuit of justice and human rights much more consonant with the Sermon on the Mount that he frequently cites. Such is the case when, as indicated schematically in the first part of "The Vocation of Christians in the French Union," a number of Catholic friends and intellectuals with irrecusable firsthand knowledge provide dramatic testimony about the massacre of Moroccans. Protesting in reaction to French provocations, they were fired

1. Flower, *François Mauriac, journaliste*, 1.

upon by French tanks in early December 1952, during the very days when Mauriac was in Stockholm receiving the Nobel Prize. The loss of life was heavy: officially some 50 and unofficially 1,000 to 1,200 Moroccans had been killed. Once aware of the severity of the crimes committed by French forces in the colonies, Mauriac responded with one of his most eloquent and powerful editorials, as he denounces the self-interested nationalism that too often blinds people to historical crimes committed in the name of their country. Mauriac's outspoken condemnation of the violence and injustice of France's colonial presence in Morocco caused a considerable uproar, not only among the staid, well-to-do readers of *Le Figaro* composing the bulk of its subscribers, but also in high-ranking political and military circles taken aback by such a frank assessment.[2]

The Vocation of Christians in the French Union

Le Figaro, January 13, 1953

I have received several letters from legal scholars but also from ordinary lay people regarding the young Alsatians who have been on trial in Bordeaux these days, and almost all leaned in the same direction.[3] I believe just as they do that the principle of collective responsibility is unbearable, and that justice must deal solely with individual cases, without any consideration of race or nationality. But the trial is underway: now we can only remain silent and wait. But what I note from these letters for today is the deep anxiety that they express and which points to more than just a remnant of justice, or at least that's what I hope. Yes, I can see that this is an awakening.

The horror of what the name of the little town of Oradour shall forever convey to us shall not keep us from looking squarely at the evil of which these young men, be they Alsatian, Prussian, Bavarian, or Saxon, were both the instruments and the victims.[4] We have eagerly condemned this essential injustice, this hideous contempt that might

2. See Lacouture, *Mauriac. 2. Un citoyen du siècle 1933–1970*, 245–61; Barré, *Mauriac. Biographie intime, 2. 1940–1970*, 244–55; Granger in Mauriac, *Journal: Mémoires politiques*, 1070nn2–3.

3. The first four paragraphs of the article as presented here were not included in Mauriac's *Mémoires politiques*.

4. Shortly after the Allied landing in Normandy on June 6, 1944, German tank units elsewhere

feels for the defenseless, this cowardly criminal attack on justice, on the holy and sacred wellspring of life, on women and children, perpetrated by an anonymous authority in Germany, in Russia, and in the United States, where we are moved by the plight of Blacks. Our half-willing ignorance is maintained by two opposing types of propaganda. On the one hand, we deny the validity of everything from communist sources, everything that we know to be orchestrated, directed, and subject to the demands of their tactics. On the other hand, we give in to the facility of accepting official accounts of events.

We do not do this out of moral turpitude, but like poor children who cannot bear for certain abominable acts to be attributed to their mother and who refuse to admit that certain men were capable of committing certain deeds in the name of France. We do not want to believe it, and we do not want to know it. The bad faith on the part of the Communists is a convenient pretext for us to reject everything without examining the facts, even the facts that the rest of the world believes it sees and, rightly or wrongly, condemns.

And then it happens that witnesses who are not Communists suddenly appear, witnesses who do not belong to any political party and whose testimony we cannot fail to hear if we are Christians and they are our brothers in Christ. It is an excusable weakness for private citizens to accept the official story without critical examination. But for the one whose mission it is to inform and enlighten fellow citizens, it is the most egregious failure. Whether we like it or not, it will soon no longer be up to us to keep silent about what really happened in Morocco (to speak only of Morocco), the day when the truth will be sifted out of the presently contradictory accounts from those on site. For the moment, I would simply like to remind the French people that there is a Christian community over there, and not only the one consisting of administra-

in France rushed north to join frontline troops. One of these was the Second SS Panzer Division, "Das Reich," which included a number of forcibly conscripted Alsatians. On June 10, 1944, they swept into the little village of Oradour-sur-Glane, south of Limoges, and, intent on exacting reprisals for Resistance strikes elsewhere in the region, massacred some 643 men, women, and children. The tragedy quickly became the very emblem of Nazi atrocities in France, particularly since a group of women, children, and the elderly, having sought refuge in the village church, had been burned alive inside. See "Oradour-sur-Glane, massacre" in Gordon, *Historical Dictionary of World War II France*, 267–68.

tors, civil servants, politicians, industrialists, shopkeepers, and business people. There is a Christian community that has taken root in this land of Islam, and which is not the enemy of Islam, but on the contrary understands and loves Islam. It is among those people that we would look for witnesses if ever we were asked to account for the bloodshed and if it were proven that such bloodshed had been unjustified.

I have here before me an admirable letter that Monsignor Lefèvre, vicar apostolic for Morocco, sent to his priests concerning the obligations incumbent on the faithful in the land of Islam. The tragedy of Casablanca has now given this text a significance that goes well beyond its meaning for the Christians in Morocco. It concerns the French Catholic Church in its entirety. The role of witnessing doubtless belongs first of all to the Christians in Morocco, as does also, if needed, that of "repairing" in every sense of the word: that means praying, healing the wounds, and restoring between the two communities the ties that have been brutally broken. But the duty of the entire Christian community, including Catholics and Protestants in the colonies and in mainland France, is to unite in opposition to this racism stemming from lucre and fear, and engendering collective crimes.

The fact remains that the public authorities responsible for maintaining order often let themselves be driven by motives that are not known by good-faith witnesses. They hold information that the public is not aware of. We do not have the intention of judging or condemning anyone on the basis of reports that, although not motivated by self-interest, are nevertheless impassioned. We simply want to get to the bottom of this bloody incident. We won't just sit back and let the page be turned.

Like the preceding piece, "The Crux of the Issue" was prompted by an incident of bloody repression. Jean Touzot points out that the "tragic shooting of July 14" occurred when French police brutally dispersed a demonstration organized in Paris by Algerians in protest of the detention of Messali Hadj: the violence claimed the lives of seven Algerians and wounded forty-four others.[5] Messali Hadj had been the first to organize Algerian Muslims in

5. Touzot in Mauriac, *La Paix des cimes*, 422n1.

view of acquiring not only equal rights but also independence. He founded several organizations which were disbanded by French authorities, including the Etoile Nord-africaine, the Parti du Peuple Algérien, and the Mouvement pour le Triomphe des Libertés Démocratiques. Up until the insurrection beginning in November 1954, he insisted on peaceful means of winning hearts and minds over to the cause of the Algerian people.[6]

However, Mauriac steps back from the immediate political context to focus on the cynicism that has also proved willing to use virtually any and all means, perpetrating horrendous violence and sacrificing countless human lives for a cause supposed to be just, in order to achieve the political ends that presumably justify such acts. Thus couching the urgent issues of the day in terms of universal history, Mauriac once again cites the biblical narrative of Cain and Abel as the paradigm of the inescapable human responsibility for such crimes.

The Crux of the Issue

Le Figaro, July 21, 1953

Monsieur Albert Camus has just sent to our sister paper *Le Monde* a letter in the sharpest terms about the tragic shootings of July 14: he denounces "a racism that does not dare say its name." I would like to lift the debate above all elements of partisan passions.

Why does a tragedy like that which has just cast a shadow over our nation's Bastille Day stir up such virulent and diametrically opposed reactions? It seems to me that the crux of the problem is situated beyond the question of racism. I understand very well that the racial question is tragically posed in all parts of the world today: this is the global liquidation of the policies imposed by the white race during the nineteenth century. But we must go deeper: what divides minds faced with these demonstrations of force, and, especially in France, stems from a certain idea of human beings, whatever their skin color may be?

A whole family of thought is cynically and magnificently expressed

6. Alain Ruscio, "Messali Hadj père oublié du nationalisme algérien," http://www.monde-diplomatique.fr/2012/06/RUSCIO/47882.

in the words that Balzac lends to Catherine de Medicis, and in which I believe he reveals his own most secret thoughts: "Over two hundred lowly peasants, you are all led to shed the tears that you refuse to cry over the sufferings of a generation, a century or a world. You are forgetting that political liberty, the tranquility of a nation, and knowledge itself are presents for which fate deducts taxes in blood."[7]

This already Nietzschean cry is answered by the eternal protest of those touched by the resounding words spoken from the earliest ages of the world: "Thou shalt not kill" and "What have you done with your brother?" Christ came and added the sublime paraphrase of the Sermon on the Mount, which promises blessed happiness for the meek, those who mourn, the merciful, the peacemakers, and to those who suffer persecution for the sake of justice.

Those are therefore the two opposing spiritual families. What complicates the problem, however, is that it has sometimes been the case that the cynical words that Balzac attributes to Catherine de Medicis appear wise (when they are reworked a bit) to a certain family of Christians and even to some seasoned theologians insistent on orthodoxy. At the same time, some people on the extreme Left who are distant from any and all religious belief are on the contrary still permeated with the leaven of the Gospel. And the Marxists in the Kremlin have no more doubts than did Catherine de Medicis as to their right to collect a tax from the people in the form of blood, the most onerous ever paid by humanity, in order to ensure their happiness in spite of themselves.

While apparently so complex, this problem should appear simple to us French. For if Catherine were in a position to judge French politics today, she would doubtless think that what is useful from now on is no longer "to sacrifice two hundred lowly peasants," but on the contrary to spare them and to be on the side of those for whom human life is sacred and who consider the lowliest of all people to have an absolute value. The fact that the respect for human rights has become the sign of political wisdom even among the members of parliament

7. "Sur Catherine de Medicis," in Honoré de Balzac, *Oeuvres Complètes*, vol. 16: *La Comédie Humaine* (Paris: Calmann-Lévy, 1879), p. 649.

who are the least inclined to have a heart in deciding matters of state illustrates the truth of that approach.

In "Playing a Double Game with Double Standards," Mauriac demonstrates that his focus on the "deeper" issues raised by the French police's killing of Algerian demonstrators does not serve as a pretext for ignoring the more immediate, concrete, and pointed matters of race and social justice that have been dramatically brought to a head by such severe abuses carried out both on the French mainland as well as in North Africa. He thus denounces the double standards of racist views that on the one hand lead to a more panicked, fearful, and therefore implacable repression of urban uprisings, while on the other hand tending to embolden those who, fearing no sanctions or reprisals, engage in shameless exploitation. The double standards allow Europeans to dominate and defeat Muslims in a double game.

At the same time, this very specifically targeted editorial points to a set of wider questions facing French intellectuals engaged in politics. Led by Sartre and *Les Temps modernes*, the Parisian intelligentsia of the postwar period, following Hegel and Marx, presumed events such as the momentous episodes of the Second World War to be the visible manifestation of a dialectical process ultimately leading to a classless society. They thus insisted on the primacy of history and the urgent necessity of *engagement*, or political commitment to actively participate in the march of history. In addition to Mauriac's leadership of the France-Maghreb Committee in trying to bring the French public and the French government to put an end to the violent repression and injustice in North Africa,[8] his editorials prove him to be as attentive to history as any of his counterparts, and just as firmly committed as anyone to political action. Although keenly attuned to political issues stemming from the major, ongoing historical developments following the Second World War, Mauriac refuses to engage in a Machiavellian, Nietzschean, or Marxist approach to human affairs that would emphasize collective political strategy to the point of aban-

8. See Lacouture, *Mauriac. 2. Un citoyen du siècle 1933–1970*, 276–84; Barré, *Mauriac. Biographie intime, 2. 1940–1970*, 260–78.

doning ethics focused on the dignity, worth, and well-being of the human person. At the same time, his adamant reaffirmation of the infinite value of each human life does not blind him to the fact that certain Christian institutions and individuals, as he grimly acknowledges, have resorted to the same cynical approach to events. Finally, Mauriac insists here in these articles, as he will throughout the war in Algeria, that since it is actually in France's long-term interest to allow the colonized the rights they demand and deserve, good ethics in fact make for good politics.

Playing a Double Game with Double Standards

Témoignage chrétien, July 24, 1953

"The French police would not have dared to fire on you!" North Africans tell their French friends. What shall we answer? That a North African crowd frightens the security services more than another? It may indeed be that those who died on July 14 were victims of the fear that the workers of their race arouse, and understandably so when they lash out (and we owe justice to all men, even to the policemen injured while doing their duty). But on another level, perhaps, the Algerians were victims even more of the fear that they do not arouse, because they have the fewest resources and they are the weakest, the least armed, and the most abandoned of all workers. Our counterparts in the press agreed on what was to be said of them: these virtuous considerations were by consensus the wreath that the French press laid on the corpses of July 14.

But that cannot suffice and does not wrap everything up. The North Africans who arouse both more and less fear than their fellow French workers are losing on both ends: hence the necessity of our protests. It is important to persuade those in charge that firing on a dark-skinned crowd constitutes an act that is just as grave as firing on a crowd with white skin. And then, perhaps, they will develop the technical means to disperse a riot, however dreadful it may be: tear gas, water cannons, whatever (I am told that only the security police are equipped in this manner). It is better to make people cry, it is better to shower them

> with water than with bullets. And that, it seems to me, is a reasonable opinion: it is very strange that those higher up had not thought of it earlier. It is of course too late for those who were killed in Casablanca and those who died at the Place de la Nation in Paris, but not for the living who may again gather in public. We demand that the authorities give to the police, whose duty it is to maintain order, the means to disperse people without killing them and to cause tears to flow artificially instead of really shedding blood.

"Malagar, Thursday, March 18, 1954" marked Mauriac's official debut as the star writer and intellectual penning a regular column titled the "Bloc-notes" ("Notepad") for the young Jean-Jacques Servan-Schreiber's recently launched news magazine, *L'Express*, featuring a distinctly modernist, stridently progressive bent.[9] All of Mauriac's articles in this series, which continue up to his death in 1970, carry the date, and occasionally the place, of their composition as the title. Mauriac thus links the content of his editorials to their form in a distinctive manner, connecting the anecdotal to the epochal, the local to the global, the biblical to the contemporary, the individual to the collective, and the personal to the universal, while at the same time relating not only his own experiences to the events and issues at hand, but also viewing the crises and scandals of the moment in light of countless events, personalities, and cultural landmarks having left their imprint on the history of France and the world. In the immediate political context of 1954, Mauriac, along with the other contributors to *L'Express*, threw his weight behind Pierre Mendès France, whom he admired for bringing peace to Tunisia and negotiating an end to French presence in Indochina. Mauriac points out that far from leading to quietism, his religious faith compels him to speak out in the face of the violence and injustice not only in recent history, but also in France's current affairs.

9. Malagar was the name of Mauriac's ancestral home in the Bordeaux region.

Malagar, Thursday, March 18, 1954

L'Express, April 10, 1954

I couldn't wait for Easter. I have come here to hole up and clam up. Spring is not here yet and I couldn't care less. Silence is what I am after. My declining years are not at all what I had thought. I am finding a deep peace within, but what violence there is without! It seems as though now all the attention that I had been paying to myself as long as I still felt a few sparks of youth, with my desires, and my dreams, has finally turned away from this heart now free from worries, and that I can no longer ignore the criminal reality of what is going on in the world.

Nothing is farther from my experience than the Marxist notion that religion prevents us from seeking justice here on earth. God has never dominated my life without reopening a wound, without maintaining a certain pain, a feeling of shame for the complicity that I had allowed to reign in me ever since I began to play the game of society. My own story is over, but the story of world history is continuing and has become my own.

I doubt, however, that there are many writers my age who have experienced the same thing. The amazement and the worry, if not the scandal that I have stirred up make me aware of my singularity. I don't play the game. Perhaps the socialites are right not to forgive me for enjoying high society while at the same time betraying their interests.

Never before had I realized just how rare—and dreaded—is someone who thinks aloud. I nevertheless only say what I see, and I only see what is in plain sight for everyone else to see as well. But people dread my articles precisely because what I denounce in them is so obvious. In the realm of politics, for example, what jumps out at you is the game that people are playing openly and shamelessly. A very small number of people are in the loop and pass the ball back and forth among themselves and are still in cahoots even if they hate each other. This team holds the power whether or not there is a ministerial crisis. And the crisis always plays itself within the team: the dictatorship remains invulnerable, intact until the next elections. And then the logic of elections will kick in and put the same team back in charge, unless . . .

"Monday, March 29, 1954" seeks to undermine the smug moral assurance and material privilege that has long allowed the upper-class bourgeoisie to exercise economic and political domination. Mauriac thus continues to attack bases of comfort that serve as a shelter from the urgent questions of society and politics. We also find clear signs of his disillusion with the Christian democrats of the MRP (Mouvement Républicain Populaire) that he had so eagerly supported in the immediate postwar period.[10] Now an enthusiastic backer of Pierre Mendès France, Mauriac leans to the left in the references that frame his commentary on current events, beginning with his quotation of the philosopher Alain (Emile Chartier), known for his stridently anticlerical rationalism. Mauriac then compares the plight of the working class in the 1950s to that of nineteenth-century France, which was periodically rocked by revolutionary outbursts in Paris in 1830, 1848, and 1871. He thus ponders the social and political developments that have allowed for greater stability even amid continuing and flagrant economic injustice.

Then, turning to the growing crisis in North Africa, where the killing of French policemen has been answered with torture, judicial irregularities, and executions, Mauriac warns his compatriots not to ignore the signs of colonialism's demise. As one of the very first to speak out against the use of torture, Mauriac once again denounces the double standards of a justice system that is lenient with those who torture and kill when they are members of the French forces of order. Intent on removing sources of moral comfort and apathy, Mauriac warns his readers to be skeptical of the official narratives of violent confrontations.

10. Founded by prominent Resistance leaders Maurice Schumann and Georges Bidault, the Mouvement Républicain Populaire party was a Christian democrat political formation that played a prominent role in virtually all of the postwar governing teams up until the mid-1950s. See "MRP," http://www.larousse.fr/encyclopedie/divers/MRP/134250.

Monday, March 29, 1954

I am pondering two of Alain's writings. First, "The common people, children of Aesop, are never besotted, nor are they asleep, they are only abandoned." And especially the following: "The enslavement of some people, the conceit and ferociousness of others are things that are so clear that all that is needed is to mention them." So I ask myself the following question. Where do we get this calm that we are enjoying? What is the basis of this tranquil order that constitutes the law and the prophets for bourgeois society, however unjust that order may be? There are several explanations. First, the living conditions for the working class are no longer strictly unbearable as they were under the July Monarchy, when the excess of dire poverty drove the common people to barricade streets in Lyon and Paris.[11]

But I wonder if the working class's hard-won achievements of progress by labor unions and their enrollment in a powerful party might have, by a sinister paradox, ended up ensuring the political reign of big business. The Communist Party has disciplined the common people and accustomed them to obeying with mechanical docility. It has killed the spontaneity within the working class, the instinct for movements that in 1848 and in 1871,[12] however, led to senseless massacres and an intensification of dire poverty. The fact remains that, in spite of failure, our last two historic days on the sixth and seventh of February, 1934 (the first of which was of bourgeois fascistic origin) showed that the crowd came very close to prevailing.[13] The heartbeat of successful revolutions had always been at the outset, passion, a movement,

11. The July Monarchy consisted of the reign of King Louis-Philippe d'Orléans, which began in July 1830 following the Paris insurrection of June 27, 28, and 29, known as "les Trois Glorieuses" (the Three Glorious Days). Louis-Philippe was himself overthrown in the democratic revolution of 1848.

12. The radical left-wing insurrection known as "La Commune" rocked Paris from March 18 through May 27, 1871, at the outset of the Third Republic. It was brutally crushed by troops loyal to the conservative bourgeoisie, who, in putting down the uprising, massacred some 30,000 people.

13. On February 6, 1934, some 200,000 right-wing demonstrators converged on the Place de la Concorde and attempted to penetrate into the National Assembly. Widely regarded as an attempted Fascist coup, the riots left twenty dead and hundreds injured and sparked the political coalition known as the Popular Front, headed by Socialist Léon Blum. The Popular Front was swept into power in the May 1936 legislative elections.

and a drive of the masses of people suffering from unemployment and hunger. Without putting an end to it, we have made poverty bearable, because now it is tolerated. Such is the great victory for order.

Social progress has replaced the jumps and starts of the common people's instinct with a strict order serving the policies laid out by the Kremlin. Strikes are regulated and carried out without anger and without the fury that exceeds all limits. But what is an ordered revolt worth? The bourgeois government has an interest in seeing that it is impossible for the working class to try anything without the permission of some party, be it the Communist Party, and without blind obedience to the labor unions' directives. The party and the labor unions tend to discipline the common people, making it poorly adapted for becoming a tidal wave. And the following factor also enters into consideration: with their technical progress, the police no longer have to use military troops. Today, Louis-Philippe could hold out.

Simone Weil: "History is nothing but a compilation of the depositions given by murderers on the subject of their victims and themselves."

I had scarcely finished writing the word "murderers" when they brought me the newspaper. I open it and run across the story that I have been looking for and dreading for eight days: "Three executions in Tunisia." Not to minimize the awful assassination of French and Tunisian policemen in Mokrine, but that was a crime committed by a crowd out of control: no arrest immediately followed the riot. I only know about the Mokrine affair from three lawyers. Perhaps they have misled me. I wish passionately that they had misled me, that their clients had not confessed under torture by electric shocks and dog bites. I wish that the examining magistrate had not, as they stated, been transported to the police department, and that he had not, against all rules, interrogated the suspects in the presence of the policemen, without the assistance of any lawyer. Yes, I wish that for the sake of the president of the Republic. I wish it for the sake of this member of the Council of Magistrates, who belongs to the Mouvement Républicain Populaire: I took it upon myself to write him personally, recalling the facts (we had been schoolchildren together). He has not bothered to respond.

Now I have seen this same Mouvement Républicain Populaire within other walls, overflowing with the most indulgent comprehension for the French citizen who had tortured and killed, who did not deny his crime, and whose life was not at stake: it was only a question of wearing an official decoration. Double standards? That's the least one could say. And yet what if the eternal Standard Setter existed? You Catholics of the Mouvement Républicain Populaire, what if what you profess with your lips were true, and what if every drop of innocent blood that was shed by your doing or with your complicity fell back on your head forever? Others cause bloodshed by the law of their species, but you?

Let's turn away from feelings that you shrug off. But are you so blind as not to see colonial empires breaking apart everywhere? Are you so stupid that you fail to recognize this asset, or what is left of it, in your hands, which is what France still means for these peoples whom you stupidly and stubborn think you can hold in check with the use of terror?

Taking stock of the impending defeat of French forces at Dien Bien Phu and the insubordination of Marshal Juin in "Thursday, April 1, 1954," Mauriac declares himself nauseated and repulsed by so much needless bloodshed and political turpitude. He again insists on spiritual values as the impetus for political commitment. He points out that he cannot withdraw to any safe intellectual or spiritual safe haven, since, first of all, as a Christian, he is committed to justice and respect for human dignity, and second, as a citizen he shares responsibility for the actions of France's military forces, as he would state so forcefully in his "Bloc-notes" entry for the following day: "Even should I want to, I am not allowed to disregard or turn away from the shedding of all this innocent blood, since those speaking and acting are doing so in France's name."[14]

14. François Mauriac, *Bloc-notes, tome I. 1952–1957*, edited and annotated by Jean Touzot (Paris: Les Éditions du Seuil [Points-Essais], 1993), 127 (hereafter, BN, with appropriate volume and page numbers).

Thursday, April 1, 1954

I'd like to be in Paris to get this scoop: Marshal Juin, a right-wing man, rebelling against a right-wing administration. That in no way means that those opposed to the European Defense Community are grouped around him on the political scene. I shall have to wait to get back in order take stock of things.

The horror in Indochina is at its peak. How much blood has been wrongly shed there! I feel suddenly nauseated and tempted to flee such a sight in order to escape from this "imbroglio of errors and violence," as Goethe defines politics ... I feel I have a right to eternity, which at my age begins on this side of death. As in the theater, when we get there early: behind the curtain that has not yet gone up, we hear the muffled sounds of what is happening in the realm of the timeless. We are already getting our minds into the play that has not yet begun. An old man is allowed to turn his heart and mind away from what constitutes absolute evil. In the political order, the war in Indochina is spiritually the absolute evil. Ah! I understand why Charles Du Bos[15] loved Keats's verse so much: "The soul is a world of itself, and has enough to do in its own home."[16] Yes, but it is too late: I have committed myself in the material sense of the word, as a soldier who has signed up for active duty. Even if I let myself get carried away or led astray by political passion, the fact remains that I am committed to these problems here below for reasons from on high.

"Monday, May 10, 1954" foregrounds the annual student pilgrimage and the cathedral at Chartres where they gathered and presents them as tangible signs of France's rich, diminished, yet still vibrant spiritual heritage now threatened by the ominous developments of the colonial crisis dramatically evident in the bloody defeat at Dien Bien Phu. Once again, Mauriac intimately associates his Christian faith with his political preoccupa-

15. The essays and journal of Charles Du Bos, 1882–1939, stressed the primacy of the inner spiritual life. See http://www.larousse.fr/encyclopedie/personnage/Du_Bos/117197.

16. Letter to John Hamilton Reynolds dating from August 25, 1819. See http://www.gutenberg.org/files/35698/35698-h/35698-h.htm#Page_282.

tions. His references to Péguy,[17] Lacordaire,[18] and Jaurès, three of France's most eloquent, outspoken advocates of humanism, generosity, and social justice, serve to underscore the thematics of silence, a silence emblematic of the absence of clear, decisive leadership at the very moment when France was facing a grave crisis. Allusions to the Tomb of the Unknown Soldier, created in memory of the 1.4 million French soldiers killed during the First World War, and to the words Jesus spoke in response to those who urged him to quiet the crowds acclaiming his entry into Jerusalem further heighten the unsettling implications of this silence.[19] As would be the case for Americans in the 1960s, the French youth would soon find themselves literally on the front lines of the colonial wars, as the military contingent sent to "pacify" Algeria following the outset of the insurrection that would break out on November 1, 1954, would eventually number some 500,000 troops, most of them young conscripts. Not coincidentally, Michel Winock notes that the Catholic student organizations would prove to be some of the most active in organizing opposition to the war in Algeria.[20]

Monday, May 10, 1954

Yesterday R. took me to Chartres where we were preceded by twelve thousand students having walked forty kilometers. Was it because I participated less closely than last year, or because I no longer feel a sensation of surprise? As moved as I was, and in total unity, of course, with that huge crowd of youth who were praying and suffering, I nevertheless felt a bit unsatisfied this year. Dare I say why? What silence greets these twelve thousand young French men and women gathered here just after Dien Bien Phu, in Péguy's cathedral, under the most illustrious vaults of Christendom. I thought for a moment that the stones

17. Charles Péguy, 1873–1914, represented a rare combination of a Catholic, Socialist, and Nationalist writer who used his eloquent pen in defense of Alfred Dreyfus. He was killed in action during the first phase of World War I.

18. Jean-Baptiste-Henri Dominique Lacordaire, 1802–1861, was known for his stirring oratory and his fervent support for republican democracy and social justice. See the online *Catholic Encyclopedia*, http://www.newadvent.org/cathen/08733a.htm.

19. Mauriac is alluding to Luke 19.40: "I tell you, if these [people] were silent, the very stones would cry out."

20. Winock, *Le Siècle des intellectuels*, p. 520.

would cry out! The cardinal did not fail to deliver an excellent address in the very words he should have spoken. But a different, nonofficial voice should have spoken out ... What voice? Alas, there were generations of Christians crowding around Father Lacordaire's pulpit, just as, whenever they were disheartened, generations of Socialists were stirred back to their feet by the great voice of Jaurès. What silence there is everywhere in this bewildered France of 1954! We should shed tears of blood over the Tomb of the Unknown Soldier, for today it is he who is remaining silent.

After the dinner at the Grand Monarque restaurant, the cathedral was literally revealed to us in its glorious body by the indirect sunlight. We went down into the basement where there was nobody except for a student on his knees, leaning his forehead against the holy table. The sexton walked by jingling his keys, but instead of crying out "We're closing," he said to us softly, "You still have a little time," as if he knew the infinite value of a sole minute of prayer.

Growing Unrest in North Africa and the Outbreak of the Algerian War

In "Friday, May 14, 1954" and "Sunday, May 16, 1954," we see that Mauriac's position as president of the France-Maghreb Committee clearly leads him well beyond statements of principle, as he gains detailed firsthand accounts of the widespread, sometimes violent unrest in North Africa and Madagascar and of the brutal and often extralegal means used in response by French authorities. Observing the convergent signs of a widespread revolt against French colonial power, Mauriac warns that intensifying the use of force against anticolonial militants will only lead to a vicious circle of escalating violence. He then rhetorically asks what enduring heritage France intends to give to these youth in North Africa, who are demanding their fair share of "*liberté, égalité, fraternité.*"

Lucidly assessing torture as only exacerbating anger and frustration, and thus only intensifying the motivation and recruitment of future terrorists, Mauriac anticipates the scenario that would so tragically play itself out in Algeria. In 1957, the systematic use of torture and summary executions by French forces would "win" the Battle of Algiers, but ultimately solidify popular support for the FLN (Front de Libération Nationale), which was ultimately victorious in its fierce struggle for independence. Mauriac's warning of a long-enduring anger and resentment among North African youth has sadly continued to prove true not only in North Africa, but also in the poor suburbs plagued by high unemployment, drugs, and juvenile delinquency in present-day France.

Friday, May 14, 1954

Yesterday evening I., having just come back from Madagascar, reported to us what he could about the sultan without breaching the confidentiality imposed upon him as a lawyer. He had found the sultan transformed by the ordeal, but very serene. I. put into proper perspective the question of the sultan's fortune, which the sovereign himself cannot administer: a dahir can take it away from him at any moment, and its proceeds have to support thirty people. The sultan still has to pay for everything himself. If they had continued to make him travel around the world, he would have had to pay for it. The police are well-behaved, quite different from the police force in Corsica, who would gorge themselves at his expense.

At the end of the day, he remains our interlocutor. In Morocco and Tunisia, that's the big problem. In Tunisia, nothing can be done without reaching a direct understanding with Bourguiba: our plight in this area hinged on Monsieur Martinaud-Déplat's veto![21] The news was bad on that side. The easing of tensions was only due to Monsieur de Hautecloque's departure! The next elections risk reopening the era of terrorist attacks. The bey is unpopular.

I came home at one in the morning. And this evening, there will be the dinner for *L'Express* where, with Mendès France, Armand, and Robert Schuman, I will speak to delegations from the *grandes écoles* and respond to their questions.[22] The hours leading up to these sorts

21. Habib Bourguiba, 1903–2000, leader of the Tunisian independence movement, became the first president of Tunisia, remaining in office from 1957 until 1987.

22. The *grandes écoles* are the highly elite, most prestigious institutions of higher learning in France, such as the Ecole Nationale d'Administration, Polytechnique, Hautes Etudes Commerciales, and the Ecole Normale Supérieure, that lead to the most prominent careers in business, industry, and government.

of taxing experiences remind me of the times in my youth when, the day before examinations, I could not take any nourishment other than cold milk. But those were mandatory tests. Now that I am at the age of retirement, what demon drives me on?

I have been living through North Africa's ordeal hour by hour, and I remain haunted by what I heard yesterday evening. It is an unbroken chain linking two forms of terror that feed off each other, with the terrorist bombings provoking the repression, and the repression leading to more bombings. As related by newspaper reports, this tragedy has an everyday, routine aspect, that of a monotonous detective film in several episodes. But this woeful affair has another, hidden face. Even if they are released, suspects that have been arrested and often cruelly interrogated do not keep their resentment to themselves. They have friends, companions, brothers, and, above all, children. This generation is being born, schooled, and raised in a climate poisoned by these two forms of terror: for them, those that we call thugs are martyrs. In spite of everything, their parents to some degree still find France venerable. But what will France represent for this generation that is growing up so quickly, for these children who are already adolescents? These children of wrath already hate France.

That's what we must have the courage to warn our country about. There is no expression in our language that is more deceptive and that we are more inclined to use and abuse than that of "gaining time." In politics, to gain time is literally to waste it: it is to ruin beforehand the time that our children, along with Moroccan, Tunisian, Algerian, and all the African children will live through when our generation has passed the baton to them.

In these countries, whose plight is linked to ours and with which we have been entrusted, we are at this very moment shaping the everlasting face of this adolescent humanity that has not yet been initiated to public affairs. Tomorrow they will take on the form that we are giving them today. When we see the French in Morocco taking measures without, for lack of imagination, we suppose, envisaging the aftermath, we feel like banging our heads against the wall. For these sorts of crimes are crimes of stupidity. "This tremendous stupidity, bull-headed stupidity" of which Baudelaire spoke is essentially the stupidity of the police.[23] Do not they see this huge, silent crowd of children reaching adulthood among the peoples under our protection? These people are noting what they see and hear, and from day to day they are taking in the lessons of history, and not only of the events that are happening at their doorstep ... They do not need to be able to read in order to decipher and interpret these events.

Sunday, May 16, 1954

Coincidence: this morning I received a letter from a Kabylian colleague, who echoes what I was writing yesterday about the younger generations in his native region: "It is not a lost cause," he told me, "when we are dealing with men of my age: France is within them, and they would not be able to renounce France without perishing. There are, however, these young men and women for whom France is emphatically not represented by the face of Marianne or by the woman sowing grain as seen on coins, but rather by the ugly mug of a cop."[24]

23. Mauriac is citing Baudelaire's "L'Examen de minuit":

Nous avons, pour plaire à la brute,
Digne vassale des Démons,
Insulté ce que nous aimons
Et flatté ce qui nous rebute;
Contristé, servile bourreau,
Le faible qu'à tort on méprise;
Salué l'énorme Bêtise,
La Bêtise au front de taureau;
[We have, to please the brute,
Worthy servant of the Demons
Insulted what we love
And flattered that which we find repugnant;
As servile executioners, we have saddened
The weak ones we wrongly despise
And greeted the enormous Stupidity
Bull-headed Stupidity;]

The French text is from Baudelaire, *The Flowers of Evil*, http://fleursdumal.org/poem/306; the English translation is my own.

24. Marianne refers to the effigy of the French Republic, whose bust is in every city hall.

In "Thursday, June 10, 1954" and "Sunday, June 13, 1954," we once again find Mauriac the writer deploying his literary arsenal to target his political opponents, with Foreign Minister Georges Bidault receiving the brunt of this salvo. Bidault would later take a hard line, refusing to accept Algerian independence, and even joining the group of French army officers organizing terrorist attacks: they thus aimed to sabotage all talks with the FLN and impose a military rule on both France and Algeria. Quoting from Macbeth to mock Bidault's vain ambition, Mauriac could have also invoked the well-known line "All the world's a stage" in this corrosive portrait of various figures who mount the podium to address the French National Assembly, in close proximity to the Place de la Concorde. Both of these famous venues thus represent "the permanent setting for a drama in which too many walk-ons have usurped the main roles and are now sabotaging the play, prohibiting the young troupe from acting their parts."

We also once more find Mauriac linking the personal and religious to issues of a collective, political dimension: he characterizes himself as "someone who was late to empathize with the victims, and whose heart had remained stone cold over so many years." While acknowledging his own previous insensitivity to the plight of the colonized, he depicts the spiritual communion among those of several cultural origins gathered for prayer and meditation in the cathedral as a model for peace. Nevertheless Mauriac points out that in the course of French history, many *Te Deums* honoring imperial conquests had also been celebrated at Notre Dame de Paris.

Thursday, June 10, 1954

Yesterday, I attended the session of the National Assembly. It had been many a year since I last peered into that vat: I hate its dim light and sooty atmosphere, worthy of a second-rate historical painting. One gets the impression of observing through a microscope the humans that gesticulate within. As we keep repeating to our younger colleagues, "Ah, if you had heard Sarah Bernhardt[25] or Mounet-

25. Henriette Rosine Bernard, who went by the stage name "Sarah Bernhardt," was known for her highly original, captivating interpretations of classical plays, not only at the Comédie

Sully,"[26] we sigh. "Ah, Jaurès and Briand were of another category."[27] Did I actually hear them that much? Once or twice, maybe. I hardly ever came into this chamber of parliament, even when the show was worth the trouble.

Shall I go ahead and say what I really think? For me, this podium will never again be the one where Clemenceau, overwhelmed with joy, stood up to speak on November 11, 1918.[28] It shall remain the podium where the obscene person of Rosenberg dished out his lesson to a desecrated France.[29]

"The Minister of Foreign Affairs has the floor." I had not seen him for two years. How I pity him! When he so much endeared himself to his students in the lycée at Reims, did one of them whisper "You shall be king" in his ear? And certainly, the Georges Bidault of that time would have deserved to hear the words of Lady Macbeth:

> yet do I fear thy nature;
> It is too full o' the milk of human kindness
> To catch the nearest way: thou wouldst be great;
> Art not without ambition, but without
> The illness should attend it: what thou wouldst highly,
> That wouldst thou holily ... [30]

Human, all too human Bidault!

Française but also within her own theater company. Bernhardt's performances were acclaimed throughout the world, including in Great Britain, the United States, and Australia, from the early 1870s through the first part of the twentieth century.

26. Jean-Sully Mounet, known by his stage name "Mounet-Sully," was a highly admired artist and actor who performed memorable roles in tragedies at the Comédie Française, often with Sarah Bernhardt, from the early 1870s through the first decade of the twentieth century.

27. Aristide Briand, 1862–1932, who served many years in the governing team of ministers of the Third Republic, is most remembered for his efforts to put an end to the arms race following the First World War; he was among those at the 1925 Locarno conference who initiated the Kellogg–Briand pact, signed in 1928. See http://www.larousse.fr/encyclopedie/personnage/Aristide_Briand/110180.

28. Clemenceau was the famed French statesman, known as "the Tiger," who was premier when the armistice ending the First World War was signed on November 11, 1918.

29. Alfred Rosenberg, 1893–1946, played a key role in the formulation of Nazi ideology. His infamous Einsatzstab Rosenberg engineered and carried out the looting of art and other valuables possessed by Jews throughout Europe. See http://www.yadvashem.org/odot_pdf/Microsoft%20Word%20-%206287.pdf. In November 1940, Rosenberg lectured the National Assembly on the "errors" of the French Revolution, the Enlightenment, and democracy. See Daniel Cohen, *Lettre à une amie allemande* (Paris: L'Harmattan, 1998), 694. He was later tried and executed at Nuremberg.

30. William Shakespeare, *Macbeth* I.V.16–21. See http://shakespeare.mit.edu/macbeth/full.html.

What an astonishing destiny is his! I can still see him in the very first days of his reign, arriving late for a lunch at the Ritz, and spouting out furiously, "*He* already named an ambassador without seeking my opinion!" "*He*" was the General. And I can still hear Bidault, imitating de Gaulle: "As for Bidault, we'll brush him aside! And we'll send him to teach ninth-graders in the Carpentras middle school!" Bidault was not swept away. It was the other one whose ark came to its ultimate resting point on some obscure Mount Ararat, and it is the little history teacher that fate has charged with writing a new chapter of our History. What a chapter! We shall not throw the first stone. Was it possible to win the day? Is it a lost cause?

His speech was entirely scripted. He made a serious and skillful plea in defense of the Geneva peace process. As if that were the real question, instead of the road that was followed for ten years and that led us straight to Dien Bien Phu! Rightly or wrongly, he is pleased with what he is accomplishing right now at the bottom of the abyss where he is floundering about. But who precipitated us into this hole? Not he alone, let us grant him that: many others had a hand in it and the whole country was complicit.

His adversary Pierre Mendès France had too easy a hand to play: Indochina, North Africa … The difficulty consisted of covering all of these points. The various ingredients of his speech seemed good, but the sauce did not blend together well. He first dealt with Geneva and Indochina, and then started over with another speech on North Africa. He should have provided a coherent synthesis of the catastrophes that the Quai d'Orsay has been orchestrating for ten years. I hurried out as soon as there was a break in the parliamentary session and walked over to *Le Figaro*'s offices at the Place de la Concorde, which is the permanent setting for a drama in which too many walk-ons have usurped the main roles and are now sabotaging the play, prohibiting the young troupe from acting their parts.

For my reading before I go to sleep, I open at random a volume of Mme de Sévigné's *Lettres*. What callousness! No trace of the mawkishness that will put itself on display a century later: "The other day, when going into a dance, a nobleman from Brittany was stabbed by two men dressed as women: one of them held him, the other kept piercing his heart at will. At the site of the crime, the little d'Hartouis was frightened to see this man that he knew well all stretched out on the floor, still warm, all bloody, entirely dressed, and totally dead. . . ." And the good lady continues right on: "Mme de Valençai's son, such a dishonest man, died of an illness, just when he was about to attack them all in court: his death made everyone happy. It seems to me that people have not taken the habit of dying when so many others wish them to." Never was less care taken to disguise one's feelings than in the century of Tartuffe. Never were people less ashamed of what they felt. We are the ones who think ourselves to be brutes and try to handle things with kid gloves.

Sunday, June 13, 1954

Yesterday evening, I attended a prayer vigil at Notre Dame de Paris, from 9 p.m. until 11 p.m., in order to obtain amnesty for France's political prisoners overseas. The cardinal had given his consent on the condition that attendance should be by invitation and that there should be no publicity. That must have earned him many insults, but also our eternal filial gratitude. There were nevertheless several hundred of us crowded around the Virgin.

If the men and women who, on the occasion of this vigil, sent me reproachful or insulting letters had been able to see that faithful flock standing perfectly still in deep prayerful contemplation, if they had heard the mysteries of the Rosary meditated one after the other in the Madagascan tongue, then in the dialect of the Ivory Coast, then chanted by some Vietnamese, and finally in the Kabylan language and in Arabic, they would have understood that they were not themselves absent from our communion: it was for them also, the French residing in the colonies, that we were engaging in this struggle. For what is it all about, if not to break the unending chain of reprisals? But what change could be imagined without political amnesty? That's the key to everything.

As someone who was late to empathize with the victims, and whose heart had remained stone cold over some many years, I bear no grudges against these people who were insulting us: I ponder that while listening to these poor brothers chant their prayers with somber faces. The sacred names rung out softly through their mysterious dialects.

With what intensity we experienced the brotherhood of all men in Christ during these two hours, at the feet of Notre Dame de France, in the dark and immense vessel where in the course of history have rung out so many *Te Deums* that must have horrified the sacrificial Lamb!

"Tuesday, November 2, 1954" is the first of a long series of incisive articles that Mauriac devotes to the Algerian War. Stemming from decades of injustices, humiliations, and violent repressions, and initiated by a handful of determined militants, this colonial war was arguably one of the darkest chapters of French history: terrorist attacks on cafés, cinemas, casinos, and racetracks were answered with ferocious repression in the form of mass arrests, displacement and detention of large groups of Muslim civilians, executions, systematic torture, and disappearances of suspects. When the reality of an independent, Muslim Algeria loomed unmistakably on the horizon, a group of Europeans led by a handful of army officers spearheaded an underground paramilitary organization, the OAS (Organisation de l'Armée Secrète), and began conducting their own terrorist campaign. On several occasions, the Algerian War brought France to the brink of civil war and military dictatorship. It also prompted Mauriac to pen some of his most spirited and eloquent editorials, which on the one hand inspired admiration for his denunciation of torture, and on the other, provoked a host of insults and death threats for having upset the established order in Algeria.

Known now as the "Toussaint rouge/sanglant," or "Red/Bloody All-Saints' Day," November 1, 1954, was the occasion of a series of violent attacks, as some thirty bombings, intentional fires, and assassinations left ten people dead in Algeria, including two Muslims and eight European French citizens. Coordinated by a coalition of several groups determined to fight for an independent Algeria ruled by the Muslim majority (there were approximately 8 million Muslim noncitizens and 1 million French citizens of various origins living in the country at the time), these attacks marked the beginning of an insurrection that would soon escalate into the Algerian War, a bitter, ugly, highly traumatic conflict that would last almost eight years before resulting in the creation of an independent Algeria on July 5, 1962.[31]

Although the events of November 1, 1954, are now recognized as the moment when the Algerian war broke out visibly, most people in France took little heed of what was occurring on the opposite shore of the Mediterranean. Attuned, as we have seen, to the highly dangerous and untenable situation created by a long legacy of colonial violence and contempt in North Africa, Mauriac lucidly foresees the frightful bloodshed about to occur, shudders at the waves of repression and reprisals, and warns that whatever may come to pass, the French police must at all cost be prevented from using torture on their prisoners in this war.

Tuesday, November 2, 1954

I did not believe that the worst was so close. Those who have gone on the attack in Algeria could have no doubt as to the response of the French government, since today it is no longer up to anyone to change the fact that Algeria is legally part of the territory of the French Republic. Do not expect me to reproach men, even if they be government ministers, for having done what it was impossible for them not to do, without betraying the duties under their charge. But my friends know that I am crushed.

The fellagha's responsibility in the immediate situation in no way extenuates that which has increasingly weighed upon us from generation to generation for a hundred and twenty years. The horror of what is going to be unleashed must be mitigated right away by a concerted offensive against low wages, unemployment, ignorance, and dire poverty, and by structural reforms that the Algerian people are calling for. And at all costs, we must prevent the police from torturing.

I want to try to believe still that, as disappointed as we may be, the present administration remains the last chance for us who love the

31. See Michel Winock, "Algérie: un état des lieux en 1954," http://www.ldh-toulon.net/spip.php?article101.

peoples of North Africa and whose last desire, when we no longer desire anything, will be to see their union with France preserved.

Our policy in Morocco makes one think of a man who is surrounded and who pretends to hesitate to pick out one of several paths of escape, while the only path open is staring him in the face. Sultan Mohammed ben Youssef himself could not, if he wanted to, renounce what he embodies, or else he would then immediately become the object of execration and contempt for these people who, today, venerate him, that is for these millions of Moroccans who love him more than their own lives.

It is strange that these same ones who, by dethroning and exiling him, have made him into a living symbol and a sacred victim, now act as if their doings were negligible and claim not to take them into account.

That the authors of the terrorist attack of August 20 should be the very ones whose opinions now appear to prevail is an enigma which I do not seek to solve. It remains for us to cry out along with Pascal: "It is an incomprehensible magic spell and a supernatural slumber."[32]

We can size up all the better what it cost the French nation to delay for one year Pierre Mendès France's installation as premier.

At the time, nothing was set and determined. It was during the fateful year that followed that the irreparable harm was done. I am wrong to write "irreparable." Let's say what the administration did not resolve to set right for reasons that escape us: from that point on, each passing day reduced the few chances still remaining. As for me, I am like a runner who, just when he is about to reach the finish line, throws his arms around thin air. But what do you expect? That's the rule in politics. One must keep on endlessly repeating the often cited saying of William of Orange, "who did not need to hope in order to undertake nor to succeed in order to persevere," especially since, in the end, he won, and out of despair, he achieved success. In Morocco, our pre-

32. Mauriac cites from Pascal's *Pensées* (Brunschvicg 194, Lafuma 11): "c'est un enchantement incompréhensible, et un assoupissement surnaturel." Pascal was decrying the inordinate attention given to trifles coupled with insensitivity or even indifference to what should matter most.

mier is not going down a straight road: a sudden change in direction may surprise us at any moment.

Protesting against State Torture in Algeria

"Friday, January 14, 1955" represents one of Mauriac's most haunting, soul-searching reflections on the grim reality of the use of torture by French police and military forces in Algeria. Mauriac was the first to denounce torture in the French press, beginning with the November 2, 1954, editorial translated above, and he was arguably the most eloquent of those who spoke out on the matter. In it, he transforms a highly detailed typewritten report on torture and judicial abuses into a poignant dialogue between a lawyer committed to exposing a long series of grave violations of human rights and a hesitating, unsettled writer protesting his inability to influence events.[33] The resulting conversation provides a dramatic survey of the grim situation in North Africa while offering an unblinkered assessment of Europe's claims to any sort of supposedly higher "civilization" and humanity. Mauriac attacks the widespread cultural attitudes that so often served as the basis or pretext for racist colonial pretensions in Algeria and elsewhere in the colonies.

Unlike the "Bloc-notes" that he was regularly writing for *L'Express*, this article carried its own special title, "La Question," the archaic term for torture. Some three years before Henri Alleg's famous book published under the same title in 1958, Mauriac conspicuously denounces the hideous practices that government and military authorities were desperately seeking to cover up. Another indication of the exceptional importance that Mauriac gave to this article is the fact that he placed under the shocking title a double epigraph, one text taken from Matthew 25.40, "You have done it to me," and the other from Montaigne, "By temperament and by judgment, I cruelly hate cruelty as the extreme of all vices."[34]

Mauriac thus links current abuses in North Africa to medieval practices, while at the same time grounding his condemnation of torture in the most venerable discourses of Christianity (Matthew) and French hu-

33. Touzot in BN I, 237n2.

34. Ibid.

manism (Montaigne). An entire series of references to the past, first to the Ancien Régime (the torture of Brinvilliers and Damiens), then to the Third Reich (Himmler's use of "common law" criminals to police political detainees), and finally to the Aztecs, serve to place the human rights abuses in France's colonial war in the context of history and of the seemingly endless chain of violence and injustice so often invoked in Mauriac's editorials.[35] He ultimately presents such political crimes as integral components of human society itself, going so far as to declare that "every civilization reposes on hidden horrors," again denying any pretension of cultural superiority.

Friday, January 14, 1955

" … you have done it to me." (Matt. 25.40)

"By temperament and by judgment, I cruelly hate cruelty as the extreme of all vices." (Michel de Montaigne, "Of Cruelty," *Essais*, Book II, Chapter 11)

"Only you can speak out … Only you."

I turn away my head. How often have I heard this "only you!" My enemies think that I am giving in to my urge to be in the limelight. I sigh:

—"We'd have to have proof. There's never any proof."

—"I saw for myself," the man says.

I steal a glance at him. I am well familiar with this look in his eyes: it's the same as that of my friend R., and of the priest from the French Mission who works in the Constantine region. It is the gaze of those who have seen with their own eyes, and who can now think of nothing else: all the flowers of the world are now faded for them. Sure, they are obsessed. I myself am beginning to feel this obsession, but a writer is good at slipping away. I persist in declining, almost begging:

—"What good is it to denounce torture, since 'it' doesn't leave any traces!"

—"They haven't stopped using bludgeons, you know! And how about the bathtub, or rather the bucket of filthy water in which the head is dunked to the point of asphyxiation, and the electric shocks

35. See Bracher, *Through the Past Darkly*, 55.

under the armpits and between the legs, and the fouled water forced into the mouth with a pipe until the patient faints ..."

—"That's not possible," I said.

—"But it is, just as it was for la Brinvilliers[36] and Damiens.[37] ... It indeed scarcely leaves a trace, no more than the bottlenecks forced into ..."

I interrupt:

—"I know ... others have told me about it. But why? Why?"

—"It's a matter of getting suspects (and I certainly don't claim that they are all innocent) to confess to their direct or indirect participation in terrorism. But above all, they are expected to turn in their comrades. I recall one suspect who had finally given in: he was beside himself with shame and despair: 'I have been dishonored,' he moaned, 'I delivered them over ... Only three.' Keep in mind that these torture sessions are interspersed with interrogations that continue on for hours, and they almost always let them go without food. So they'll sign anything."

—"But how about the judges?"

—"Oh, before taking them to the courthouse they make their victims presentable ... a little sprucing up, you see! The fact remains that at the beginning of November, these court appearances were taking place either very early or very late so that there would be no witnesses. At seven in the morning on November 12, my wife, who was on the lookout, nevertheless saw some young men who were still bloody going in to see the judge."

—"Without a lawyer? I thought that the presence of a lawyer was required by law."

—"They inform us neither of the date nor of the time of their court appearance. In order to have some chance of assisting a client, I too had to post myself on the lookout at the judge's door: for eight straight hours, as a matter of fact ..."

36. Marie-Madeleine d'Aubray, marquise de Brinvilliers, was burned at the stake in Paris in 1676 for having poisoned her father and brothers. See *Petit Larousse Illustré* (Paris: Editions Larousse, 1994).

37. Robert François Damiens was tortured, then quartered in Paris in 1757 for having stabbed King Louis XV with a pocket knife. See ibid.

—"So the police have the right to detain an individual for more that twenty-four hours without bringing him before a magistrate? I had nevertheless been told . . ."

—"Article 114 of the Penal Code does indeed ban arbitrary sequestration."

—"But there again, how do you prove it?"

—"Oh, that's easy! All one has to do is to compare two dates: that of the arrest and that of the warrant for incarceration or the release order.

—"Well, then why not press charges?"

—"Do you believe that the victims refrain from pressing charges? Countless charges have been filed! Not one has ever been investigated. Do you hear me? Not one, at least not to my knowledge. Poor 'French citizens!' They have no more means of legal recourse than do our Algerian 'wards.'"

—"Look, I remember at least one time when you were wrong. The France-Maghreb organization had taken up the case of Moulaï Merbah, the secretary general of one faction of the MTLD.[38] The minister of the interior found proof that there had been a mistake, and that this suspect had not been tortured.

—"Yes, and Mitterrand was acting in good faith.[39] It was he who was fooled. I'm quite familiar with the whole story: Moulaï Merbah was not taken before the examining magistrate until November 5th, and it was on the 9th that his lawyer, who had been in Algiers for five days, was finally able to communicate with him and learn firsthand of the torture that he had had to endure. His back was covered with wounds that were still open or scarcely closed. A prison guard stated that the accused had been in that condition when he was locked up. But the forensic pathologist who was brought in to examine him was of the opinion that Moulaï Merbah was in excellent condition: it was his certificate that the Minister of the Interior had in his possession."

38. The Mouvement pour le Triomphe des Libertés Démocratiques (Movement for the Triumph of Democratic Liberties) party.

39. François Mitterrand, 1916–1996, who would later serve as president of the Republic from 1981 until 1995, was at the time of Mauriac's article minister of the interior, responsible for ensuring law and order and overseeing police forces.

—"You see! Indisputable proof will always be lacking."

—"No! For many cases, we have witnesses. My wife saw Abd el Haziz's wounded chest. The judge agreed to call a forensic pathologist, but not to have the medical examination take place in the presence of a professor from the school of medicine of Algiers. I could tell you the story of Adad Ali, on the Algiers city council: the reporters, lawyers, and magistrates in the corridor when they brought him in witnessed the fact that he was in a daze. Marks from the blows that he had received were visible on his face and on his legs. The judge immediately called for a doctor. And how could we doubt Laichaoui, the friend of Mrs. Mounier, Domenach, and Mandouze, when he tells us of what he had undergone?

We keep silent for a minute. He ponders things for a minute, then says:

—"And then, detention constitutes a torture in itself. People talk about Oudjda: if only you knew about the prison at Tizi-Ozou! Seventy-one detainees are penned up in rooms of 105 square meters. They are forbidden from opening their mouths, even to pray. 'Common law' criminals guard over them: these are methods worthy of Himmler! What a legacy to follow!"

After another moment of silence, I once again hear the incessant refrains: "Only you ... If people only knew ... people will believe *you*."

I shake my head:

—"They most certainly will not. On the contrary, they get upset when they are forced to see what they have resolved to ignore. They accept the fact that every civilization reposes on hidden horrors: prostitution, the sale of women, vice squads, reform schools, jails for the insane and the mentally handicapped, every kind of torture. It's a necessary evil. Woe to anyone who dares speak openly of these things! The Aztecs sealed away body parts in the stones of the temple built to the glory of the Sun god."

—"But we aren't Aztecs."

—"No, of course not! We are the French, and, from one generation to the next, the brightest and best of France's children have understood and put into practice the Sermon on the Mount better than any other people. We are the country that proclaimed human rights to a euphoric Europe."

—"... Yes, and to think that, for most of those suffering under us, France still remains that country of idealism and human rights!"

—"The perpetrators of these crimes won't even have the excuse of leading a conquest, for it is not by means of force, but by its message of humanism that France remains a conqueror: by dishonoring their country, they are leaving it defenseless."

He sighs: "The perpetrators will lose everything!" He gets up, shakes my hand, hesitates, and says timidly:

—"Have you read my book on the people of Madagascar?"

I bow my head. He keeps on:

"These members of the Madagascan parliament ... they're innocent, you know! They've been suffering for years. One of them is growing weak and may die. These are your fellow Christians, your brothers. You should ..."

"Yes ... yes ... ," I reply. I escort him to the door. Then I find myself alone again. I absentmindedly open a record album of Mozart's piano sonatas performed by Gieseking, the album that J. brought back from New York for me. I pick one out ... Only three. But no, it's not possible. The horror of what I have heard still fills the room. This music is not for me. I am like a man who has unwittingly taken part in a crime and who now hesitates to turn himself in.

Mauriac continues in the same vein in "Friday, July 5, 1957," penned at the height of the phase of the war known as "The Battle of Algiers": when the FLN decided to bring the war home to affluent Europeans in Algiers with a series of ruthless bombings randomly targeting civilians gathered in public places for entertainment and social pleasure, French authorities responded by giving full power to the elite force of six thousand paratroopers commanded by Colonel Jacques Massu. The latter lost no time in utilizing mass arrests, torture, and summary executions against the urban guerilla terrorists. Others were arrested, tried, condemned for their actions, and guillotined. Such was the context for fellow Nobel laureate Albert Camus's eloquent call for the abolition of the death penalty, which prompted Mauriac to deliver a grim assessment of Europe's record of historical crimes over the preceding twenty years, including the Stalinist purges, the slaughter of the Spanish Civil War, Vichy, and the Holocaust, without forgetting the diffuse violence of social injustice entrenched in the continuing politics of social class. The problem of capital punishment only represents the tip of the iceberg, argues Mauriac.

Friday, July 5, 1957

What Albert Camus wrote in the *NRF* in opposition to the death penalty, I have always thought and believed.[40] So why do I get this unsettled feeling when I read it? I now gauge how hard it is to have lived through this history that has been ours over the last twenty years, the story of the white Christians who have inherited Christian civilization.

I deny them the right to declare themselves for or against the death penalty. They are no longer at that point. Only the forms of justice subsist in their society. Human rights abuses are proliferating everywhere behind the worm-eaten facades of old laws. As if the issue were really that of the death penalty!

The white race has supplied the protagonists of the Spanish Civil War; it has hunted down, tortured, and burned to death millions of Jews, including hundreds of thousands of children, in order to punish them for the crime of being Jewish; it is still using the concentration camp regime; in more than one place on the planet, those executed at Nuremberg remain its leaders and inspirations; it has reestablished torture, and the practices formerly entrusted to specialists have now become the hobby of citizens no more wicked than others; it has familiarized itself with the notion of political crime and uses it, especially in Russia, every time that it needs to make a clean slate (and we French have shown under the Vichy regime and during the Purge what we are capable of in this area). The white race no longer holds the right to reflect on the death penalty: they have flouted and violated all the principles that could serve as reference point or norm in this debate.

40. *La Nouvelle Revue Française*, one of the most prestigious publication venues for writers and intellectuals in France.

Moreover, what's the point? If the death penalty were removed from the law, it would continue to rule in our mores, or rather it would continue in the practice of police killings that are so widespread everywhere and which, by comparison, restitute the dignity and honor of the death penalty.

Even if you erase it from all the legislative texts where it still subsists, innocent people would still be legally slain, "for having tried to flee," for example, and in Russia and elsewhere, human beings will nonetheless die from starvation and exhaustion in unknown camps.

Martial law and the granting of special powers would moreover reestablish the death penalty by applying it to innocent people every time it so pleases politicians.

You are only rekindling the debate over the death penalty in order to give yourself the illusion of still belonging to a community worthy of taking up the issue: you wish to escape the unbearably obvious fact that from year to year all our notions of justice have become more and more murky, especially over the last twenty years. Dictatorial regimes have accelerated the decomposition initiated by the Great War.

I fear that discussing the death penalty relieves noble souls from dealing with the most burning issues. It lets us believe that we are part of a world in which the life of a human being, whatever the color of skin, remains sacred.

How I would like to go up and stand at the podium in the National Assembly, the day when the head of the government will ask that his discretionary powers be extended to mainland France! Just what is this French Parliament where I wish to have a hearing? An assembly of men who, as Camus recalls, know that alcohol-related crimes make up 60 to 72 percent of the total, and that impoverished shacks quite naturally (and with what regularity and abundance!) produce abused children; these men in the National Assembly have, on the order of those that they serve, made our great nation the first among nations for the consumption of alcohol and the fifteenth for construction.

The abolition of the death penalty should be the supreme achievement of an entire set of laws that no military or civilian police force would be able to violate any more. We know how it goes at present.

What refinement there is for the type of people we have become to respect human life even when guilty of great crimes. We are really being dainty! We should not reach this point until we have made an effort at the regeneration that we have not even begun to undertake. Let us wait until we are worthy before abolishing the death penalty.

Abolish the death penalty when we are reinstating torture? Come on Camus, be a bit logical!

Also penned at the height of the Battle of Algiers, "Sunday, July 14, 1957" represents one of Mauriac's most corrosively ironic editorials targeting military bravado. We find him juxtaposing the French armed forces' traditionally ostentatious display of pomp and circumstance on the Champs-Elysées for the July 14 Bastille Day celebration with the somber reality of judicial malfeasance that is evident in the conviction of a group of Christians who were first tortured and then put on trial in Algiers for having tried to shelter Algerian militants from similar torture and prosecution. Once again, Mauriac places current crises in the broader context of European history unfolding over centuries, as he links television coverage of the military parade to the sinister musings of Herman Goering as well as to the spiritual contemplations of Saint Bonaventure and Etienne Gilson.

Sunday, July 14, 1957

In my capacity as an "exhibitionist of the heart and mind,"[41] I refrained from going to the Champs-Elysées. I was content to watch the paratroopers parading on television. I can even boast of taking in the spectacle in a more leisurely manner than I would have if the president of the Republic had seated me on his right-hand side. At times, the television screen became a living tapestry of faces viewed from as close as one can come without bumping into them. If they so cared, viewers could indulge in the pleasure of comparing different types of people. What differences there were between one corps and another, and within the same unit! There were indeed individuals of a noble

41. As French Premier Robert Lacoste had charged.

and of a vile sort. On that score, I made a few of my own reflections that wisdom counsels not to share with anyone!

The truth is that, by eliminating prancing horses, motorized vehicles have killed military parades.

Let's leave aside the heart and the mind in order not to offend Monsieur Robert Lacoste, who would be capable of drawing his revolver like Goering.[42] There remains common sense, which as we all know is the most commonly shared commodity in the world,[43] even among foreign diplomats. I saw one such diplomat taking in this parade. What were his thoughts on the matter? Even though he said nothing to anybody, and especially not, I suppose, to Mr. President of the Republic or to the premier, I believe I figured it out. This reasonable man was thinking that any instrument should be fitted to its intended purpose. I don't know what nuclear warfare would do to the pretty plaything whose band "was making heroism well up in the hearts of city dwellers."[44] I do know quite well, however, what guerilla warfare does, or rather does not do to such a force.

To be fair, the gnat has not yet overcome the lion, as in the fable, and

42. The Nazi Hermann Goering is often cited as having supposedly said that whenever he heard the word "culture," he reached for his revolver.

43. As Descartes famously asserts in *Discourse on the Method.*

44. Mauriac is citing from memory the words from part three of Baudelaire's poem "Les petites vieilles" ("Little Old Women"):

> Ah! que j'en ai suivi de ces petites vieilles!
> Une, entre autres, à l'heure où le soleil tombant
> Ensanglante le ciel de blessures vermeilles,
> Pensive, s'asseyait à l'écart sur un banc,
> Pour entendre un de ces concerts, riches de cuivre,
> Dont les soldats parfois inondent nos jardins,
> Et qui, dans ces soirs d'or où l'on se sent revivre,
> Versent quelque héroïsme au coeur des citadins.
> [Ah! how many of these women I have followed!
> One, among others, at the hour when the sunset
> Makes the sky bloody with vermilion wounds,
> Pensive, used to sit alone on a bench
> To hear one of those concerts rich in brass,
> With which the soldiers sometimes flood our public parks
> On those golden evenings when one feels new life within
> And which inspire heroism in the townsman's heart.]

Baudelaire, *The Flowers of Evil,* trans. Aggeler, http://fleursdumal.org/poem/222.

I don't think that he will ever get the best of him.[45] But the lion will continue to switch his sides with his tail without doing much harm to the gnat. That is what must be feared, and it is not this dazzling parade that will reassure those French citizens who are capable of thinking a bit.

Of course, we can always continue in the same manner. We cannot say that there is no price to pay: as high as the cost may be in terms of human life and billions of francs, the easiest thing is to stick with the method that consists of closing our eyes and refusing to think. The immortal words of Monsieur Lacoste's oration have laid out this method for centuries to come: "Here I am, well in place, still there, and I will do everything in my power to remain there." Which in fact means, "I'll let them do whatever they want so that they will leave me in power." For whose hands are tied tighter than those of this phony proconsul? They say that at times he lets out a yelp.

Ah! Let's switch it off! The TV viewer is a masterful god who can at any second interrupt a spectacular parade such as this one.

July 14 ... But even the fourteenth of July is a window onto the timeless. Every year, the storming of the Bastille leads our thoughts away from the admirable saint we celebrate today: Bonaventure, the seraphic doctor, Saint Augustine's disciple, spiritual heir of Saint Francis, and strongly unfavorable to Aristotle. Following my heart, I decide to devote this afternoon to the celebration of his memory, and so here I am looking for Gilson's thick volume on "Saint Bonaventure's philosophy." I shall read the first and last chapters.

To escape into the realm of the timeless ... But there is this letter from a lawyer in Algiers that was sent to me about two weeks ago and to which I have not responded. I would like to join Francis of Assisi and his spiritual heir Bonaventure on the heights of Mount Alverne, but there is this letter from a lawyer in Algiers. However, we must deny that there is any contradiction here: "We reach all things through Christ and through all things we come back to him ...," says Gilson in his commentary on Bonaventure. I therefore take up the letter again:

45. Mauriac is alluding to Jean de la Fontaine's version of Aesop's fable "The Lion and the Gnat." See http://www.musee-jean-de-la-fontaine.fr/jean-de-la-fontaine-fable-uk-162.html.

"My dear friend, the trial of the so-called 'conspiracy of radical Christians in Algiers' has been slated for July 22. I have seen many a trial over the last two years, but never any like this one. For there was never a hint of any conspiracy. After being physically and psychologically tortured, these people have waited in prison for months to go on trial. The only thing they did was to bear witness to the fact that they were Christians through individual and spontaneous acts of brotherly love: 'by this they will recognize that you are my disciples. . . .'[46] [. . .] No one dared modify the first indictment for a 'criminal attempt against state security' although they are in fact being prosecuted for 'harboring criminals.' By 'criminal,' understand any Muslims on the run or thrown into panic by the paratroopers' house to house searches, anyone who was seeking to hole up anywhere they could, knowing that if they were caught, they would be tortured. No one dared dismiss any of the charges, even against those who have clearly done nothing wrong and who had for that very reason been released on their own recognizance. The whole cartload has been sent before a military tribunal.[47] [. . .] You must enter into the public arena not only for the sake of the thirty-four accused, but also because beyond them there is an entire way of thinking about life and human relations that must triumph."

I ponder somberly over the matter, and return to Gilson's book on Bonaventure: "Bonaventure is filled with anguish when he sees that what has been created by a God and restored by a God's blood is undone every day, as if, out of foolish blindness, all that can choose between nothingness and being made the choice for nothingness."

The choice for nothingness: that is what is in command here. Captive to an old illusion, he was playing soldier on the Champs-Elysées this morning, deaf and blind to the world that is going to be constructed without us and against us, although our calling had been to become its living thought.

46. Mauriac is recalling the words of Jesus in John 15.

47. The image alludes to the cartloads of prisoners taken to be guillotined during the Reign of Terror.

As is often the case for articles penned at the conjunction of a feast day and a political drama, Mauriac deploys the full range of his editorial talents in "Tuesday, December 24, 1957," a Christmas Eve meditation far removed from conventional sentimentalism and devoid of "holiday cheer." With devastating rhetoric, he points out the scandalous contradiction between the habitual indulgence in champagne, lavish cuisine, and elaborate decorations on the one hand, and the birth of a poor child destined to end up ignominiously tortured and executed as a common criminal on the other. This stark juxtaposition moreover provides a template for a relentless indictment of some of the most heinous historical crimes, including the genocidal conquest of the New World and the use of the atomic bomb on Hiroshima, two acts committed by those claiming to carry out divine will. Thus continuing his unsettling reflections on the link between the violence in Algeria and an often criminal past, Mauriac examines not only the legacy of French and European politics and society, but also the implication of Christian individuals and institutions in some of the major crimes of history.

Tuesday, December 24, 1957

Tonight, the Western world is stuffing itself. In whose honor and for what reason are all these champagne corks popping? There was this moment in history, this night among all nights, this birth of one male child among billions of others. How many of us are there, even among Christians, who know what this night has meant for the generations who have come before us? How many of us believe it?

Perhaps it is not good for me to reflect on this subject. Some readers will get irritated and shrug their shoulders: "Just talk to us about politics!" But after all, this is Christmas Eve. Do you believe that this night had nothing to do with human politics? If you who are rejoicing no longer know the reason for your joy, why would I, who have not forgotten, not remind you?

You eat and you drink in the midst of your hope that is dead, or that you believe to be dead. Yet it is still breathing. If nothing were left of it, Christmas would be an ordinary night for us. To you as well, you who no longer believe or have never believed, this little Child was given. You carry him clumsily like men who do not know how to carry children. But what does it mean for us, we faithful who press him to our bosom and who believe all that was written concerning this holy night? And how can we make these things understood by those outside our faith?

This Child-God will grow rapidly within us. Liturgy concentrates a thirty-year story into a few months. Of the wailing little creature of this night, nothing will remain on the evening of Good Friday but the dead body of an adult, a tortured body similar to all bodies tortured before and after him, tortured by all guards and police forces, with the permission of all the Pontius Pilates, and in the midst of the approving silence of the scribes. Yet a day and a night, and then this man will be alive once more. He will walk along a road next to us at the time when the shadows grow longer, for it is evening and life is over. But his wounds will not even then be closed. We with Thomas will be able to put our fingers on them. These wounds will be unendingly renewed everywhere in the world right up until now, here at arms' reach, despite protective parliamentary committees. For these are indeed the same wounds: "Truly I say unto you, you have done it unto me."[48]

For us, he is still living. We are no longer alone: that is the Christian hope. He is present in us by his Grace, but also, according to his promise: when two or three of us have come together in his name, he is in the midst of us. And finally, he is the living Bread, but that is inexpressible. We are no longer alone. "Someone is in the midst of you that you do not know." Christians of all times and of every standing, and not just the priests, have received this word and their vocation is to announce this news. They have only come into the world for that, and to the extent that they have failed to do so or have shirked the task, the evangelization of the world has partly failed (and that's putting it mildly): we are the witnesses to that failure but are also responsible for it.

And certainly, if the world has refused the light, it is because "their

48. Matthew 25.40.

deeds were evil and they preferred darkness," according to what is written in John's Gospel. The fact remains that it is also because those who believed in the light did not love the light alone. At times, without their knowledge, or with their complicity, they were used by the will to power of Empires. The word of God was profitable to Mammon.

Millions of champagne bottles are being popped open tonight throughout all the night spots of the Western world, in honor of a poor little child born 1,057 years ago: this misunderstanding sums up all of Christian history. Today as in the first days, the kingdom of God comes down to a few measures of yeast in the dough.

Throughout history, most of the politicians who have claimed allegiance to the little Child of that night were in reality his executioners. In his name, the Catholic king's conquistadors destroyed entire races. The "most Christian" kings made a mockery of the term, and the hands that just recently dropped the atomic bomb on Hiroshima, annihilating 200,000 of God's children in one stroke, were the hands of Puritans.

And even here and now, as I write ... But what good is it to talk? We know very well that we are liable for part of what is being done and that in democracy no one is free of responsibility. So you see that I have tumbled back down from the lofty heights and jumped feet first into politics again. The other world does not lead committed Christians away from this world. On the contrary, it leads them back here, ties them to this world, and forbids any and all escapes. Such Christians must seek the kingdom of God and its justice right here and now on this earth: they must seek the kingdom, even though they already possess in their hearts the kingdom of the little Child who was born this evening.

"Monday, January 27, 1958" displays the courage and moderation that Mauriac brought to bear on the events and protagonists of the Algerian War, as he pleads for clemency in favor of two elementary school teachers, a Frenchwoman married to an Algerian Muslim, convicted of having planted a bomb intended to destroy the headquarters of a natural gas company. Without condoning their actions, he implicitly concedes the validity of the Algerian Muslims' desire to write their own history, that is, to take command of their own destiny by shaking free of those who have dominated, exploited, and humiliated them ever since the French conquest began in 1830.

Monday, January 27, 1958

The parish priest of Uruffe will not be sent to the scaffold.[49] Abdelkader and Jacqueline Guerroudj, the two elementary school teachers from Algeria who were condemned to death, will be sent to the guillotine unless they obtain a pardon. For what crime? This French national, this mother of five children, and this Algerian man are Communists affiliated with the FLN. That is true, and it is equally true that she gave Iveton the bomb that he placed in the Gaz d'Algérie building. But the device had been set in such a way that it could only go off after the personnel had left. There were no victims, and it was not possible for there to have been any victims. The court admitted that this was not an attempted murder: these strange criminals had premeditated to shed no blood. So why such a pitiless verdict, unless it was because Iveton was for his part executed? It is as if this miserable fellow had demanded that the two schoolteachers join him and that it were necessary to appease his ghost!

Who would deny that their deeds deserved severe punishment? But the death penalty! Guerroudj's own noble declaration before his judges was a testimony to the agonizing split of allegiance in a man torn between race and culture, the same dilemma that Jean Amrouche confided to us. The entire war in Algeria can occur in one single person. The blade of the guillotine does not constitute a valid answer to the question posed to the French people by one of these men who have learned our history: it wasn't theirs, and they have resolved to have one. They are writing it at this very moment. And the role that we should play in it is not the one whose horrible mask we are made to wear because of Robert Lacoste's policies.

49. He was convicted for a nonpolitical double murder, according to Touzot in BN I, 24n1.

5 ∽ THE ERA OF CHARLES DE GAULLE

The General Returns

The failure of France's government ministers and its National Assembly to meet the challenges of the Algerian War led to a carefully orchestrated threat of a coup d'état. The attempted putsch also signaled the demise of the Fourth Republic and occasioned the return to power of General Charles de Gaulle, who a few months later introduced a new constitution, which once adopted, granted the president of the Fifth Republic extensive powers in directing foreign and domestic policy. Encouraged and assisted by activists, journalists, and politicians who presented de Gaulle as the only recourse for recourse for restoring peace and keeping Algeria under French control, a group of demonstrators protested the inauguration of Pierre Pflimlin, rumored to favor a negotiated peace settlement with the FLN. These activists ransacked and occupied the seat of the French government in Algiers on May 13, 1958, demanding that a Public Safety Committee headed by army generals Jacques Massu and Raoul Salan assume full control of civil and military affairs in Algeria.[1] Massu and Salan in turn called for de Gaulle to return as France's leader.

Announcing his willingness to lead the French Republic, de Gaulle nevertheless organized a press conference in Paris on May 19 to declare that he would refuse to receive power from the hands of the generals calling on him in Algiers. When the representatives of the French National Assembly balked at approving de Gaulle's return, the military leaders of the coup in Algiers threatened to use paratroopers to take control of Paris and impose their own authority over France. Then on May 27 de Gaulle announced that he had begun preparations for the formation of a legal governing team under the Republic. President René Coty legalized the process on June 1 by officially calling upon de Gaulle to do so.[2]

As is amply evident in the editorials from the 1960s, Mauriac would prove to be one of de Gaulle's most ardent and faithful advocates. He was nevertheless shocked by the attempted military coup that enabled the general's return. Mauriac's commentary from May 13–14 thus expresses relief in seeing the Republic maintain at least the formal signs of legality. He also voices his ardent desire for a brisk revival of the French Left, which must stand up to the would-be military junta in Algiers, since the Right had shamefully revealed its complicity with the generals' mutiny.

Mauriac's reaction to de Gaulle's May 19 press conference focuses on the complexity of the political situation and the dubious alternatives facing France. Speaking openly of his own rather contradictory position with respect to de Gaulle's return to power in such murky circumstances, Mauriac displays an intellectual honesty and a faithfulness to the complexity of events that are all too rare in politics. On the one hand, Mauriac acknowledges that the attempted military coup had in fact flouted democratic institutions but was never rebuked or disavowed either by the National Assembly or by de Gaulle. On the other hand, Mauriac also admits that he finds de Gaulle's prestige and charismatic aura irresistible, to the point of being "possessed." He clearly understands the very personal and authoritarian manner in which de Gaulle will conduct affairs of state. Indeed,

1. They referred to "un Comité de Salut Public," the term used by the revolutionaries Danton and Robespierre for their own ruling entity during the French Revolution.

2. For a more detailed account of these events, see "13 mai 1958, Alger se révolte," http://www.herodote.net/histoire/evenement.php?jour=19580513&ID_dossier=9 .

Mauriac aptly characterizes exactly what Pierre Mendès France along with so many others found so unpalatable, if not unacceptable, in a state claiming to be a liberal democracy: "a French Republic turned authoritarian" and "Marianne [with] this big mouth, this grand style, this power stemming from pride, indifference and contempt." Yet Mauriac insists that de Gaulle represents France's best hope for ending the frightful violence and the systematic practice of torture, as well as for a just and peaceful relationship with other peoples and nations.

Night of May 13–14, 1958

The Republic goes on. Paris did not capitulate in the face of Algiers. The installation granted to Monsieur Pierre Pflimlin has in the end spared us this latest shame. And now, in the face of the *pronunciamento*, the French Left has to revive: we must have no other political thought. Nothing can change the fact that, over this past night, the Communists in the National Assembly sided with the defenders of the Republic against the Right that was complicit with the Generals who had mutinied. On the basis of what imperatives can you now exclude them from the national community? Socialist ministers must immediately take the place of the farmer-independents who, in abandoning the premier, showed their true colors. The government ministries thus reinvigorated must govern, using the support of all of the Left, without conceding anything to the agitators.

We are still hoping for de Gaulle, but not a de Gaulle who would answer a call of the likes of Massu. The grandeur of de Gaulle is to belong to the entire nation. May he not say one word, nor make one gesture that would link him to the generals behind this attempted coup.

Monday, May 19, 1958

"May General de Gaulle not say one word, nor make one gesture that would link him to the generals behind this attempted coup." Those are the last lines of the last "Bloc-notes," written during the night of the thirteenth to the fourteenth.

Events move fast. Today these words no longer have any meaning. The fact is that "the generals behind this attempted coup" have not been outlawed. Far from treating General Salan like a rebel, the government solicited his reports and pretended not to judge his intentions to be suspect. The government delegated its powers to him. This great deployment of a defense of the Republic that resulted in the passage of the emergency law concerns us French who live on the mainland. But, at least as far as I know, it did not seem urgent for anyone in governmental circles to clearly define the act of generals who create public safety committees with the plainly stated intention of removing an elected representative from power and imposing the arbitration of a military leader.

We know already that the state no longer exists. But this obvious and sinister reality is all the more unavoidable when we see official declarations punctuated by a fist pounding on the table. General de Gaulle does not have to be more respectful of the institutions of the republic than you. He asked you a question: why would he treat these soldiers, for whom you are apologizing and with whom you have conspicuously refrained from breaking, as dangerous agitators? How do you respond? By saying that it is his fault? That he himself gave the example eighteen years ago?

It is certainly nonetheless true, as Maurice Duverger writes this evening in *Le Monde*, "that there cannot be any arbitration between legality and rebellion without the former being flouted and the latter officialized." That is true, but whose fault is it? And must we lodge a complaint against the arbiter, especially against this arbiter who is proposing, not imposing, his services?

I have several times in this very column cried out toward General de Gaulle. Now that he is at the gates, am I going to stand up against him? I would be capable of overcoming all within me that stems from the area of sentiment, all that makes him forever dear to me. It would not be without effort, certainly, but I could manage to do so, it seems to me. But there is another consideration that for me is unavoidable. It began to haunt me during the press conference, when General de Gaulle said: "Algerians are at present giving a magnificent display of a tremendous fraternization that offers a psychological and moral basis for the accords and arrangements of tomorrow, *an infinitely better basis than combat and ambushes*." What a resonance these words found in me! And I am still listening to them, I am as if possessed.

Upon my return, under the blue skies of Paris, two friends accompanied me as I walked under the chestnut trees in the Jardin des Tuileries. One is Algerian: he wants what the FLN wants for his country. The other is a great friend of the peoples of North Africa. Both are of the opinion that the present French government would only intensify an endless, intractable conflict and that, in the immediate future, General de Gaulle brings us a chance for peace in Algeria, and, in the longer term, the promise of a federation in Africa. In their view, even if there exists a degree of artifice and theatrics in these gatherings of Muslims and French in the Forum in Algiers, there is no doubt that, by taking power, General de Gaulle has probably caused something unexpected to happen on this scene.

Will we lose this chance to give the tasks of peacetime back to French youth, to halt the agony of these Algerian people, who have for years been caught in an atrocious crossfire. I am not among those who say, "Let a nation perish rather than a principle." What a hypocrite I would be if I pretended not to be moved by this soaring hope that blood should no longer be shed, that French soldiers may come back to France, that the poor folks in the little Algerian villages should no longer experience any other misery than that of being poor and without anything, that we should never again hear of torture, that not one soldier of ours ever again have the occasion to say what General Massu confided to my fellow journalist with *La Croix*: "That's all you talk about, torture. But I am indeed obliged to engage in it: how else could I manage?"

If General de Gaulle shows us "how else to manage," if the French and the Algerian people are reconciled under his leadership, in an autonomous Algeria where both flags will fly, never again to be separated, well, I will get over the sight of a French Republic turned authoritarian, I will accept the fact that Marianne may suddenly have this big mouth, this grand style, this power stemming from pride, indifference, and contempt, and which can be offensive. After all, when General de Gaulle speaks to Europe in the name of France, France will no longer be humiliated. What a relief! Don't you see that we are overwhelmed with joy?

Now of course I am not blind: if the frogs who are asking for this king get him, I suspect that they will not always croak for joy. "I had rather be their servant in my way, / Than sway with them in theirs."[3]

Those are the words that Shakespeare places in the mouth of Coriolanus. General de Gaulle will have us decipher the meaning of those words! I measure the risk. If it were only up to me, I would run it.

"Sunday, June 8, 1958" responds to a rapidly evolving situation. Immediately after being officially designated as France's premier, de Gaulle visited the Forum in Algiers where Salan, Massu, and the Public Safety Committee had claimed control of Algeria and issued their demands. Facing an enthusiastic crowd, de Gaulle declared, "I get your message.[4] I know what happened here. I know what you tried to do. I see that the road you have opened up in Algeria is the road to renovation."[5] In retrospect, de Gaulle's words appear to have been a shrewd exercise in ambiguity, if not ironic equivocation. While most of those intent on keeping Algeria under French control took them as an endorsement of their demands, de Gaulle soon concluded that maintaining France's domination was untenable both domestically and internationally, and initiated a process that, though slow and tortuous, ultimately led to Algerian independence.

Unlike the crowd in Algiers, Mauriac seems to have more accurately interpreted de Gaulle's declaration as a reprimand directed at those who had been tempted by military dictatorship. Indeed, Mauriac points out that despite its proud heritage of reason, logic, and humanism, France was no more immune than Spain had been to the threat that he designates by its most unsettling name, "Algerian Fascism," the blunt term he had already used in his repeated condemnations of judicial malfeasance, torture,

3. Shakespeare, *Coriolanus* II.I, http://shakespeare.mit.edu/coriolanus/full.html.

4. "Je vous ai compris" (literally, I have understood you).

5. "13 mai 1958 Alger se révolte," http://www.herodote.net/histoire/evenement.php?jour=19580513&ID_dossier=9.

and summary executions. But instead of joining those who had marched to the Place de la Nation in Paris to criticize the unsavory circumstances having resulted in de Gaulle's installation as premier, Mauriac is intent on convincing his friends on the Left that de Gaulle, as the Ariel having tamed Caliban (that is, the military junta), represents the only viable chance for the integrity of France and the Republic.[6] The clever touch that Mauriac salutes in his closing paragraph consisted of de Gaulle's having selected men from a wide variety of political affiliations to serve in his governing team, which included not only Christian Democrats and Socialists, but also such notable personalities as Antoine Pinay of the CNIP (Centre National des Indépendents et Paysans, popular in rural farming areas) and André Malraux, the renowned literary figure and adventurer.

Sunday, June 8, 1958

"I get your message!" The general had scarcely opened his mouth, and all was said in these four words. What French citizen listening to the screaming crowd in the Forum did not repeat for himself or herself this "I get your message"? We had been condemning Fascism in Algeria for years, but our knowledge of it had remained abstract. We recalled the conquest of Spain by Franco and by his Moorish guards as one speaks to children of the bogeyman, without believing that it could ever threaten the native country of Descartes and Pascal. It took this crowd screaming in our ears and 30,000 shock troops at the gates of a France that had already been surrendered by those whose mission it was to defend it: then our eyes were opened. In this spring of 1958, the French Republic seemed nearer to being strangled than in 1937 had been the Spanish Republic, whose people were unanimous and, if armed, would have held up against Franco if not for Hitler's Messerschmitts. But as for the people of our Republic, I marvel at the fact that some were reassured to see this huge, peaceful crowd gathered at the Place de la Nation in Paris. It doesn't take many submachine guns to disperse a hundred thousand citizens armed with grand principles.

6. Men such as Pierre Mendès France and editor-in-chief of *L'Express* Jean-Jacques Servan-Schreiber, who would remain adamantly opposed to de Gaulle's exercise of power.

Yes, I marvel at these passionate defenders of the Republic who reproach Monsieur René Coty and Monsieur Pierre Pflimlin for not having surrendered to Caliban, these unarmed citizens along with this betrayed and dismantled state. But what have these defenders of democracy themselves done to reconcile the two working-class parties? Would they have agreed to arm the common people? They should have the decency to admit it: by cutting themselves off from the extreme Left, they made the initiative from the president of the Republic and Monsieur Pierre Pflimin inevitable.

From now on, it's a fact of history: if General de Gaulle does not fail, and even if he only half succeeds, no republic, ever since there have been republics, has ever been saved by one man as ours will end up being saved by General de Gaulle. You can treat him like an adversary all you want: you know well that through him fate has granted you a reprieve in order for you to get a grip on yourself. For a few days, a few weeks, or a few months? As I write, the radio is announcing that General Massu has fallen back in step and that the Forum will once again become quiet. This is Caliban submitting to Ariel. But we would be wrong to rely on it. Don't blast Ariel any more.

As my youngest son, who was on the trip to Algiers with de Gaulle, had to give his name for the inspection of passports after coming out of the plane, the stunned official recomposed almost word for word the cry of Phaedra: "What name came out of your mouth!"

From Bordeaux, I learn of the positive resonance that Pinay's name has found in the depths of that unfathomable province. The same batch of mail brings me a letter from this young man from Bordeaux, Philippe Sollers (a "drop" in the New Wave): "Malraux in a government ministry is Romanticism in power!" The more I contemplate it, the more this conjunction of names, Pinay-Malraux, appears to me as one of these bold moves that are the felicitous strokes of genius. De Gaulle had all the time he needed to compose his "imaginary museum" at Colombey-les-Deux-Eglises. What is more, this big fellow is clever. May God bless him!

Throughout the next ten years of what is commonly called his "reign," de Gaulle would continue to be a shrewd, effective, and highly popular political leader who fully exploited the possibilities of mass communication created by radio and television networks. Mauriac's articles of late June and early July 1958 express the basic tenets of the unswerving loyalty to de Gaulle that he would maintain throughout the 1960s. Embarrassed by the seizure of two news magazines, Mauriac invokes the legacy of the Resistance and again insists that de Gaulle, respectful of France's long heritage but also of human rights, remains France's best protection against an ongoing Fascist threat.

Friday, June 27, 1958

Shall we hold the premier accountable for this seizure of two weekly news magazines? We shall then have to pretend to be unaware of this struggle for power behind the scenes, between those who usurped power and those who have been legally installed in office without yet holding their power fully in hand. The conflict between Algiers and Paris is the tragic reality of the events that we are experiencing. As long as de Gaulle is subjected to this situation, he will not have won out. He is the first to be struck by blows that strike us, as in the case of this seizure of *L'Express*. No offense against liberty spares the premier: he remains our last chance to remain a free people.

He has come and placed himself between us and the shock troops commanded by leaders who were determined to rein in mainland France: if he had not been there, these men would today be our masters. They have not given up: their accomplices are everywhere. And who would not have been resigned to accept such a situation? Their shoulders were already bending to accept the yoke. We knew that most writers would not cry out and that after the coup, they would continue unperturbed, writing articles about highway traffic.

What is surprising, when one reads certain declarations emanating from military circles (I am thinking here of the officer's letter published by *Le Monde*), is to discover that this ambition of theirs seems legitimate to them: why would the army not have the right to work for the restoration of the state, if some military leaders believe they have the remedies for the ills from which the state is suffering? Yes, but they also have planes and automatic weapons. The members of this new party intervene in the political battle holding a submachine gun in their hands. Their arguments suffer no reply. One would have to submit or die.

I ask these officers, if they are in good faith: does not this threat mark a regression in France's political history, one that horrifies every unfettered mind? Do these officers not believe that the French Left (whose shirking of responsibility in these times of crisis should make the politicians who remain responsible die from shame) would once again become involved in the ordeal? No, men and women of the mettle of those who from 1940 to 1944 waged their combat in silence and in darkness have not become extinct. "Never were we more free," wrote Sartre. "We had lost all our rights. They were deporting us in droves ... because of all that, we were free."[7]

De Gaulle's grandeur stems from the fact that, while born into an aristocratic milieu, trained in the same subjects as the other French military leaders, and inclined by tradition and by personal affinity to listen to lessons from prominent nationalists, he has never committed the crime against the state that some of you are thinking of. He has never attempted to cripple this France that has been wrought by the centuries, the France of the Crusades, but also the nation of human rights. It is not a crime (even if it is a mistake) to want to eliminate political parties, but it is criminal to set out to destroy what is expressed through them: the demand for justice that all persons born Christian and French carry within and that you will not snuff out.

"Sunday, June 29, 1958" once again unblinkingly points not only to the reality of Fascism in the France of the late 1950s but also to its particular appeal to young men. Mauriac underscores the grave violations of human rights, including the torture and secret executions that prompted groups of Algerian women to come to the Forum in Algiers, pleading to obtain "at

7. Sartre's bold affirmation of freedom at the very beginning of his article "La République du silence" was first published in *Les Lettres françaises* on September 9, 1944, two weeks after the Liberation of Paris. The essay can now be found in *Situations III* (Paris: Gallimard, 1949), 11–14.

the very least" some information about the men who remain missing. Yet at the same time he joins de Gaulle in invoking France's grandeur, insisting that justice and human rights remain indispensable to France's honor and prestige.

Sunday, June 29, 1958

Among the well-to-do of society, adolescents are Fascists by instinct. All the testimony from the social workers that I know concurs. Their hearts are inclined to follow Massu more than de Gaulle, for better and for worse.[8] The worst does not shock these privileged sons: one does what he has to. "They are tough!" sighs a friend of mine who came to spend an hour with me this evening: he is a young teacher exhausted after a year spent working in a boarding school. "They are tough." And they are simple. Fascism is simple, too. It can adapt to these childish minds, and it is perfectly suited to the pitiless age.

As for leftist intellectuals, they are not simple. Their dialectical verbosity relieves them of a sort of irrepressible urge. Yes, one would say that they write more for their own deliverance than in view of convincing. Their writing is prolific and obscure. They are only speaking to the best students in the class. But those are the last we would need to convince that it is a shame for a great nation to be at the mercy of its soldiers.

And it is first of all to these soldiers, to these young, intelligent leaders who have thought about it and perfected their methods, that you should speak, not with insults in your mouths nor contempt in your hearts, nor as those with superior intelligence, nor as if you ignored the measure of heroism and quite often of charity that many of these fighters have displayed, even though it is they who have ended up being the first victims of the policies that we have condemned.

8. Jacques Massu, 1908–2002, was the general in charge of the French paratroopers brought to Algeria in 1957 to put down the insurrection and the terrorist bombings in Algiers. Though notorious for his use of systematic torture, he was frank about his methods, which he later came to publicly regret. See Michael J. Kaufman, "Jacques Massu, 94, General Who Led Battle of Algiers," *New York Times*, October 31, 2002, http://www.nytimes.com/2002/10/31/world/jacques-massu-94-general-who-led-battle-of-algiers.html.

Speak to them as if you recognized that they were worthy of realizing that the French citizens who had stood against the use of torture are not bad French citizens and that it is France that is crying out when they cry out. Some young leaders could come to concede that the France for which they are fighting, willing to risk death, is also and above all a people among whom there will always be a few "free spirits," refusing to accept what Henri Alleg suffered and asking questions about the fate of five thousand French citizens (since Algerians are French citizens!) who have disappeared. They have vanished into thin air, and not even their loved ones have thought they could seek to know what had become of them. Jean Lacouture writes that groups of Muslim women have come to the Forum this morning to ask for the liberation of their husbands, their fathers, and their brothers, "or at the very least for information about them." Stop and think for a moment about what is horrible in this *"at the very least."*

To yearn for a France that is great is to yearn for a France that is just. The civilization of any people can be gauged by the status of its justice. The young leaders of the army might be won over to these truths. As well as to a few others. Take this one for example: with armed force, you might indeed seize power in a state that is dismantled and no longer defended. But once in control of things, what would you have done? What would you have done, faced with this university, these labor unions, these countless liberals, and everyone that you brand as "progressives" and "defeatists"? You know very well that these labels designate not some egregious error nor any will to betray, but a certain conception of humanity, one that has been an integral part of France's international influence and prestige. You won't deny that this ideal of humanity is part of the spiritual heritage for which you have fought and suffered, and for which so many of your men have given their lives.

And we put one last question to you: what could the best constitution imaginable do against the evil of having the army control the state? What constitution would be so perfect that it would not be at the mercy of a commando linked with the police forces?

"Saturday, July 5, 1958" refers to a solemn Mass celebrated on the rather marginally recognized tenth anniversary of the death of the Catholic novelist Georges Bernanos, known for his scathing condemnations of Franco's brutality and his uncompromising criticism of political hypocrisy. The Mass prompts Mauriac to string together a series of seemingly disparate yet thematically linked meditations, which lead the reader from the anecdotal observations on those gathered at the church to memories of Bernanos's novels, on to the striking, sharply contrasted passion for eternity as expressed first by Nietzsche, then by Berdayev, and finally on to Mauriac's own reflections.

Mauriac proceeds from the eternity presumably enjoyed by Bernanos to the "*France éternelle*" so passionately invoked by Charles de Gaulle. On the one hand, Mauriac clearly observes that de Gaulle's view of France's past as an epic saga of civilization and democracy does not correspond to the historical record, but instead results from a fanciful construction realized through a number of major exclusions and denials. On the other hand, Mauriac cites Chateaubriand and Proust to express his admiration for de Gaulle's vision, and voices hope that it will spur the French to achieve the ideals fictitiously projected onto the past.

Saturday, July 5, 1958

There was a Mass this morning at Saint-Germain-des-Près for Georges Bernanos on the tenth anniversary of his death. There were some people in attendance, but not a crowd. There were many women, of the sort that were the last ones to remain at the foot of the cross and around the empty tomb. There were few young people, it seemed to me. But thanks to a few faithful, both young and old, he is still there, and that is what matters: the soul is ageless. At the end of his life, Bernanos was a young person more alive than most twenty-year-old young men that I know.

Except for the one celebrating Mass, I did not catch sight of any priest at this anniversary Mass, at least not in the chancel. Bernanos, creator of so many priests in his books, was on this day surrounded only by those that he had thought up: Donissan, Chevance, Cénabre, and others who have no name in Bernanos's novels. I kept seeing their black, shiny robes fall in heavy pleats on big, muddy shoes covered with the dirt from all their dead parishes, and wearing around their thin necks a stole, similar to a halter: but it is love that pulls on the rope and leads them there where Bernanos himself has arrived and where he remains. Ten years? But for a person who has been delivered from time, what do these anniversaries mean?

"I love you, Oh Eternity!" I had forgotten this cry of Zarathustra, which I had found so striking in my youth and that I met up with again this evening, cited by Nicolas Berdayev in his *Dream and Reality: An Essay in Autobiography*. I claimed this cry as my own during this Mass, letting it be penetrated, however, by the light to which Nietzsche blinded himself: for the eternity that he loved was not that which Georges Bernanos possesses forever.

I have a hard time imagining this eternal Bernanos uninterested in the time from which death delivered him, and in which the history of this France that he loved so much is being written. But does he still see these French people in the same way? That boils down to wondering if France is really the way that Péguy and Bernanos saw it to be, and the way that de Gaulle demands that it should be. Or has their love (as does all love with the beloved) invented and recreated France in its own image?

I must confess that throughout these last ten years, I have at times believed that in the real world, not a single trait corresponded to that heroic idea of France, and that such an idea had only existed in the passion of those few individuals who touched up history to make it mean what they demanded, and who crossed out and erased everything that contradicted this set of quaint images glorifying the great nation.

That is what makes de Gaulle's latest "experiment" so moving. Don Quixote is only mad because Dulcinea does not exist. If Dulcinea existed, Don Quixote would be the most reasonable of men. De Gaulle believes in the France of his own French history. He acts as if he believed in it, and in so doing, he lifts it out of the fictional: it becomes true, thanks to him. If de Gaulle should fail, it would once again be the annihilation of this great dream. It is not easy for me to entertain such a thought. The aging Chateaubriand wrote the following words just before dying: "To break with what is real is nothing, but with memories! One's heart shatters when it is separated from dreams, for there is so little reality in a human being."

In a letter that I still have, Marcel Proust thanked me for having pointed out these words from Chateaubriand.

The Brave New World of the '60s: Urbanism, Media, and the Dawn of Consumer Society

While the dramatic events of the war in Algeria and the collapse of the Fourth Republic spurred Mauriac to throw himself unreservedly into the momentous debates of the day and thus become the most widely read editorialist of the time,[9] matters of politics and history, however compelling and inescapable, did not exhaust his interests. During the last decade of his life, the questions of personal and religious identity that had always infused his novels regained prominence in the "Bloc-notes," as did the strong sense of national identity that had always informed his politics. The editorialist now writing for *Le Figaro Littéraire* directed increasing attention to the disappearance of "*la vieille France*" (old France) in the wake of belated, but rapid industrialization, the advent of consumer society, and the Americanization of culture as experienced by a Frenchman who had come of age in a society whose institutions and *moeurs* still belonged to the nineteenth century.

Mauriac provides a firsthand account of what we now understand as the radical transformations of "*les Trente Glorieuses*" (the Thirty Glorious Years), the term coined by Jean Fourastié to characterize the three decades of economic expansion and prosperity following World War II.[10] In this

9. Jean-François Sirinelli, "Mauriac, un intellectuel engagé sous la IVe République," in *François Mauriac entre la Gauche et la Droite*, ed. André Séailles (Paris: Klincksieck, 1995), 146–53.

10. Jean Fourastié, *Les Trente Glorieuses, ou la révolution invisible de 1946 à 1975* (Paris: Fayard, 1979). Fourastié's term was a play on words associating the postwar era of the baby-boomers with the revolutionary uprising against King Charles X by the people of Paris on July 27, 28, and 29, 1830. These events inspired Delacroix's famous painting *Liberty Guiding the People*.

context, Mauriac aims not so much to teach the lessons of history as to resuscitate the past, to preserve from oblivion the seemingly ephemeral experiences of his childhood, and to recall the rich legacy of humanity inscribed on the countrysides, landscapes, and edifices testifying to the triumphs as well as the crimes of previous generations. For Mauriac, a uniquely human identity is constituted on a personal, social, and national level precisely by the accumulation of experience over the years.

Mauriac's many references to the past thus serve not only as a filter through which contemporary events and issues are to be interpreted but also as one of what Pierre Nora has famously called "*lieux de mémoire*," or places of memory that have become an integral part of French identity. The tendency to project the controversies of the present into the past, and vice versa, is indeed not specific to the writing of François Mauriac, but on the contrary widely cited as a distinctive trait of contemporary French culture. As the industrialized, urban France of the twentieth century moved farther and farther from the time-honored traditions, rituals, and gestures that had structured everyday life in a largely rural, agrarian, Catholic France, the French turned to the past with ever-increasing frequency and passion, seeking to retrieve what had virtually disappeared from the last four decades of the twentieth century. As Nora explains: "a place of memory's fundamental reason for being is to halt time, block the process of forgetting, freeze one state of things, make the mortal immortal, make the immaterial material in order to . . . enclose the greatest amount of meaning in the smallest number of signs."[11]

The setting of his childhood and adolescence, Mauriac's ancestral estate at Malagar and the surrounding Bordeaux region furnish a rich nexus of memories which he so often uses to reenchant the dreary modern world of the automobile, urban sprawl, consumerism, and mass culture. Traveling from a rural setting to an urban center and vice versa thus occasions a journey back through time, as is the case in the following piece, "Malagar, Friday, May 29, 1959," a text full of nostalgic depiction of the magic

11. Pierre Nora, "Entre mémoire et histoire: la problématique des lieux," in *Les Lieux de mémoire,* vol. 1: *La République,* ed. Pierre Nora (Paris: Gallimard, 1984), xxxv. These three opening paragraphs have been adapted from "In Search of Times Past," in Bracher, *Through the Past Darkly,* 145–46.

of childhood and rich local color. Returning to his ancestral home in the Bordeaux region, Mauriac associates the rural landscapes with his childhood memories and his most treasured pieces of music. Mauriac's rich prose treats the reader to distinctly Proustian strains of a remembrance of things past, as he presents the names of the villages surrounding his childhood home invested with the lyrical transports that he had for so long sought after and found lacking, or at least inadequate, in the aesthetic domain: while even Mozart's sublime music (to which Mauriac elsewhere ascribes metaphysical status) and opera cannot abolish the "thick barrier of times past" and recapture the magic of Mauriac's childhood world, the names and places of the "litany" of villages recited here bring about, for him, just such transports.[12]

Malagar, Friday, May 29, 1959

Yesterday we left Malagar at dusk. It was an evening "golden and blond like a peach" such as the one that, in his *Elegies*, Francis Jammes describes one evening in this city of Bordeaux to which we are heading. Each village in this valley of the Garonne river has a name that resonates within me. I gave the name Virelade to the family in *The Unloved*.

Here we see the town where I was born, and houses where my family lived ... Here we see the Grand Théâtre and the steps that I climb up in my daydream. Not even Mozart's Concerto in B Minor played by Clara Haskil can make it through the thick barrier of times past, whose exact dimensions are provided to me by this delightful hall. What an abundance of landmarks there are here known only to me! My eyes seek out a particular place in the gallery. One of my brothers and I had secretly gone up into there one day. It was the first time I had been inside a theater. We heard the first act of *Mireille*. What had I imagined? I remember my overwhelming disappointment, and it has lasted all my life.

So many of the people I know have put the infinite in theater (and

12. Cf. Bracher, *Through the Past Darkly*, 167.

today in cinema). It always seemed to me that they were being deceived, and that I was the only one who knew that it was a case of deception. I have always thought that, as far as I am concerned, the experience of religion devalues theater. In worship and in the breaking of bread, we participate in the sacrifice that we take in. This is not a show; something is really taking place, even though, as in the theater, it happens through the words, the gestures, and the chants. As sublime as the ceremony may be, however, I prefer the silence of a Low Mass. In the end, we prefer silence to all else.

If religious faith is a "mental illness," at least it preserves us from all other mental illnesses. What member of a Catholic contemplative order ever resorted to drugs?

Except for *Don Juan* (where the "holy and terrible voice" resounds in the music), what opera escapes the pitfalls of puerility, absurdity, and silliness?

Such were my thoughts in the car that was taking us back to Malagar, through the sleepy villages watered by the Garonne river: their names compose one of the secret litanies of the vacations I had in the happiness of my childhood: Villenave-d'Ornon, Beautiran, Virelade, Cérons, Barsac … Music beyond all music.

In "Saturday, March 14, 1964," a spring vacation trip from Paris back to Mauriac's ancestral country estate at Malagar becomes even more emphatically a voyage through time, providing another Proustian symphony of souvenirs, sensations, and literary associations. Proceeding from the teeming metropolis through the picturesque provinces on to the rolling vineyards of the Bordeaux region, Mauriac ponders the sedimentation of history that has left its traces not only on France's landscape and architecture, but also on the contours of his personal memory. Paris and Malagar represent opposite poles in Mauriac's temporal geography. The "Bloc-notes" often associate the bustling metropolis with the modern world's inhuman onslaught of highways and concrete, while Mauriac's provincial home is linked to a rich network of accents, manners, and practices having remained largely unchanged over the *longue durée* of the French rural world. He accordingly welcomes the prospect of traveling from the capital city back to his country dwelling as a voyage through the past, one that will bring him back into contact with the humanity still radiating from the hearth, the focal point of a vitality transcending differences of age and social class.

But even such a heavy dose of nostalgia does not dissipate Mauriac's deep-seated misgivings over the socioeconomic forces that he observes so rapidly transforming longstanding rhythms and patterns of life. Beyond the obvious contrasts between Paris and Malagar, urbanism and rural life, Mauriac sees a dramatic confrontation playing itself out in the contemporary world between, on the one hand, the steamroller of consumerism and technology, and on the other, the web of relations tying humans to their habitat in both Paris and the provinces. Such a network has been accumulated over time and retained in the web of memory, as we see when the Auteuil train station connects Mauriac with the world of Verlaine.

In Mauriac's eyes, the gradual depopulation of the rural habitat signifies the disappearance of that rich network of life and culture. While his perspective is privileged in every sense, and not totally free of an unwitting paternalism, it nevertheless testifies to the anxiety accompanying the radical cultural and social evolution brought on by the massive movement of rural inhabitants to urban centers in France, an anxiety that will ultimately be experienced not only by this bourgeois Catholic member of the Académie française (as his critics and rivals would paint him), but by the entire spectrum of French society.[13]

Saturday, March 14, 1964

I am once more about to climb into the car one morning and experience the joy of driving down a familiar highway, knowing that I will not stop before reaching the threshold of a certain kitchen … I can see this kitchen in my mind just as it has been since my childhood, and I can breathe its delightful smell. We never entered by any other door, and this is the most human place in the house, perhaps not so much because of the sacred fire in the hearth and the flames of the vine branches that make it flare up when meat is being grilled, but more because of the many poor women who have busied themselves over

13. Cf. ibid., 150–55.

the fire throughout the last one hundred and twenty years. I remember a verse of Jammes' poetry: "A lifeless woman servant with the docile smile. . . ."[14] There was always one such woman that the children loved.

How distant this kitchen seems to me as the car barely reaches the Auteuil train station, where, every Sunday, Verlaine would watch Lucien Létinois descend the steps "like an angel along the celestial ladder"![15] I think of them, not each time I go by the station, but each time that the station becomes the first stop on a trip through times past: the departure for the vacation period.

I am traveling through a past woven from just as many and even more woes than those we have "right here and now." The fabric of history and the story of my own past join seamlessly together in me and at the same time a shout goes up—or rather a symphony only I can hear. But everyone listens to their own, at least if their ears are sensitive enough to tune in this music of destiny.

It is therefore not that the world should have gotten worse, only that I am no longer in tune with it. And through the sun-filled mist of a spring morning, or perhaps through the windshield trickling with tears, I shall seek to remember the road the way it used to be, for it has changed a lot. It is no longer the road for horse-drawn coaches nor lined with elm trees, a few of which remained just a few years ago. I remember the plane trees at this crossroads: I saw them one morning as they lay bleeding in the ditch. New shortcuts deprive us from crossing villages that we loved. Vivonne and Croutelle are over and gone for us: we will never pass by there again.

14. Mauriac is citing from Francis Jammes, "Élégie," in *Mercure de France*, October–November 1898, 338–39 (the English translation is my own):

Et le soir glissera dans le jour qui vacille
Dans la cuisine noire où semble encore assise
Une servante morte au sourire docile.
[And, in the vacillating day, the dusk/Will slip
into the dark kitchen where seems to be still sitting
A lifeless woman servant with the docile smile.]

15. Lucien Létinois was Verlaine's *compagnon* from 1878 until 1883. See "Biographies: Verlaine," http://alphonse.daudet.pagesperso-orange.fr/lettres/romances/rspctxts/verbio.htm. Mauriac is citing from Paul Verlaine's "Lucien Létinois XVIII"; see Paul Verlaine, *Selected Poems* (New York: Oxford University Press, 1999), 164, for the original French text along with Martin Sorrell's English translation.

Once we have crossed the Loire, I gaze more attentively: for me, the area begins long before we have really reached it. The Charente region already features the same smell and light effects. As I survey this dead rural area, I at times somberly rejoice at its death. Paris will someday be enormous. The few large cities in the provinces will suck in all that remains of the human population around them. In the end, however, this empty countryside will subsist, with these lonely fields where those capable of loving it will always find refuge …

No! That is an intellectual view. In fact, a deserted rural area becomes a corpse. The Landes region, the remote area native to me as a child, appears quite wild and uninhabited. Yet the reason it remains alive in my memory is because in reality it was the site of a human story in history: in the most obscure sharecropper's house the farthest from any village lived a family. As far as we might penetrate into the Landes region through highly inaccessible marshes, we could always hear the sheep bells ring, a shepherd's guttural cry, and the herd's trampling hoofs. In that time, the Landes was a populated wasteland. Now the sharecroppers' houses that have not burned down are for the most part abandoned. Neither the fields nor the herds are there anymore. A rural area deserted by humans is dead. Those who have disappeared have taken with them a language (this regional dialect that I loved as a child and that all the women used to speak with their servants), as well as the mores that used to order all occasions in life, especially weddings and funerals.

It is because this land was alive that I, who was born from it and would have been nothing without it, have been a living writer. And my novels owe everything to the sandy loam and the clay in which they take root.

For consolation, I tell myself that the earth cannot die, that it does not change. These are no longer the same pines: rather, others have grown that are similar. The pines in the park where I would go for summer vacations are moreover still there: the last ones are holding up, in spite of having been devoured inside. And time can do nothing to change this stream. And on its banks these are not the alder trees of fifty years ago, these alder trees that I used to call "*vergnes*." The prairie that it watered has become a swamp. Nevertheless it is the neverending stream where I would stretch out with a book and the snack that I had brought from home: when I kneel down on its banks, it is easy for me to understand why the first humans considered springs to be divine:

> Nature awaits you in its austere silence;
> At your feet the grass raises up its evening cloud . . .[16]

God! How far I feel from all that is being written and translated into images on the screens nowadays! And how everything on these screens appears to me to be drained of its living substance! . . . This living substance, this lifeblood used to circulate through all the books and through all the paintings. Their infinite diversity did not prevent them from all being tributaries of this living circulation that was connected with living beings and trees and the earth itself. I used to suffer from a rural area deserted by humanity, but now humanity has also deserted writing and painting . . .

In "Saturday, July 16, 1966," concerns over the destruction of natural habitats and an acute sense of mortality prevail over Proustian remembrance, as Mauriac contemplates the disappearance of people and places that he loves. Speaking of the soon-to-be-razed landscape in terms of a person dying of old age, whose facial features have slowly faded away and whose very soul is being violated by the designs of technocrats, Mauriac underscores the humanity painstakingly etched into the rural habitat by countless generations over the course of time. The references to Péguy and to "a story of history which is no longer visible" illustrate Mauriac's fervent desire to preserve this fabric of humanity woven into the countryside, which clearly constitutes a key "place of memory," since it is an integral part of the history that has fashioned France's identity.[17]

Mauriac treasures both the urban and rural landscapes, including the natural habitat with its living organisms as well as human constructions:

16. Mauriac is citing lines from "La maison du berger (I)" by Alfred de Vigny. See http://poesie.webnet.fr/lesgrandsclassiques/poemes/alfred_de_vigny/la_maison_du_berger_i.html.

17. Cf. Bracher, *Through the Past Darkly*, 148–49.

their unique, irreplaceable character appears as the cumulative imprint of generations. Although famous poets, Parisian monuments, and "great moments" of history remain irreplaceable for Mauriac, his writing also testifies to the intimate connection of the physical habitat to the lives of unrecognized everyday people, and to a whole web of humanity left by the wayside in the wake of the implacable rural exodus underway in the France of the late 1950s and early 1960s.[18]

Saturday, July 16, 1966

"Love that which will not be seen a second time."[19] In his poem "La Maison du Berger" ["The Shepherd's House"], Vigny places immutable and impassive nature in opposition with the ephemeral character of his beloved and her "loving, suffering" smile. If this verse comes back to my memory at the instant I return to my garden north of Paris, it is because I am on the contrary applying it to nature and not to a face. It concerns namely this house and this garden, which have been slated for destruction, as has moreover the countryside that surrounds them. Over the fifty some years that I have known this landscape, its traits have slowly been erased: on the plain there used to be avenues of old pear trees that have all ended up cut down. And now the superhighway has just sprung up.

But the countryside is tough: it takes many years for it to die of old age. This one would have held up even longer if its demise had not been willfully inscribed in the plans for the airport at Roissy-en-France. To remodel the land is to wound its soul, even in this northern suburb of Paris, in these dead parishes where Péguy heard his last Mass.

I tell myself that after all, this future airport with its supersonic airplanes will testify day and night to human life at this moment in time and will not erase one single trace of a story of history no longer visible on this plain now leveled by the intensive growing of crops. On the other hand, I fret over it when voices in the know tell me discreetly, "Versailles is threatened, and not only Versailles. If you want

18. Ibid., 150.
19. Mauriac is citing a line from "La maison du berger (III)"; see note 16.

to go meditate and pray at Port-Royal one last time before dying, make haste. Get informed about what is being planned for that sacred place of solitude."

The press doesn't say anything about it. Moreover, who would be upset if it did? Am I not myself resigned to it? I have outlived too many trees not to notice that places die as do human beings, that in places where the earth was a beloved face, their traits get worn away. In my *Nouveaux mémoires intérieurs,* I describe this lost area of the sandy moor south of Bordeaux from where my family originates and where, after the most recent fires, nothing remains.[20]

The buildings at Versailles can be kept up and restored, but it's hardly a matter of buildings! And then what is left of Port-Royal? A few stones, of the kind that forever cry out: "... if these were silent, the very stones would cry out."[21] At Port-Royal one finds trees and paths other than those dating from the time of the recluses, although there remain earthen stairs that Pascal climbed and descended. There is nothing else here other than a solitude that is the opposite of abandonment. At Versailles and in the Chevreuse valley, those living in the present have managed to set aside a sort of privileged ground for the story of the past, not the history of battles, but of ideas. This cemetery of Port-Royal that was profaned by Louis XIV and the Jesuits has become a living desert at the gates of Paris, laden with all that overflows from within us when we come to meditate here. What is being plotted against Versailles and against the Chevreuse valley?

I protest, I worry, and I know that my protest is to no avail. It is not only all flesh that will fall into nothingness: earth as well has only successive faces that will often be worn away before our demise. When certain traits of these faces remain, their apparent fidelity makes us more keenly aware of the distance that separates me, for example, from this oak on which I pressed my lips as a schoolboy: it is true that it is still standing, surrounded by a few pine trees and having survived

20. Published in English as *Inner Presence: Recollections of My Spiritual Life,* trans. Hera Briffault (Indianapolis, Ind.: Bobbs-Merrill, 1968).

21. Mauriac is citing Jesus' well-known words on his entry into Jerusalem, as found in Luke 19.40.

the most recent equinox storm, its extended branches blessing me one last time. It is no longer the gauge that can measure the depth of time.

"Love that which will never be seen a second time …" I sense quite well what is absurd about this demand when it involves my own humble destiny and the landscapes familiar to me. But I believe that it is legitimate when we are no longer dealing with me, nor with the footprints that I have left in the sand at one instant, but with France and its illustrious history. Even within the confines of Paris: think of everything that has been destroyed there at the time of Haussmann and even since I have come here! The year of my arrival, the dismal Boulevard Raspail was finishing off the Abbaye-aux-Bois convent, where my wife was one of the last to attend school.

And to think that it is under the reign of de Gaulle that people have concocted the worst criminal attacks against this France of which he maintained a certain idea only because he had formed a certain image of it when he was a child,[22] perhaps just as I myself had done, led on by Alphonse de Neuville's illustrations in Guizot's *Histoire de France*.

Each stone seemed precious to us under the Occupation: the balustrades of the bridges in Paris, the only ones not destroyed by the catastrophic defeat of June 1940, were the old parapets that Baudelaire and Rimbaud used to lean on at dawn. There is no stone nor any tree in the Paris region that may be touched without respect. But above all, there are zones of silence around Versailles that have been miraculously preserved, as if history had intimidated those who make a profession of erasing the traces of the past, putting in its place the gloomy ugliness of high-rise public housing and getting rich. Now they have overcome their timidity, and history no longer scares them …

"Friday, November 18, 1966" represents one of Mauriac's most explicitly Proustian articles. Once again linking one of his keenest personal preoccupations to an important phenomenon in French society, Mauriac places

22. Mauriac is alluding to the famous words at the very beginning of Charles de Gaulle's *Mémoires de guerre. L'appel, 1940–1942* (Paris: Plon, 1954), 5, which became the watchword of his "politics of grandeur": "Toute ma vie, je me suis fait une certaine idée de la France" (All my life, I have maintained a certain idea of France).

his own passion for retrieving, retaining, and reinvesting a bygone world in parallel with similar interests demonstrated by the general public. Such is the case with the visitors thronging to the Orangerie museum in Paris, where they hope to glimpse the privileged moments of beauty and harmony that artists such as Vermeer, Chardin, and Cézanne have managed to capture in their paintings. Reflecting back on Proust's *Remembrance of Things Past*, Mauriac suggests that the featured painters of yesteryear offer us a refuge of humanity amid the dull routine of everyday life and the anxiety of the atomic age. Thus relating the public's ostensibly aesthetic enchantment with these paintings to the unsettling context of the Cold War, he gives powerful expression to the pathos of the 1950s and '60s while at the same time pointing to a crisis of human identity.[23]

Friday, November 18, 1966

Vermeer is on exhibit in the Museum of the Orangerie. We didn't need Paul Valéry's warning to know that civilizations are mortal. Even if the Arno river and its waters polluted with fuel oil had not just destroyed or irreparably soiled so many paintings, books, and manuscripts, I would have, standing before the Vermeer paintings in the Museum of the Orangerie, perhaps felt this deep anxiety that the painful death of masterpieces creates in me: it is the element of death that has already entered into their "conservation." Is it I who have changed since I saw them and fell in love with them? Have they been touched up or poorly revarnished? Have they undergone certain treatments? Have they been restored to their original luster, and is each painting just as it was in its original state, such that what would make it suspect to me today is to have been cleaned of its centuries old grime?

Nevertheless, this delightful pleasure that I no longer receive from the Vermeer paintings (I'll leave aside the portrait of the young girl in the blue turban that is so moving for me, since it reproduces the face of one of my granddaughters right down to the last trait), I now receive anew when I stand before paintings by Chardin, Le Nain, and Cé-

23. Cf. Bracher, *Through the Past Darkly*, 163–64.

zanne, with which I was not familiar (*Bridge over the Marne at Creteil*). Yes, those canvases are still throbbing with their authentic life.

I wonder whether *View of Delft* was known to me before I read *Remembrance of Things Past* and Swann spoke of Vermeer to me: to my mind, Marcel Proust has forever hung this masterpiece inside his own. My first priority this morning at the Orangerie was to once again locate on that painting "the little yellow stretch of bare wall" that struck Swann's eyes when he was about to die, and then I sat down like Swann on a bench, feeling this grief that I knew I could escape, since I believe with Charles Baudelaire in the testimony to our dignity that these great painters have given.[24] What other dignity, if not that of being the children of God?

Why this daily rush to see an exhibit such as the one in the museum in the Orangerie? This is not the snobbery of inaugural cocktail parties. These poor folks have not come to be seen, but to see. To see what? Infinitely more than what is displayed for them. They know that the subject matters little and that one must not attach any importance to what the picture represents. But then what are they seeking? Like Proust, whom they have perhaps not read, they are unknowingly engaged in a search for the time that must be retrieved: the time of Vermeer or of Chardin has been miraculously fixed onto a bit of canvas and has held up over centuries: a time on a human scale, to which we all hark back, and which has been brushed aside by the atomic age.

Vermeer, Le Nain, and Chardin all entrust each of these visitors with the same secret: poetry arises out of everything. It can well up

24. Baudelaire's poem "Les Phares" ("The Beacons") honors Rubens, da Vinci, Rembrandt, Michelangelo, Watteau, Goya, and Delacroix as prime examples of painters whose art attests to human dignity:

> Car c'est vraiment, Seigneur, le meilleur témoignage
> Que nous puissions donner de notre dignité
> Que ce long hurlement qui roule d'âge en âge,
> Et vient mourir au bord de votre éternité!
> [For truly, Lord, the clearest proofs
> That we can give of our nobility,
> Are these impassioned sobs that through the ages roll,
> And die away upon the shore of your Eternity.]

Baudelaire, *The Flowers of Evil*, trans. Aggeler, http://fleursdumal.org/poem/105.

from the least object or gesture or anything bathed in light, for all it takes for us to desperately sense the nothingness of our own life is one light ray forever fixed at a certain hour, on a bowl or on a servant's hand, unless . . .

The question that would be raised at this point can no longer be posed in a world that has deliberately chosen to be atheist. Light has come into this world, you no longer know it, but there we see its reflection offered to you: beyond the material light, something else fascinates you, which is in time and not of time, something which both enchants you and leaves your hunger unsatisfied. For after all, these are only paintings on a canvas, at the mercy of wartime destructions or a flooded river. And yet we do indeed feel what Baudelaire heard in "The Beacons": we too hear this cry repeated by a thousand sentries, this cry of hunters lost in the great woods. You have to plug your ears not to hear it.

Perhaps these waves of people continually flowing up the ugly new stairway in the Museum of the Orangerie reveal a most singular anxiety that no other era had ever experienced. What fascinates today's living beings in the work of Vermeer, Chardin, and the Impressionists is actually a secret suddenly lost. It had been handed down without interruption from century to century up until Pablo Picasso; then all of a sudden one link was missing, the spell was broken, and there was a seismic shift somewhere. In reality, we know the artist who is responsible and who enjoys an almost god-like status among us. It takes two palaces to celebrate the most ingenious destruction that art has ever suffered. Will it experience a renaissance? The question raised by the great Picasso converges with what the worshipers of Vermeer are asking themselves. It is not post-Gaullism that constitutes a problem: in the political realm, Gaullism is both an outcome and a point of departure. But what comes after Picasso? Yes, that is the problem: the grass will perhaps never grow again where Picasso has passed by.

For what painter that will come after him can you imagine in the year 2000 an exhibit that could retrace his work and offer the crowds of that day a bit of what they are receiving today from Vermeer, Chardin, and Cézanne? I am struck by the fact that nowadays the Western world is gaining an awareness both of the need for self-discovery and self-recognition through colors and forms, and of its sudden impotence that, for the first time in five hundred years, makes it drop the brush of Vermeer, Poussin, Watteau, Manet, and Cézanne.

It took a genius to break off and perhaps put an end to the most sublime of stories. You are certainly not wrong to give the Luciferian Picasso an exceptional place. But we are not the ones who will have the last word about his work: it will be judged by the generations coming after ours which, thanks to him, will be free of all the old molds and commonplaces, but condemned to everlasting rubble. The other evening I was listening to André Malraux speaking to us on television about Picasso as constituting the greatest epoch in the history of painting. Yes, just as the hour of our death is the one that counts the most in our life.

The Apogee of Gaullism: Ecstasy and Agony amid the Politics of Grandeur

Throughout the 1960s, no one would prove to be a more fervent and unswerving supporter of de Gaulle than Mauriac, who parted company from Jean-Jacques Servan-Schreiber and *L'Express* in 1961 in protest of his colleagues' ceaseless attacks both on the general's politics and on his very personal exercise of presidential power, which they denounced as an affront to democracy. Mauriac adamantly defended de Gaulle, pointing out that he had finally established an orderly, coherent governance that brought an end to colonial war, maintained unprecedented domestic prosperity, and restored France's international prestige. Among the numerous articles that Mauriac devoted to de Gaulle's "reign," the following highlight key aspects of the decade marked by his presidency.

In "Monday, January 9, 1961," Mauriac not only surveys the various reactions to the massive (75 percent) approval of de Gaulle's referendum granting Algerians the right to determine their own status and future, but also underscores the importance of de Gaulle's television appearances, which seemed modeled after John F. Kennedy's media success. In addition to Mauriac's eloquence, lyricism, and erudition so evident elsewhere, he here displays his keen political acumen, observing that, while worrying or annoying other political leaders, de Gaulle's singular appeal to make the issue a personal question between him and each individual voter had clearly struck a chord with the public. He moreover points out that such a capacity for establishing "direct" contact with voters would now be crucial, as television was bringing politicians right into family dwellings.

Monday, January 9, 1961

Of all the French people listening to the radio yesterday evening, those on the Left who voted "no" should be the most elated: never have the losers had more reasons to be happy, for they barely escaped with their skins. Think about it: it is now an established historical fact that under the Fourth Republic, the Left steadfastly and diligently carried out the politics of the Right in Algeria. It really would have been too much this morning if History had had to record this new confirmed reality: it is to a great extent the French Left that delivered a fatal blow to self-determination in Algeria. You can say what you like: the victory of your "no" votes would have had no other meaning than that.

If ever there were creatures of this world who ran at a dizzying speed away from what they desired, it is certainly you, my friends on the Left![25] Your luck is to have been forcefully brought back by an old nation of people who are more reasonable than you.

It is true that the event does not give a very grand idea of the importance that the common people grant you. But I would like to emphasize one singularity about this referendum: the French people did not just say "yes" to de Gaulle over your heads, but over the heads of all French political leaders and in spite of the instructions given by their parties. I was struck, as were many people, by a sentence in the Gen-

25. Mauriac cited a similarly worded prayer by Saint Teresa of Ávila as an epigraph to his novel *The Knot of Vipers*: "Dieu, considérez que nous ne nous entendons pas nous-même et que nous ne savons pas ce que nous voulons, et que nous nous éloignons infiniment de ce que nous désirons." (God, consider that we do not understand ourselves and that we do not know what we want, and that we stray infinitely far away from what we desire [translation mine].) See Valentine Lesenko, "Une lecture pascalienne du *Noeud de vipères*," in *Pascal-Mauriac: L'oeuvre en dialogue*, ed. Jean-Francois Durand (Paris: L'Harmattan, 2000), 273.

eral's last talk, which I cite from memory: "Beyond all intermediaries, this is a personal matter between each one of you and myself."

This elimination of intermediaries is something new in politics. While those around me displayed shock, I was on the contrary touched and moved more than I could say, although I am starting to believe that I am a rather singular sort of democrat. Yesterday evening on the radio, politicians in favor of the "yes" vote and who were gloating over the results nevertheless commented rather tartly and even bitterly on de Gaulle's words. You have to agree that the event gives them special significance.

If I am to believe people around me, General de Gaulle was supposedly struck by the determining role of television in President Kennedy's success. Direct, familiar, and repeated contact with the mass of voters does not favor all politicians, only those who have an ability to enchant. Television would have been of no use to Poincaré, for example, whereas it would have served Aristide Briand quite well. That has far-reaching implications. De Gaulle understood that what was happening between him and the crowds during his trips could be extended, maintained, and renewed on television. So what good are the intermediaries?

The poor intermediaries! The fact of the matter is that they are no longer in tune with the music. Mounted on tired old warhorses, they gallop after the chariot of the state now converted into this strange, accelerating machine steered by a hero, and they cannot catch up. The distance between it and them will increase up until the day of some unforeseeable accident.

Don't think that I am gloating about it. It is today that the real contest begins. The playing field has been leveled, and no longer will the army or the crowd gathered at the Forum in Algiers serve as an excuse for scheming. One unique obstacle stands opposite de Gaulle: the GPRA.[26] The anxiety stems from the question that arises: does there exist within the GPRA a shared will that can be articulated? Or is there only a mix of conflicting tendencies that cancel each other out? Is

26. The Gouvernement Provisoire de la République Algérienne formed by the rebels.

what General de Gaulle is from now on confronting alone and freely sitting on hard rock that nevertheless can be shaped, or is it an elusive cloud?

No, I am not in the mood to gloat. I have received in the mail an appeal from Serge Groussard and a bitter, despairing letter (written before the referendum) from a friend of the French people of Algeria who is also my friend. Believe me, dear Yves and dear Serge Groussard: your friends in Algeria thought they had been deceived by de Gaulle, but de Gaulle is precisely the only living politician who will not compromise on what they deserve. Remember what I am telling you. I do not believe that events will prove me wrong.

Although the bloody Algerian conflict ended with a negotiated settlement that was finalized in March 1962 and that led to the independence of Algeria on July 5 of the same year, the last two years of the conflict were marked by a particularly ruthless campaign of terror carried out both in Algeria and on the French mainland by the OAS, a group of hardliners refusing any and all concessions to the Algerian rebels. The same period was also marked by acts of severe brutality and massacres committed by French police, who killed a (still) unknown number of Algerian demonstrators in Paris on October 17, 1961, and by the bloody incident at the Charonne métro station in Paris. It was there that nine of those protesting peacefully against the violent tactics of the OAS ultranationalists seeking to maintain French control of Algeria at any price were crushed to death by the charge of antiriot police forces.[27] In the face of such disconcerting episodes of violence still continuing in the heart of Paris over three-and-a-half years after de Gaulle retook the helm of the ship of state, Mauriac offers a frank assessment of events in all their complexity, without trying to make the facts conform to de Gaulle's vision or even Mauriac's own political commitments.

Clearly shocked by the French police's repeated use of ruthless brutality, Mauriac begins by reflecting on the role of the writer living in a time of civil war. As was the case when he found himself disheartened by the

27. See "8 février 1962. Manifestation tragique au métro Charonne," http://www.herodote.net/histoire/evenement.php?jour=19620208&ID_dossier=9.

frightful bloodshed produced by France's attempt to quell anticolonial uprisings in the early 1950s, he reflects on the seemingly unending chain of violence characterizing French history and finds himself tempted to take refuge like Montaigne in the timeless world of writing, or even, like monastics, in spiritual contemplation. Once again, he insists that his vocation as a Christian is to seek the divine among human beings by plunging into politics in pursuit of peace and justice.

At this political level, Mauriac acknowledges his predicament. Although unsettled by the de Gaulle government's mendacious claim to be quelling two opposing extremisms and by its unavowed complicity with the provocations of the OAS, he nevertheless attempts to explain why, even at this particularly troubling moment, he believes de Gaulle represents the best hope for France. It is here that Mauriac candidly assesses the enchantment that de Gaulle exercises over him and over so many of his compatriots.

On the one hand, Mauriac clearly states that the Gaullist narrative of French history as an epic of grandeur is an artful construction that simply omits countless episodes of civil war and political crimes. The concluding words of this editorial are astoundingly honest and apt: "De Gaulle is the heart and mind of a great nation rallied together, a great nation one and indivisible that does not exist." Yet as fanciful as it may be, de Gaulle's "certain idea of France" wins Mauriac's endorsement as a political strategy for integrating the disparate elements of the nation's past into a coherent project for the present. Hence Mauriac's assertion that de Gaulle "embodies the France of history; he gives a flesh and blood reality to what was only an idea."[28] That such a formulation better befits the exercise of power by a monarch than by the president of a liberal democracy was of course hardly lost on either de Gaulle's detractors or Mauriac's political adversaries.

Saturday, February 10, 1962

Montaigne began writing his *Essays* in 1572, the year of the Saint Bartholomew's Day massacre.[29] Plutarch's *Moralia,* translated by Amyot,

28. Cf. Bracher, *Through the Past Darkly*, 186–87.

29. On August 24, 1572, in the context of France's religious wars, some 200 Protestant nobles were executed in Paris upon the orders of the Catholic monarchy, which was keen on consoli-

were published the same year and became his breviary.[30] I don't believe this was a coincidence: Montaigne was seeking refuge in writing. For him, it was a matter of escaping the horror of living in a kingdom perennially divided against itself. Four centuries after the religious wars, we have not gotten out of this state of affairs: the pretexts change, but not the hatred nor the criminal attacks. Petty crimes committed in the name of grand principles: that pretty much sums up all of French history.

We too, whose profession it is to write, dream like Montaigne of escaping events and of making our honey from them with our essays. And for us Christians who by God's grace have a sensitive heart, there is another temptation: the one that stems from our capacity for fleeing on high. Yes, a temptation—and we must not yield to it. The saints who flee the world for the cloisters suffer and die there for the world. As for us laypersons who are not saints, our vocation is not to flee human beings in God, but on the contrary to find God in human beings, be it in the thick of a miserable political situation.

We must therefore resume our commentary on the sordid, monotonous, everyday story of history without presuming, on our own humble level, to make from it a work as durable as the *Essays*, for nothing is more ephemeral than France's domestic politics: the mud dries quickly and turns into dust, and so it goes with the writings that report on it. It would seem that our nation is ashamed of it and in a hurry to forget.

But this is hardly a question of posterity! We agree to work in the immediate present and for the immediate present, if this work is an attempt to see clearly within ourselves in order to enlighten others, and if it serves to untangle the knot of our own feelings, which are a reflection of the most mixed up political juncture that ever was.

I hold tightly one end of the thread, which is my admiration for de Gaulle, the trust that I still reserve for him, and the certainty that he is

dating its power. Seeing this officially sanctioned slaughter, the Parisian populace took to killing any and all Protestants it could find. The massacre spread to other major cities in France, ultimately claiming the lives of some 30,000 Protestants. See http://www.herodote.net/24_aout_1572-evenement-15720824.php.

30. Plutarch's *Philosophy,* commonly called the *Morals*.

France's good fortune, that he is reaching the goal, and that he is going to win, as we will win with him. But at the other end of the thread, I am just a poor fellow who bristles at the declarations made by the minister of the interior: his words have this irritating quality of being correct in theory while flouting the humble reality of lived experience. For it is true, as the minister said, that it is up to public authorities to fight against disorderly agitators, and that adding to the disorder only plays into their hands. We remain convinced of it, and he had no trouble persuading us. But the minister did not recall what we know and what we have most bitterly experienced: namely, that the public authorities have really not been acting in good faith over the last few days or at best the last few months, and that throughout this time their laxity looked like complicity, and according to some (I am thinking of Gaston Deferre) was indeed complicity. They let the evil turn into what it did. Even within the outer circles of power, they were soft on it. Edmond Michelet left, others came: you could tell the difference and come to your own conclusion.

If, by our consent, they should make fools of us, the Gaullists on the Left, our love for de Gaulle has never blinded us to the behavior of some of his servants. As soon as the three fateful letters appear vaguely in the watermark of an official document, our immediate fear is that the French nation might remain as dull as it seems to be, but our hope remains that we shall finally see it come out of its slumber. It would be hypocritical for us to pretend to be worried because this nation should have finally righted itself.

This old nation whose political education was completed two centuries ago has such a long history behind it that it is a grave offense to tell people stories and to think that one can make them believe fairy tales such as the supposed equivalence of the two extremes, which is in essence what the minister was saying. That is such flagrant nonsense that we were embarrassed to hear and see him say so. Every criminal attack is the doing of one side. The entire world sees that: hence our anxiety at seeing the Left lie flat on its face. If they did not wake up after getting hit like that, who could ever awaken them?

Now we see the Left again, staggering a bit, but on its feet. I am not as happy about it as I said: that would be an insult to those who are mourning their dead. We are not happy about it on the political level either, even though we had hoped and believed that this awakening would happen at the behest of de Gaulle and that, as at the time of the Resistance, the Left would unanimously rally around the man capable of leading French politics back onto its true course.

Why try to deny it? We are not being consistent with ourselves. The split within us is due to a twofold fidelity: fidelity to de Gaulle who, alone and against a world of armed, powerful adversaries, has in three years succeeded in achieving France's political goals, whereas all the politicians on the Left had proved to be incapable or unworthy of doing so. We also maintain our fidelity to the people who, as on other historic days, once again are marching somberly down the avenue between the Place de la République and the Place de la Nation.

These two fidelities are on a collision course within us, and I see quite well what is preventing and what shall always prevent us from overcoming this contradiction: the fact is that it stems from the heart of de Gaulle's destiny. He embodies the France of history; he gives a flesh and blood reality to what was only an idea. As long as he is breathing, thinking, and acting, this France has the appearance of existing. Thanks to him, France has a tailor-made foreign policy that fits its place in the world. And since France sees through the eyes of de Gaulle, its vision carries a long way, too far for the actual nation and its confused mass of dark desires and interests compromised by events. The rumblings of this confused mass reveal the nation such as it really is to the outside world, such as it appears to other nations as soon as it is no longer de Gaulle that they are seeing and hearing.

Against these forces that are hostile to him and torn by infighting, de Gaulle is still prohibited from having recourse to certain components of the nation, even the working class neighborhoods, unless there were a military coup. If this calamity can be avoided, the chief of state will, out of a necessity in his very being, not have any particular ties to any single faction, nor to any single class, nor to any single religion or mindset. He will remain unmoved, as no other leader before him ever was, and that is his grandeur in all his popularity. De Gaulle is the heart and mind of a great nation rallied together, a great nation one and indivisible that does not exist.

The "Bloc-notes" of "Wednesday, May 9, 1962" reacts to the horrific acts of violence perpetrated by the OAS against women, children, and hospital patients. These acts of terror were a desperate attempt to sabotage the recently (March 19, 1962) concluded peace accords leading to Algerian independence. Beginning with a sort of prose poem associating changing landscapes with the affectivity of the writer, this signature editorial formulates a maxim on the passage of time and the resulting vanity of human attachments. Instead of lingering in melancholy contemplation, however, Mauriac plunges more resolutely than ever right back into the thick of history and current politics, issuing an unequivocal condemnation of the coldly calculated terrorism preying on the most vulnerable among the Algerian Muslim population. In the face of France's crimes, Mauriac's eloquence is matched by his lucidity in denouncing both the tacit complicity of the European population in Algeria and the ultimate goals of "the Fascism" and the OAS "cutthroats in Algiers." In the end, however, it only reinforces his support of de Gaulle as the sole rampart against both anarchy and military dictatorship.

Wednesday, May 9, 1962

I had expected this late Easter to be wonderful, but since spring has not come on time, my hopes were for naught: April has turned out to be a chilly month of March. I was really counting on seeing the roses this year, but the only one I picked was on the morning I left, just before getting into the car. The previous day at dusk, I had been reassured by a few birds I heard warbling off and on: the nightingales were there but did not sing during such a cold night. Thus it is that things betray us: we must not count on them any more than on living beings. Affection for trees and stones is betrayed, as are all loves.

Yet nothing can change the fact that history goes on. "I am in deep, deep solidarity with this world where flowers and wind will never bring us to excuse all the rest ..." (Albert Camus, *Journal*). I suddenly think of a letter that I received: as fond as I am of a house and a piece of land, even though I only spend three months out of the year there, I should be more sympathetic than I let on to the wrenching separation imposed on those who had to leave behind their homes in Algeria. Reading Camus's *Journal* gave me a sense of that Algerian land and its power of enchantment. What does my apparent insensitivity stem from? For it is only an appearance. Whenever I fix my mind on a particular case, I can easily share a similar anxiety.

What distances me from the anxiety of those Europeans who had to leave their homes in Algeria is this big pile of dead bodies growing wider and higher every day: these are corpses of the poor, of children, of maids, and every evening their bodies cover those who were killed the day before. Although chosen at random, these victims all belong to the same group of people: those who have been the poorest, most humiliated, and the most insulted for a hundred years. I know quite well that not all the Christians who have humiliated and insulted them have taken part in today's abominations. Many condemn these acts. Nevertheless, eyewitness accounts are all in agreement: these crimes are carried out with absolute impunity, not almost always, but always. I am willing to believe that fear might have a lot to do with it. Still, all other ordeals pale in comparison with the one inflicted on this group of people; all other injustices seem minor in comparison with this uninterrupted, mechanically regular string of crimes on such a huge scale.

The killers belong to a known type of people, a fauna that has appeared at various times in history. In the past, however, the phenomenon occurred at events such as the Saint Bartholomew's Day massacre, with a beginning, a middle, and an end, or else during one of the insurrectional days of a revolution. I doubt that in any other era or at any other time there has been anything similar to the events that have been going on for weeks and months in the cities of Algeria and are still happening today: actions are being carried out in broad daylight and according to a preconceived plan.

This butchery is the product of cold calculation. It has been carefully and consciously thought out. And even if there are not many

French people, not even on the right, who approve of it, there are, however, a good many willing to absolve the killers and blame their crimes on the man who, according to them, has made these actions possible by a policy that they hate. For it is true that a policy is judged on its results, provided that it has not suffered a sabotage that deforms it. And if you say that it is the policy itself that provoked the sabotage, and that it must therefore be held responsible, that is a mockery: for what is opposing the Evian accords in Algeria is not another conception or another view of things that might correspond to what this particular juncture demands. If those who command these killers were in charge of things, they would not be able to establish anything today in an Algeria that has tasted the strong wine of independence, pride, and victory, and which has one hundred thirty years of humiliation and contempt to avenge. Moreover, what difference does it make to these murderers? What interests them is Paris, this overprivileged and overfed metropolis, these dull people who are only drawn out of their slumber for a day by salary matters, and this Left which has sold out to the bourgeoisie.

They believe that all they would have to do is to reach out to the other side if de Gaulle were not there. With him pushed aside or taken out, everything would become easy. But does it occur to them to ask who or what is supporting de Gaulle? The killers in Algiers, or at least those who use them, cannot avoid being struck by this fact: the writings of journalists on the Left, Claude Bourdet or Jean-Jacques Servan-Schreiber, are cited with approval and without the insults that only recently were customary in these militant papers. Although of course not intentional, this objective alliance compels us to face our political destiny: that takes courage, because this destiny is horrible.

If de Gaulle were taken out of the picture, there would only be two mutually exclusive possibilities. The first is that in the immediate, if not long-term future, Fascism would win and cutthroats of Algiers would rule in Paris through their cronies. After all, our fellow journalist and writer Jules Romains would look good in André Malraux's armchair, and why would he not have the right to enjoy these delights before dying? The cutthroats will easily find a Bidault or an André Morice for each government ministry. The second possibility is that this old nation that does not know what it wants, but knows very well what it does not want, will spew them back out. Then it would come back to what it had vomited up previously, namely the Fourth Republic and the folks who have been idle since its demise. For no one new will step forward, and we will find them all once more, showing their hungry teeth and licking their chops even more conspicuously than before. And the whole circus will crank up again in its usual disorder.

"Thursday, September 13, 1962" once again begins with a lyrical description of the landscapes, skies, and seasons at Malagar, as Mauriac ponders the accelerating pace of change and searches for havens of continuity in nature and history. If on the one hand he remains strongly attached to the rhythms and gestures that have for ages characterized life in these rural provinces, he skilfully lays out the subtleties not only of de Gaulle's proposal to have the president of the French Republic elected by direct universal suffrage, but also of the rising prominence of media in public life.

Thursday, September 13, 1962

At the very height of the drought, the day before yesterday was a scorching hot day, the likes of which I had never seen in September. For the first time, the dusk will not deliver us from the heat. I frightened the children by saying that the earth, since it was already cracked, was going to quake. Toward the middle of the night, fog finally stretched out over the vineyards, and the dew of daybreak soaked the wilted grass.

Today the weather has become milder. Elsewhere, it must have rained, but the storms are not for us. The halcyon moon rising from behind the hedges is no longer the one worshiped by the first humans, nor is it the moon whose light flowed into my room when I was a child who would get up to open the shutters. Tomorrow, robots will be its masters.

It is nevertheless the case that the little farm boy who this afternoon was carrying from house to house the fox that his father had killed was placing his steps back into the steps made for centuries by all the little farm boys whose fathers had killed a nasty beast. Thus I eagerly seek out the slightest signs of a permanence of times past: what has withstood the years, what will hold up a little longer against a humanity crazed with technology.

The colonization of the moon leads my thoughts back to politics and to de Gaulle's plan for the election of the president of the Republic by the people and to journalists who are clouding the issue. I am surprised that these clever folks do not see what should jump out at them, namely, that neither the Parliament's disrepute nor the parties' paralysis are de Gaulle's doing, any more than was the loss of the empire or the mutation of the army. It is unbelievable, and yet it is true that a brigadier general turned out to be the only French politician capable not only of fathoming what the now clichéd expression "acceleration of history" means, but also of adapting his vision and his policies, while the others, all the others faced with this reality on the Right and on the Left have only had emotional reactions as stupid as that of Xerxes who had the sea whipped.

It is true that de Gaulle counters such gut reactions with an indifference that seems a bit inhuman. The thousands of French women and French men who, thanks to Nazi Germany, learned in their flesh how far human beings can push their contempt for other human beings, and what a ferocious intelligent beast is hidden within, did not carry an ounce of weight that could have delayed the reconciliation with Germany decided by de Gaulle, just as the army's furor never exerted the slightest influence on his policies for Algeria. He goes through the worst obstacles to the truth as it emerges from the facts. The others are dominated by it, but he dominates it and imposes his style over it.

What can the indignation of the Socialists and Radicals do against the least of these facts? From now on, nothing could prevent de Gaulle from using the radio, for example, to penetrate into the most humble dwellings or from using television to penetrate there in a visible way. Radio and television are creating a world different from the one in which Guy Mollet made his career. How can he not see it? If de Gaulle goes over your head, it's because he has the capability of doing so. It's technology and not de Gaulle that cuts you out.

Nor is it his fault that the Fourth Republic pushed the demonstration of its own harmful and impotent nature to a level of absurdity unprecedented in history. Dressed as the ringmaster Monsieur Loyal, making Georges Bidault and his fellow clowns run around the track jumping through paper hoops, poor Monsieur Coty left us an indelible image. You are indignant for the sake of a political orthodoxy that seems as outmoded as a dentist's chair dating from 1880. What a flea market one finds in French politics, from Guy Mollet[31] to Pierre Boutang![32]

As for the claim that General de Gaulle will make good on what he has decided in his mind, that's another matter. The future belongs to no one. It may not resemble what de Gaulle has decided it should be. Great men do other things than what they believe they are doing. But French politics will not return to what it has vomited up.

What lasts forever are the traits of French character that are expressed in each party. For example, the big MRP newspaper in my province pointedly refrains from attacking de Gaulle head on, as a Radical or a Socialist would, but they present the general's triumph in Germany as a staged act. De Gaulle is an actor for the members of the MRP in Gironde, and a virtuoso of the bluff. The real hero of the reconciliation between France and Germany according to them is still Robert Schuman: not the person that embodies this reconciliation today by his deeds, but the one who was the first to speak of it. It is true that at the time de Gaulle was saying no to ideas that were scarcely grounded in reality, and that he said yes when the time was ripe. Consider the man from the time when he was a theorist of the motorized army and when he intransigently refused to accept defeat in June 1940, then go on to contemplate the man who in 1945 maintained the French army on the Rhine, quelled the anarchy in the provinces without having recourse to these military forces, and prevented all-powerful allies from evacuating Strasbourg. Then continue on to ponder the decolonizer of today, standing against a pack of assassins, mutinous generals, and furious politicians, and admire the great realist and perhaps the only re-

31. Guy Mollet, 1905–1975, served as secretary general of the Socialist Party in France from 1946 until 1969, and was France's premier in 1956 and 1957.

32. Pierre Boutang, 1916–1998, was a writer and philosopher on the extreme Right, virulently opposed to de Gaulle.

alist of French politics, although I hesitate to say the only realist since Clemenceau and Poincaré, who were both fitted with thick blinders and who also obeyed imperatives handed down from great ancestors and old pontificators.

I shall once again say yes to de Gaulle, not that the election of the president of the Republic by universal suffrage appears to me to be a panacea, but because the reasons that led de Gaulle to choose such an election, and that he will explain to us on September 20, are based on an analysis of political facts by a sovereign mind that has not often been mistaken.

Whether or not he violated the spirit and the letter of the constitution is something that I do not feel myself the least in the world capable of deciding. This experiment with the referendum will in any case be decisive. If de Gaulle should lose or just barely win, the old moribund parties would run around and get all excited, and thus regain a hint of life. If de Gaulle wins, the only thing that will be left to do is to throw a few shovelfuls of dirt onto their mass grave. The French Left shall then have to be reinvented. Its hour will have come at last: Charles de Gaulle will have condemned it to revive.

Mauriac penned his "Bloc-notes" for "Thursday, March 28, 1963" in response to the incisive anti-Gaullist editorials published by the left-wing Catholic weekly *Témoignage chrétien*. He thus explains his fervent adherence to de Gaulle's vision of French grandeur, while at the same time pointing out the violence and turpitude that the general has omitted from his idealist scheme of things. Yet Mauriac also points out the significant tensions between his own views and those of the general. Reflecting on the passion for history that irresistibly draws him to de Gaulle, in spite of his own misgivings over certain chapters of French history that the general seems to ignore, Mauriac measures the disparity between de Gaulle's epic vision and the current citizenry of France. He perceives the measure of braggadocio in de Gaulle's claims to French grandeur, and makes a point of setting his own outlook apart from that of the general. It clearly takes a willful effort for Mauriac to perceive France's past as de Gaulle sees it, and even then he has to admit that, far from inspiring transports of national pride, some chapters leave him queasy. In the end, however, Mauriac admires the general precisely for his obstinate idealism, which he sees as uniting France in pursuit of a coherent political project.[33]

Thursday, March 28, 1963

Courage, my dear sir, consists sometimes of being on the side of authority: not always, of course, nor in all situations nor in every age. One hundred years ago, the Catholic bishops would have done better not to be under the thumb of Napoleon III, so I gladly approve of their present attitude. For a layman, however, and for the writer that I am, I think that today I should stand with de Gaulle and not give in the temptation to take a stance that costs so little to those who boast of it. Courage consists of refusing to write something just to give a certain idea of oneself that would meet with approval both in *Témoignage chrétien* and in *Rivarol*.[34] Courage consists of joining one's obscure individual solitude with the illustrious solitude of the leader who has on his side only his people, that is to say both an unlimited force and no one, and who, threatened as never before, hated as never before on the Left and on the Right by those who have no other hope in this world but his death, remains faithful to this idea of France which resembles so little present-day French people, yet which for him represents an irrefutable reality.

I imagine that what separates him the most from Kennedy are words such as those that the president of the United States slipped into a speech made before André Malraux the other day, I believe: "France, the greatest artistic superpower in the world." (I cite from memory.) For his part, de Gaulle believes that France is still a great nation on all levels. His adversaries retort that this notion is dated, and that his policies hark back to an antiquated nationalism. But he could care less about being seen as a nationalist. He keeps his faith, or rather he founds his certitude on facts that are based on other things than his-

33. Cf. Bracher, *Through the Past Darkly*, 183–86.

34. Just as *Témoignage chrétien* is known for its strident left-wing stances, the magazine *Rivarol* is prominently situated on the extreme right of the political spectrum in France.

tory. Let's admit it: it is easier for M Spaak to be a good European than for de Gaulle.[35]

Not that I completely share his faith. Putting my mind to it, I can see this France that de Gaulle sees, the one that Péguy saw, the same one that, when I was a youth, Barrès saw and Maurras did not see.[36] Maurras eliminated what he hated and carried out his personal civil war through history. De Gaulle, it seems to me, does not pick and choose: Robespierre and Saint-Just enter into the composition of his painting as rightfully as Saint Louis and Joan of Arc. Yes, I can see this France, but without giving it all my heart. Our history fascinates and horrifies me. If I were not fearful of making people laugh at me, I would admit that a part of me has never been consoled over the Albigensian Crusade, nor Louis XIV's use of soldiers to stamp out Protestantism, nor the destruction of Port-Royal, nor the Reign of Terror, nor the queen's trial, nor the child abuse suffered by Louis XVI's young son, nor all the rest, right down to the last act of torture and the most recent victim of torture in Algeria.

All of that enters into the idea of France formed by de Gaulle. He repudiates none of that grandeur cemented by heroes'—but also by victims'—blood, and fashioned by political thinking that has been a constant from Philippe the Fair to Richelieu and from Richelieu to de Gaulle. Although incapable of feeling what he feels (what I imagine he feels), I am inclined to believe in the possibility that history will prove him right over those who decided that France had definitively turned into a second-tier nation. I take his side in choosing not to measure our country by the citizens now living. I bet on the great nation, without repudiating Europe in the process.

My reasons are not only of the mind and spirit. It was an enemy of de Gaulle, Pierre Boutang, who wrote this morning: "The factory in Pierrelatte is in fact the most extraordinary and promising venture for ensuring the economic independence of France and of Europe. The production of enriched uranium (uranium-235) is presently an

35. Paul-Henri Spaak, 1899–1972, who had served as Belgium's premier and the secretary general of NATO, was Belgian minister of foreign affairs in 1963. See http://www.larousse.fr/encyclopedie/personnage/Paul_Henri_Spaak/145011.

36. Charles Maurras, 1868–1952, headed the virulently antidemocratic, nationalist movement Action Française and published a newspaper of the same name.

American monopoly. This uranium has a military use and must serve to equip us with thermonuclear weapons. But its civilian use as fuel in atomic reactors, both our own and those that France will be able to export throughout the world, will without a doubt be still more important." But one must read what comes next. Boutang adds: "To want Pierrelatte, whatever the immediate price may be, is to want France to exert an influence in the world and to remain a great nation, regardless of whether one chooses to accept or reject the idea of a national nuclear strike force."

"Saturday, February 19, 1966" was written in the wake of the Ben Barka affair, in which the leader of the Moroccan opposition was kidnapped and killed by two French police officers who later implicated their superiors. Mauriac's fervor for France's historical heritage and his loyalty to de Gaulle lead him to embrace some rather embarrassing notions of national identity, as he indulges in some regrettable and flagrant excesses. Although deeply troubled by the murky circumstances of the incident,[37] Mauriac adamantly refused any analogy with the Dreyfus affair that might tarnish de Gaulle. Without entering into the details of this controversy, we can observe, with no little amazement, that in defending de Gaulle, Mauriac espouses the claim that history is inherently criminal, and therefore, so is the job of governing.

This line of reasoning constitutes a stunning about-face for the author of the "Cahier noir," justly admired as a Resistance piece for its unequivocal denunciation of Machiavellian politics. It also points to an apparent lapse of conscience for the editorialist of *L'Express* who, when denouncing the torture and oppression perpetrated for reasons of state during the Algerian war, had constantly reminded his readers that history has a human face. Mauriac had indeed repeatedly insisted that neither France's public officials nor the citizens who elected them could escape responsibility for crimes committed on behalf of the government. Rather than appearing as the result of human all too human enterprises, however, the "history"

37. An ex-convict having set up the trap for Ben Barka was, at the moment of his arrest, found to have "committed suicide" in a highly suspect manner. Touzot in BN IV, 201n2.

invoked here seems to unfold implacably outside the realm of human will. Mauriac's concluding words in this effort to insulate de Gaulle from the Ben Barka affair moreover represent a veritable idolization of the general. Not only does Mauriac liken the founder of the Fifth Republic to a consul, a sovereign, and a monarch, he even depicts him here as a sort of high priest of a "religion of a French honor," raising the glorious body of the immortal French nation for all to worship.[38]

Saturday, February 19, 1966

"There is nothing interesting on earth except for religions."[39] Those are Baudelaire's words and they could serve as an epigraph for the collection Writers before God, published by Desclée de Brouwer, where Monsieur Jean-Bertrand has recently come out with a fascinating book, *Victor Hugo*. Now there's a subject I would love to meditate. What a destiny for Hugo, who was probably not even baptized and who nevertheless never ceased to bear witness to the living God! He had no need to distance himself from a church that was foreign to him. But that is hardly the question! What touches on the subject of God must not serve as a refuge for me to escape from daily reality, especially when this reality is sinister.

Maurice Clavel has brought me an article from the *Journal de Genève* (February 17). According to my Swiss counterpart, I am supposedly "torn." They say that those close to me know "that I am waiting to have knowledge of all the facts before penning a few authoritative words that would hurt de Gaulle more than all his opponents together." Well, actually, no! That's giving me too much importance: I do not have such a great power, but if I did, I would not use it against the man that I admire the most in the world and to whom I feel the most gratitude. I haven't done anything these days that does not testify to my desire for avoiding every ambiguity on this subject and to stand all the nearer to him when he is attacked the most.

38. Cf. Bracher, *Through the Past Darkly*, 193–95.

39. Mauriac is citing from Baudelaire's *Mon coeur mis à nu: journal intime* (1887), http://www.bmlisieux.com/archives/coeuranu.htm.

I am therefore not "torn." I would be lying if I pretended to be so. I am indeed saddened and disgusted by this matter concerning the police, just as the average person is. But why torn? And between whom or what? I have no need to take sides. Here there is no innocent person being crucified as there had been in the past on Devil's Island,[40] and as there are at present in Moscow. Nothing better reveals the desire of de Gaulle's enemies to take the fullest advantage of the Ben Barka affair than their attempt to assimilate it to the Dreyfus affair. What they have in common, but only partially, is the context of counterespionage. As for the rest, I don't see any forgery in the current affair; the main author of the crime is known, and it is the minister of a foreign country. The French implicated in the matter are behind bars. Figon's body haunts us, certainly, but as far back in my life as I can remember, I find dramatic events, kidnappings, and suicides, and they give rise to an inexhaustible supply of the most widely read literature in the whole world.

The fact remains that what has always occurred should not have occurred under de Gaulle. The French people have sensed that. In their surprise and indignation, de Gaulle's adversaries themselves paid unwitting tribute to the man they execrate. But as for me, I know that history is criminal and it is up to no one, not de Gaulle any more than it was up to Titus, Marcus Aurelius, or Saint Louis, throughout all these centuries, to make it innocent. Especially today, when a simple matter of a kidnapping like that one cannot escape having global ramifications. "The international backdrop of the affair" is the headline of an article in *Le Monde*, and it is enough to make us understand why the enemies of de Gaulle will not succeed in reducing the Ben Barka affair to the dimensions of French domestic politics.

History is criminal and it poses dreadful dilemmas to its elect: de Gaulle's response to the dilemma of 1940 still seems a folly to a lot of people. I imagine that in comparison to what he experienced at that time, everything afterward must have seemed anodyne to him. The fact

40. In what was intended to be an exemplary punishment, Alfred Dreyfus was deported to the desolate Devil's Island, a former lepers colony off the coast of French Guyana, where he spent 1,517 days. See http://www.dreyfus.culture.fr/fr/dreyfus-et-les-siens/les-itineraires-d-un-officier-francais/le-deporte-de-l-ile-du-diable.htm.

remains that as a soldier, his vocation was to fight, and he fought, and to give his life, and at Verdun he gave it, and took upon himself the destiny of his nation in 1940. He charged himself with France's destiny at a time when everything seemed mixed up and murky: the question of duty was so unclear that he was going to be condemned to death by court-martial. Since that day, this revolutionary has never ceased marching in a certain direction where it was not up to him to avoid the mud puddles and the pools of blood, no more than it ever was up to any prince over the course of history, however saintly or wise he may have been: "One does not govern innocently."[41] But politics is perhaps the only domain in which it sometimes becomes a merit and a virtue to turn one's back on innocence.

Nevertheless, you will say, if you are not torn, others among your Gaullist friends are. Are they really? I believe that in the face of the Ben Barka scandal they are in fact obeying their instincts as opponents, not of de Gaulle, of course, to whom they remain more faithful than ever, but to his administration. Persuaded as they are that the plight of Gaullism is linked to the presence or absence of certain men in power, how would they not have seen in this affair a chance to clear the playing field?

I will not follow them, despite my affection for them. Because in the first place neither the prime minister nor the minister of the interior, regardless of what you claim, has been compromised in the least, and secondly, if there is one area where de Gaulle must remain the sole judge of things, it is the matter of determining whom he is to trust, on whom he can depend, and by whom France will be best served. You claim to know that better than he does, you who give in to the illusion of believing that all it would take for justice to rein and for de Gaulle to receive the benediction of a reconciled Left would be to put certain new people in power.

What is singular in de Gaulle and makes him dear to me is that fundamentally he understands you, in spite or because of your passing

41. Mauriac is paraphrasing Saint-Just, who, when demanding King Louis XVI's head at the latter's trial, stated: "Nul ne peut régner innocemment" (No one can reign innocently). See Alexis Philonenko, *Essai sur la philosophie de la guerre* (Paris: Vrin, 2003), p. 95.

fancies. There is a part of him (and what a wonder when you think of what his life has been!) that has withstood the tendency to harden. His friendship for you should be enough to prove that this great politician, one of the greatest of our history, is not a politician. He is so ill inclined to be a politician that I fear some day that I will see him descend the front steps of the Elysée presidential palace, walk down the sidewalk of the rue Saint-Honoré all alone, hail a taxi, and disappear without coming back.

As long as he is there, let him proceed and trust the men that he has chosen. He would have set them aside if he had thought it was in the interest of the nation. Each of them as each of us has his strengths and weaknesses that de Gaulle is aware of and that he has weighed on scales more accurate than yours.

For my part, I do not believe that de Gaulle's prospects are hinged on choices of this sort. As long as de Gaulle is there, this old nation will maintain itself on a plateau: it is back in shape after having tidied up its clothes and wiped away the stains. And once again, it is "living up to its name," as we used to say in the provinces.

When my hope has bottomed out, I tell myself that after de Gaulle everything will get back to the way it was previously. What gives me such fears is the hostility on the part of eminent figures who nevertheless do not have reason to hate him, as do former collaborators or extreme right-wing militants. De Gaulle embodies everything that they cannot bear: a certain idea of the independence of our nation with respect to all others, and above all to the most powerful nation; the religion of a French honor to be preserved and defended, of the "French destiny" that our kings and republics have passed on from century to century right down to de Gaulle, and that he, the latest in this long tradition, raises above your furious heads.

Recounting his visit of the magnificent cathedral in "Strasbourg, Friday, June 24, 1966," Mauriac draws on the salient features of the church's architecture and aesthetics, and then compares its construction of unity and harmony to de Gaulle's construction of grandeur and unity for the French people. Mauriac thus links his adulation of de Gaulle to his ardent desire to see a reaffirmation of unity, permanence, and specific identity of the French derived from its past. The embodiment of history that Mauriac finds in the Alsatian city's cathedral is all the more striking since it follows on the heels of three paragraphs decrying the devastation of the rural habitat brought about by the construction of the Roissy airport. The venerable Gothic edifice thus appears as a powerful antidote to the dehumanized urban landscapes dominated by machinery and concrete.

Mauriac dispels his anxieties over the younger generation's historical amnesia and the dissolution of France's historical identity in describing the transports inspired by the parallel figures of de Gaulle and the Strasbourg cathedral, both of which are transformed into "places of memory" in this passage. Even the dehumanizing effects of technology alluded to in the first line are overcome by the majestic music emanating from the cathedral's architecture and the organ. Mauriac likens the construction of the cathedral to the historical magnum opus realized by de Gaulle's "*certaine idée de la France*": just as the rough-hewn stones have been incorporated into a grandiose masterpiece that preserves their particular qualities while at the same time giving them a transcendent permanence, so de Gaulle, asserts Mauriac, allies the democratic idealism of the Third Republic with Barrès's nationalist fervor, thus maintaining France's identity while reaffirming its "vocation" in a world dominated by the United States and the Soviet Union. This realization of national unity in such a dynamic synthesis is moreover reiterated by Mauriac's lyrical description of what momentarily bonds him, the "old man raised by the losers of '70 and by Barrès"[42]—in other words by the ultraconservative nationalists—to "*ces touristes*" casually wandering about in the cathedral: all have been swept up out of the shallow mediocrity of the moment and into the glorious harmony of the architecture.[43]

42. Mauriac is referring to the wealthy bourgeois and Catholic traditionalists who turned out to be the biggest political losers after the catastrophic military defeat suffered by Napoléon III's military forces in the 1870 war with Bismarck's Prussian troops. In the wake of that loss, the Third Republic, which would usher in a long series of major social and political changes, was created.

43. Cf. Bracher, *Through the Past Darkly*, 199–201.

Strasbourg, Friday, June 24, 1966

Here, for the first time, the machines have been vanquished: we no longer see or hear them. Here, it is the stones that cry out: their clamor drowns out all the rest, and history prevails.[44] People will say that all this is going on within me, in the imagination of an old man raised by the losers of '70 and by Barrès. In fact, no: the men and women wandering about in the dimly lit cathedral were no longer the tourists that they would once again become upon going out.

It was as if all had been stunned and lifted out of time, or rather incorporated into the story of history. The great organ suddenly resounded. The last time that I had heard it was when people joined in singing the *Te Deum* at the Liberation. General de Gaulle was standing to the right in the chancel. The bells were louder that the rumbling of a nearby cannon. Today, twenty-two years later, I enter the chapel where the bread of life is kept. I do not know the *Te Deum* by heart, so it is the *Magnificat* that rises up to my lips from my heart, and my heart overflows with a certitude that fully elucidates de Gaulle's political strategy: a nation is really a person who has a vocation, a particular destiny, and intercessors. How can you who have experienced the last twenty-five years not acknowledge that we have been protected and saved?

I can see once again in my mind this picture from *Le Monde illustré* of 1870 that I so often leafed through when I was a child: the bell tower of the Strasbourg cathedral in the gloom of night, surrounded by bursting shells. By what miracle has the city survived these three wars? Perhaps the two enemy nations were unknowingly reconciled in their love of a city which was born of both of their respective creative spirits and which is in their image, and so agreed to spare it.

Everything on the level of feeling nevertheless converges here with politics. The overriding question is to know whether de Gaulle is right or wrong, whether a nation's vocation still exists even though its pow-

44. Mauriac is alluding to Jesus' triumphant entry into Jerusalem, where he was acclaimed by jubilant crowds. "If the latter were silent, the very stones would cry out," affirmed Jesus. See Luke 19.40.

er has diminished and that now two huge empires are exerting a hegemony over the world. It is to know whether what subsists of this little France's influence in the world is tied to the person of de Gaulle and whether after him, France will have to fall back in formation and never again leave it, or whether the nation will remain sovereign, faithful to its friendships, but free not to follow policies imposed by others that France does not approve. And what does de Gaulle think of all that in the evening, after one of these exhausting days? I do not believe that on the downward slope of such a life he could harbor any illusion about human nature, particularly about a certain type of French political animal ... But what do you expect? From the bottom of the abyss and all along the climb out right down until today, he has managed to find as many French as necessary to resume the march of history. It is a never-ending chain that seemed broken in 1940, as in other times in history, when the king of France was the king of Bourges. But there has always been someone to repair things, in the absolute sense of the word repair.

6 ∽ FROM HERE TO ETERNITY

A History Full of Sound and Fury

Reading Mauriac's editorials, one finds the past everywhere present, as Mauriac filters his perception of current events through a vast repertoire of figures and episodes from history. History permeates his writing, informing his positions on virtually all subjects, constantly providing the essential frame of reference. Prefacing the first volume of his collected "Bloc-notes," Mauriac specifically pointed to history as the nexus of his editorials: "someone is there amid the circumstances of an ordinary life with his ideas, his tastes, his moods, and each week: he reacts to history being made under his very eyes. This confrontation of the individual with the universal is what the *Bloc-notes* is all about."[1] We should recall that the French term *histoire* not only covers the various senses of the English word "history" but also includes the meaning of "story." Surveying current events, Mauriac views them as part of an ongoing drama. The particular and the individual participate in a larger scheme of things. Instead of

1. BN I, 37.

writing about isolated incidents or random anecdotes, Mauriac considers series of actions unfolding over time, originating in the past and leading to the future. Events are interrelated: just as a new photo placed in family album is understood in relation to a larger collection of pictures, each new occurrence becomes another episode in a longer saga.[2]

In most cases, Mauriac places the present in relation to the past in order to endow it with fuller meaning. History represents an ethical and ultimately a metaphysical drama. Yet Mauriac adamantly refuses to attribute historical events to fate or any other impersonal force, such as Marx's notion of a dialectical march of events toward a classless society. But we must equally note that Mauriac also refuses to attribute the course of events to divine will: "I have never been able to see signs of divine intervention in the events of history."[3] Instead, he emphasizes the primacy of the human element in history, particularly when commenting on violence and injustice.[4]

Since he finds himself inextricably caught up in this dramatic story of history, Mauriac declares himself *engagé*, engaged by, committed to, implicated in contemporary human events no less than were Sartre, Camus, Aragon, and other French intellectuals of the 1940s, '50s, and '60s. Unlike most prominent figures of the Parisian intelligentsia, however, Mauriac is compelled not by the march of history to some new humanity, but rather by a Christianity that summons him to responsibility for the well-being of his fellow human beings. It is on that level that Mauriac aims to be an active party to events through his editorials. For history is ultimately a narrative, a story of events written and told by one human being (or group of human beings) to another. Witnesses to the events and writers of the story, such as Mauriac, thus bear crucial responsibility for setting the record straight and placing the events before the public eye. Although aware of the large-scale developments defying conscious control, Mauriac persists in viewing history as not only a human but in the final analysis a personal matter. History lies in human hands in the sense that it must ultimately be understood and communicated through narrative and therefore placed under the gaze of those who must suffer its consequences.[5]

2. Bracher, *Through the Past Darkly*, 19, 27.
3. "Thursday, June 18, 1953," BN I, 79.
4. Bracher, *Through the Past Darkly*, 46–48.
5. Cf. ibid., 53, 60, 65.

Mauriac penned "Tuesday, January 15, 1957" at one of the most dramatic moments of the Cold War, several years after the death of Stalin and shortly after the crushing of democracy in Hungary. He focuses explicitly on the question of history as posed to both nations and individual human beings keen on enjoying a large measure of control over their collective and personal lives. Like many of his compatriots, Mauriac deplores the division of the world into two hegemonic blocks, denying traditional powers such as France their accustomed autonomy. In this situation, history not only refuses to obey the conscious control of individuals, it also escapes the desires of entire nations. For France's role in the universal drama has now been scripted. Harboring few illusions as to the real range of options available both individually and collectively in such circumstances, Mauriac acknowledges that history does often call the trumps. However, he denies it holds all the cards, even if in some instances historical developments outstrip not only the private world of the individual but also the prerogatives of entire nations.

Nowhere in Mauriac's editorials do we find more powerful images of historical developments totally unsubmissive to human thought and volition. It is as if the course of history had been dictated by a preexistent text: the train of events seems to be leading France over rails laid out by two superpowers. But in the same breath, Mauriac goes on to posit the unfathomable autonomy of human beings and deny that this history has the last word. History may be inescapable, but it is not the whole story: there exists for Mauriac a part of each human being that cannot be subsumed by events, dissolved into some material process, or reduced to a chain of causes and effects.[6] Recalling Shakespeare's "tale told by an idiot," Mauriac insists that countless stories of personal lives cannot simply be subsumed into the categories of history and politics.

6. Cf. ibid., 53–54.

Tuesday, January 15, 1957

This history, our story of history, is unfolding within another one that is enveloping it, and that will ultimately determine its outcome. I don't know if there were many French people celebrating this morning as they read the newspaper headlines: "Persistent Malaise in Hungary," "Poland: Greater Hostility toward the USSR," "Threat of a Strike in Potsdam." Certainly, there is reason to celebrate the assurance thus granted us that humanity is standing up to the system, that a people really has a soul, and that it is not a myth. But there is also reason to tremble, for if this part of Europe caught fire and it spread to Berlin ...

The USSR will not back down. It cannot back down. Our hearts and minds are so much with the heroic Hungary that it escapes our attention that, as cruel as it is, Russia's repression does not constitute a crime in the style of Stalin. It has nothing in common with the abomination of the Katyn massacre, for example, nor with the trials of 1935–38. It is a political act that is neither Stalin's nor even specifically Russian: in this case, it is a matter of a normal reflex of the defense that an empire puts up as soon as it feels threatened in an area that it deems essential.

On that level, the only difference between the free nations in the West and a Marxist state is that the latter does not have to take principles into account or bother with them. It does not resort to word games to get around them, as we do when we find ourselves having to engage in repression. And above all, it does not have to handle with care that part of public opinion which, in our countries, demands that policies toward the nations that still depend on us be inspired by the democracy that we profess and claim to practice.

It is not Stalin that Hungary and Poland are dealing with at the moment. It is not even Lenin or Trotsky. It is the Russia of Peter the Great whose entire defensive system risks being challenged and will stop at nothing to prevent a breach from opening. If ever one did open, it would be plugged with as many cadavers as fate would demand.

Thus our drama unfolds, enveloped in a larger drama that contains it. Thus our little men get all excited and smash everything inside our private rail car; but it is being drawn away to God knows where on the same track along with many others.

I doubt that this total history is the only true story. Beyond this "tale told by an idiot, full of sound and fury, signifying nothing" that Macbeth speaks of, something is still at work, a ferment is acting in the substance of humanity, and this hope that overflows in the humblest of hearts is indestructible. This mysterious joy that death itself, which hounds us all our life, cannot manage to drive out, where does it come from and who is it? I believe that there exists another story besides History: my story and yours—as many stories as there are human beings. It is the secret of novelists, and each of these stories contains the makings of an irreplaceable masterpiece.

In "Malagar, Monday, September 16, 1957," we find Mauriac withdrawn to the serenity of his country estate in the Bordeaux region. Poring back over his activity as an editorialist, which has taken precedence over his writing of novels, he presents his editorials as the confrontation of his "interior life" with history in the form of current events, points to the new and still changing world order that has emerged from World War II, and observes somberly that France's political life resembles a confusing tragedy of errors and violence. He nevertheless refuses to despair of bringing France closer to its touted ideals of grandeur and justice, even if that paradoxically means creating an acute awareness of the crimes and injustices committed in its name.

Malagar, Monday, September 16, 1957

In the house not yet completely awakened from my absence, I put myself to the test of rereading what I have written in the "Bloc-notes" since the first day I began to compose it. For these pages in which a nation's political life and the inner life of a writer flow together so strangely must in the end be published. It is out of the question to include everything in this book. But the duration or continuity of such writing is what makes it so valuable. Falling back into the "selected passages" genre would spoil everything.

It makes for bitter reading, but not because of my personal failures.

Through the "Bloc-notes," I go back over the course that we have followed for five years; or rather, I look down from on high, from where my eyes perceive the unbroken chain of causes and effects. I have always thought that this long string of misfortunes is the work of men. Today, I see that it is so. A few politicians whose names are known have been and continue to be the agents of these woes, but they have certainly not acted against the will of the nation.

I suspect that here I am going to shock and sadden many friends. What holds them up and consoles them is this idea that our country is the victim of a team of members of parliament who are serving the interests of the oligarchy. Such a view corresponds with reality only very loosely. Let us dare to say the truth: the great mass of the bourgeoisie, from the least to the most prominent, has given their consent to the policies enacted, and still do. Those are the facts. I believe they consent out of mental laziness, but that changes nothing.

This laziness hardly lessens the responsibility of those who have condoned and who still condone these policies. Once the disaster was consummated, they moreover shamelessly disclaimed responsibility, trying to blame it on the only statesman who had no part in it, who for ten years never ceased to denounce these policies and predict their dire results.

As I proceed forward in the "Bloc-notes," I remain dumbfounded by the scruples to which I have sometimes yielded as a Christian. No, I certainly do not find myself guilty of any injustice with respect to these talented schemers who resorted to orchestrating the Parisian and provincial press, using another name in place of their own in order to proceed with a settling of scores, and who succeeded rather well. Just yesterday I was reading in one weekly news magazine, as if the matter were self-evident: "The damage done by Mendès and by the loss of Indochina. . . ." Today, I understand why it should be a crime to lie. No, certainly I feel no remorse, or rather, yes I do: compared with the men of Dien Bien Phu who dared broach this subject, I fault myself for being weak and soft-pedaling the issue. I regret all that I refrained from saying about them.

It is a fact that the Fascist-leaning organizations in Algeria are ruling by fear and are shaping French politics at will. But one would have to have lost all contact with the provinces and with the families of the petite, the upper, and the middle bourgeoisie who continue to believe only in the use of force in order to deny it.

There are few French people from these social milieus who display the capacity to take stock of the new world that sprang up in 1945 and summoned the colonial powers to adapt accordingly. The price we paid for saying no in Indochina and Morocco opened the eyes of only a very few. Have many people been struck by the incredible failure to recognize the real structure of power in today's world as illustrated by the Suez fiasco? I wouldn't swear by it. In that instance, one single threatening sentence from the Soviets was enough for us to call everything to a halt. In all other instances, a frown from one of the two behemoths would find us just as docile. Does daring to face up to this reality mean that we have lost hope for our nation? Those who accuse us of that are themselves defeatists who have failed to recognize the arms that France still had then and has now for maintaining her rule in all domains.

No, there was nothing inevitable or predetermined in this story of history visible in the "Bloc-notes." It would have been possible for the sultan of Morocco not to have been deposed or exiled. It was possible to negotiate a new statute accommodating the interests of both nations. A premier other than Guy Mollet could have avoided tumbling head first into the trap set in Algiers on February 6, 1956. Another would not have given in under the [barrage of] tomatoes.

When we look at things closely, the only one of our woes that no one could have prevented was the National Assembly that resulted from the last elections. Who could deny that the worst came out of the ballot boxes? For in a democracy, the worst consists of having a supposed government of the Left carry out the blindest and most deadly policies of the Right.

So what good is it to get so upset, and why don't you just worry about inventing and telling stories, since that's your job? That is probably what a good many people are thinking, and at times I ask myself the same question. But for a writer thrown into "the tangled mess of errors and violence" of politics, to borrow Goethe's phrase, no failure can prevail over this vocation: to say clearly what the writer believes to be true with no desire to go easy on any particular interest or person. That goes farther than it is up to us to measure. If I am sure of one thing in this world, it is that nothing will be lost as long as from one day to the next the truth is gleaned from this "tangled mess" and declared.

For in spite of all of our miscalculations, I have no reason to lose heart, neither as activists (my mail proves it every day) nor as citizens of France. I can see at every moment this inexhaustible capital that France enjoys in spite of all of its faults and disasters: nothing is lost for us. Even my most determined adversaries, in almost every case, sigh the name of France from time to time with a nostalgia in which love is strangely joined with hatred: I have observed this attitude in numerous encounters.

The miracle for France lies in the fact that over the last ten years we have not succeeded in destroying a certain idea of France. And what else have we to do but to lend a hand? Our vocation is to make France into a nation that resembles this image that survives in the hearts of free people all over the world. It is a living image that also is subjected to torture each time that someone is tortured by one of us, but the image survives because it is immortal.

In "Friday, September 27, 1957," the atrocities committed by the French army in Algeria lead Mauriac to relate the traumatic events of the present to the fundamental questions of humanity, as posed by the seemingly unending series of crimes and tragedies found throughout French history and as recently as the German occupation of France. As is so often the case in his editorials, but never more poignantly than in this piece, Mauriac frames the current situation with such allusions to events and figures of history: the experience of the past does not simply vanish but accumulates over the years, becoming ingrained in the particular character of persons, places, and things. He thus articulates his enduring, passionate attachment to the landscapes and people of his country who have laboriously sculpted them over the centuries. While Mauriac clearly takes solace in the physical beauty of France's landscapes and architecture, his stinging indictment of torture has lost none of its power.

Friday, September 27, 1957

The army ... in fact, we are dealing with the question of humankind; for after all, those specializing in these kinds of interrogations "that get a little rough" are not monsters. They belong to the category of everyday people. Had it not been for this war that led them to discover their true nature, they would doubtless have done nothing worse than to tear the legs off a fly in order to keep themselves entertained in class.

I kept mulling over these thoughts during a bright, hazy day, while letting my friends take in the ancient ramparts of the little towns surrounding Malagar. We went inside some Romanesque churches, unknown marvels of architecture now crumbling. On the highest hill, in the light of the fifth hour, stood the Benauge chateau with its proud walls that recall the Hundred Years' War with the English and that perhaps saw Edward, Prince of Wales, pass by in his heavy armor. There are certain moments when I can only love my country physically. That was my experience in Paris during the Occupation: the trees and balustrades in the Tuileries and the reflection of arched bridges off the Seine were more sacred to me than most of the humans in my vicinity, particularly those who were then getting rich, really getting fat [off the black market], for example the horrible couple depicted in *Au Bon Beurre*.[7] People too often forget that such folks are still one of the essential components of today's electoral majorities. These fortunes that were heaped up during the Occupation now hold and occupy us in turn.

On that subject, I note that certain critics had discouraged me from reading *Au Bon Beurre*, hinting that between Jean Dutourd and the hideous couple that he has depicted, there was a murky complicity. Now, as I have been making my way through the book these days, I have experienced a feeling of deliverance: "Finally," I kept saying to myself, "that ended up being stated after all. This couple with whom we more or less all had to deal with for four years has now been

7. Published in 1952, Jean Dutourd's novel *Au Bon Beurre* tells the story of a greedy, hypocritical dairy-shopkeeper during the Occupation years who traffics in the black market, collaborates with the Germans, and then pretends to be with the Resistance when France is finally liberated.

denounced and exposed in a pillory. From now on, this image will dominate the history of these dark years. In order to deny that the author of this fine book is a courageous man, you would have had to be totally ignorant of the cowardice that leads so many people today to opportunely close their eyes and seal their lips."

To love one's land physically is after all to love this face made in the image of humanity, the face imposed on the land by those who, over the centuries, tortured and massacred, but also by the obscure people who painfully struggled, testifying to the truth and giving their lives. And so even when I believe that I no longer cherish anything but a certain light on the hills and mountaintops, or a certain smell of wet leaves and mist, or the old roof tiles turned violet by the rain, I nevertheless cherish my country's humanity. Yes, the same humanity, for the brutes that torture have lived in every time. On the other hand, the best among those who have gone before us were no more saintly than the men and women still living today, and I know the names of a few.

It is precisely French claims to cultural and historical prestige that Mauriac invokes in "Sunday, March 16, 1958," as he seeks to drive home the shame and scandal of the crimes committed in France's name. Written shortly after Henri Alleg's *La Question* had provided incontrovertible testimony on the widespread use of torture by French military and police in Algeria, this piece denounces the banality of evil with an ironic commentary inspired by a production of Alfred Jarry's play *Ubu roi*. Intent on shaking his readers out of indifference, Mauriac cruelly underscores the traits likening Ubu to the smug, sententious middle-class patriots fiercely devoted to ensuring their own material and moral comfort regardless of the consequences for other groups of people. For Mauriac, Jarry's perversely grotesque king personifies not such archetypal heads of evil empires as Hitler or Stalin, who provide such easy and reassuring targets for this type of satire, but the silent majorities ultimately responsible for the crimes committed for "the love of country."[8] Mauriac thus undermines the ethnocentric presumptions which, as noted by Alain Finkielkraut (along with many

8. Cf. Bracher, *Through the Past Darkly*, 107–9.

others), have always served as a pretext for plunder and destruction of indigenous peoples by "civilized" Europeans.[9]

Sunday, March 16, 1958

What a little man, after all, was old man Ubu yesterday evening at the Théâtre National Populaire. Now there's somebody who has piped down a bit! As we grow old, we begin to resemble the most highly charged caricatures that people have made of us. Ubu seemed less funny, perhaps because he seemed more real, and that's putting it mildly: I found him to be less ugly than real. Neither old men nor old nations laugh anymore before this big windbag puffed up with crimes, this big beast from our apocalypse, so much more anodyne than the beast who rules over us today!

Yes, Ubu seemed dull to me and I would have liked to spice him up a bit. His smug certitude that it never costs too many human lives to fill his belly and keep a tight fist over everything that has been stuffed into his pockets is a trait that is common in our species, and widespread, not among primitive tribes, but even among an old Christian people like ours, fiercely moralistic and at times revolutionary.

As stupid, cruel, and cowardly as he may be, the fact remains that old man Ubu is not as stupid, cruel, and cowardly as some of the people driving French policy in 1958. At no time during the play do I see him hate or despise people because of the color of their skin, nor take pleasure in making somebody suffer. His machine for debraining people is after all not very original: Henri Alleg could give him a few pointers on the subject.

The real, historical Ubu is neither Hitler nor Mussolini nor Stalin: these monstrous figures have a few of the same components as Ubu, but they were builders and organizers. They had an idea. As terrifying as it may have been, it was an idea, and they shaped it into the form they desired using humans as clay. Ubu does not think: he devours and stores away. And to store away, he massacres.

9. Alain Finkielkraut, *L'humanité perdue* (Paris: Éditions du Seuil, 1996), 13–28.

> Ubu does not come out of Nietzsche. The dear old fellow has nothing of an overman. In democratic regimes, he proliferates. There are minuscule Ubus, and in the realm of the infinitely small, Ubu nebulae. This enormous beast does not in truth appear under a microscope, for it is teeming and armed with pincers more dreadful than those invented by Alfred Jarry. And if all he had were pincers! But Ubu has principles: he literally exudes the love of country.

"Saturday, March 22, 1958" shows Mauriac to be once again intent on dissipating any smug illusions that his compatriots may harbor about France's history and the nation's capacity for criminal action, as he further responds to the publication of Henri Alleg's *La Question*, in which the French Communist recounts the torture that he personally endured at the hands French forces in Algeria. Though horrified, Mauriac expresses his most powerful refusal to confine himself to literature in hopes of escaping what, borrowing from Goethe, he often termed history's "tangled mess of errors and violence." To better dramatize his distress at having continually to confront such horrors, Mauriac constructs a dialogue in which the temptation to turn away from history is voiced by a sophisticated cynic who reviews the sinister parade of crimes marking France's past and argues that Mauriac should resign himself to enlightened detachment as the most logical response to history's horrors.

Mauriac's text is clearly structured to make such indifference impossible. The enumeration of historical crimes accumulates into a sweeping flood of violence that leaves our imagination awash, and then the unbearable anecdote from Mme de Sévigné drowns any remaining claim to enlightened detachment in a sea of anguish. Determined to model the reader's response, Mauriac grapples with his own resistance to historical involvement while at the same time pointing out all the factors that make the position of a passive bystander untenable. The rapid-fire references to some of the darkest chapters of French history plunge the reader into the past, underscoring the suffering brought about by present French oppression in Algeria.[10]

10. Cf. Bracher, *Through the Past Darkly*, 101–3.

Saturday, March 22, 1958

I would very much like to turn away from France and the French and declare myself, like Lamartine, to be the "compatriot of every thinking soul."[11] I cannot: these people are my people, their history is my history. Shall I confess that I can no longer bear my position as a French citizen? I certainly do not believe that our Right is the dumbest in the world, as Monsieur Guy Mollet claims, nor that our police are the most ferocious. I do not believe that the average English subject in South Africa belongs to the elite of humanity any more that the average French citizen in Oran or Algiers. But the behavior of the latter engages my responsibility, while the behavior of the former does not.

Someone says to me: "You're mad, for history has always been a criminal affair. That hasn't stopped decent people as well as the others from going about their business and indulging in all the little satisfactions to which they were entitled or which their temperament required. On their deathbed, they never dreamed of saying their confession for the Saint Bartholomew's Day massacre, or the Palatine fire,[12] or the executions by guillotine, drowning, and firing squad, or for Red or White terror, and even less for the rather rough methods that every police force in the world has always used in dealing with the uncouth individuals who don't answer when interrogated. You're going to bore us to death with this stuff! In a letter to her daughter, Madame de Sévigné tells of soldiers in Brittany who put a small child on a skewer and roasted it for fun. She didn't stir up a riot in Europe for a trifle like that. You want to change the world, and it's a grand folly: the Marxists will get over that urge just as the Christians did. They are already starting to get over it."

What should I answer? These words are not lacking in force and it

11. The aristocrat Alphonse de Lamartine, 1790–1869, one of France's most renowned Romantic poets and a former monarchist who came to embrace democratic ideals, denounced militaristic nationalism in his poem dating from 1841, "La Marseillaise de la paix" ("The National Anthem of Peace"): "Je suis concitoyen de toute âme qui pense; la vérité, c'est mon pays" (I am the compatriot of every thinking soul; the truth is my country). See Alphonse de Lamartine, *Oeuvres complètes* (Paris: Gallimard, 1963), 1173–77.

12. Mauriac is referring to the systematic destruction of towns and villages in the Palatinate region of Germany that was carried out under Louis XIV by Turenne on two occasions, in 1674 and again in 1689. See http://www.herodote.net/Turenne_1611_1675_-synthese-441.php.

would not take much for me to give in. As I remain silent, the person presses the point: "It is not the world that has changed, it is you who are involving your conscience with what is the farthest from its domain: politics. If a political practice is bad, you are right to criticize and fight it, on the condition that it should not cost you one hour of sleep. Certainly it is necessary to save face and to use big words sometimes, and to refrain from needlessly offending, as we did in Sakhiet.[13] That is what is called international morality. One good hypocrite deserves another. There is no crime in politics, there are only foolish mistakes. Besides, why don't you just enjoy this fine evening of your life in peace?"

The one thing good about such talk is that it makes me sense how useless it is to try to make people sensitive to what is tormenting me. It is not madness to feel what I feel, but it is to demand that others feel the same way, just as it is madness to refuse to accept the fact that they can bear what has become unbearable for me. The fact remains that I accommodated myself to this situation during the greater part of my life. Yes, I am really taken aback and can find nothing to answer.

But still by myself, I look for this card that I received in the mail yesterday morning, and I reread for the tenth time these clumsy verses that someone sent to me anonymously.

> O somber people sitting at our door,
> Game prey for our prisons, hung from our crosses,
> This evening I hear crying your millions of voices.
> What good in the end is the love I have for you?
> Ismaël, heir of the deserts and the heavens,
> Son of dryness, face of sadness,
> You poor one whose only God
> Remained your only wealth!
> From this supreme love we have separated you
> And we have stolen from you even your prayer.
> You now only raise to heaven your clenched fist.

13. On February 8, 1958, French planes bombed the Tunisian village of Sakhiet near the Algerian border, in response to a series of cross-border attacks on French forces. The bombing claimed the lives of 78 people, including a number of children, and prompted a withering condemnation from Mauriac, who chastised such bombings in his "Bloc-notes" dating from Thursday, February 13, 1958. See Touzot in BN II, 29n2.

In "Saturday, July 2, 1966," Mauriac does turn momentarily away from the sound and fury of history to contemplate the deep, long-term evolutions he sees underway. No one was more attuned to the major changes which, underneath the more visible surface of political affairs, were rapidly transforming the networks of socioeconomic interaction and the fundamental texture and rhythms of daily life in the 1950s and '60s. For Mauriac, the disappearance of the agrarian society in the wake of urban development that was scarring the physical environment created an abrupt discontinuity and a sense of loss. It also constituted an acute crisis of personal, social, and human identity. Mauriac accordingly refers to these changes in terms of the most devastating of natural catastrophes: "There has been an earthquake, an enormous break between the past and the present, whereas there had been none between the past and everything that had come before."[14] Such words testify to his deep sense of estrangement from this brave new world.

Mauriac also points to another source of estrangement, stemming from the younger generation's indifference to the historical experience of their predecessors. Mauriac was born in 1885, some fifteen years after the humiliating defeat that amputated the Alsace-Lorraine region from French territory. He had witnessed as a medic the horrific human destructions wrought by World War I. It is therefore hardly surprising that he should deplore the younger generation's seemingly willful, insouciant ignorance of its elders' experience of history.[15] Passionately attached to the people and events of yesteryear, clearly haunted by his own mortality and by his increasing sense of the "vanity of vanities" resonating from Ecclesiastes, particularly now in his eighty-first year, Mauriac reaffirms his staunch support of de Gaulle, who in his eyes had finally introduced a strong degree of substance, coherence, and continuity into the governing of France.

14. BN II, 289.
15. Cf. Bracher, *Through the Past Darkly*, 158–59.

Saturday, July 2, 1966

I too am entitled to a month of silence. I am surprised that I long for it with such desire this year. It's that the writer who has been writing his editorials for fifty-six years (actually the same editorial: what I believe today is what that adolescent in his province or the student in Paris used to believe) feels slightly embarrassed and almost ashamed to still be speaking and writing when almost all of the great voices have grown silent and when there remain so few witnesses to a history and when today's generation is turning away from it. But that's somewhat of an exaggeration, for to turn away they would have had to focus their attention on it for an instant. The fact of the matter is that nothing that preceded their coming into the world has any existence for our grandchildren.

The coming of the atomic age and the conquest of space makes them feel their generation has unbounded possibilities. So they devalue our past, reducing it to the status of an interminable and pitiful Middle Age. And it is the case that in our childhood we were raised by men and women who had been the subjects of Napoleon III. I recall my uncle saying to me one evening at the variety show on my first trip to Paris: "The last time I came here was in 1869 and the emperor was there, between those two columns."

We older ones have not changed directions. The ridiculous red pants worn by the thousands of young men cut down in August 1914 were those of the soldiers of the Second Empire. There was continuity in everything. Barrès, our most revered and authoritative writer, remembered seeing the Prussians at Charmes. The fires of the Paris Commune shed a sinister light on all of French history for another of our most admired writers, Paul Bourget. We were integrated into an unbroken historical continuity.

It is true that everything started to change in the first few years of the twentieth century. But neither electricity, nor the cinema, nor the first cars, nor the first films upset life: they crept into it slowly, and at first did so without destroying anything in the old order. Such was particularly the case for the bourgeois country people that we were, rooted in a province where the peasantry had remained unchanged since before the Revolution: it had its strange mores, its witchcraft, and its regional dialect could not be understood ten kilometers down the road.

The stories that our schoolteacher would read to us in the afternoon when it got too hot were, for example, "The Last Class" by Alphonse Daudet, a story that made us cry over the loss of Alsace. This past held an obligation for us. Such was the case up until the Second World War and our last colonial downfall.

The defeat of 1870 and the annexation of the Lorraine and Alsace *départements* determined our destiny for the next forty-four years. Granted, the French of that time also thought that they had come out of the theological age. They already adored science, but they had scarcely changed since Helvétius and Condillac in the eighteenth century. They were of the same mindset as the Encyclopedists, just as we Catholics unknowingly belonged to Port-Royal. Nothing had changed for any of us for three centuries. Frequent communion was still a matter of discussion in my family. I remember very pious women who would only approach the holy table on major feast days.

There has been a seismic shift, an enormous break between the past and the present, whereas there had been none between the past and everything that had come before: Renan and Anatole France were continuing Voltaire's manner of writing well and laughing derisively. Enlightenment progress remained an unchallenged dogma even for these skeptics.

When we reread in 1966 the speech that Anatole France delivered for the inauguration of the statue of Ernest Renan at Tréguier in 1903, we feel the urge to break out in desperate laughter: "Do not ask what the city of the future will be (so speaks Pallas Athena), but know that I will build it.... Slowly but surely, humanity makes the dreams of the sages into reality." This hymn to unending progress rose up eleven years before the first slaughter, thirty years before Hitler.

One single injustice against a single Jew had just led the French Left, then all of Europe, to rise up in his defense. But millions and millions of Jews of every age and condition were going to be annihilated while the world kept silent: they were, if such is possible, more innocent than Dreyfus, who had at least been accused of a crime that he had not committed. Hitler's victims were not even falsely accused, only guilty of being themselves.

Throughout these years and all while worshipping the statue of Ernest Renan, the Third Republic created the conditions leading to the first massacre, a story of history that no longer interests anyone except me. If God leaves me enough time, I am going to republish all that I wrote from day to day in the daily newspapers and the weekly magazines now impossible to find. Shall I say that I have been a lucid witness? Well, yes, I will, because in rereading these texts, I cannot refuse this word of praise, and at my age I couldn't care less what others will think. All along the events of these years, I never ceased protesting, opposing, and saying "no." If today I say "yes," it is because for the first time during this long (brief) lifespan, a political mind is in action in a France that is sovereign and free. Today, I compare the reflections articulated by a mere writer during these sinister years in which decisions were criminal and democracies were all struck with the same paralysis, with the Gaullist mind that acts, shapes events, and creates the conditions necessary for a French political strategy: it's the proof that these huge catastrophes could have been avoided, and that no knowledge is more necessary than political wisdom, that there is no worse misfortune than for a nation to be given over to the apathetic, the incompetent, or the foolish, or what is worse yet, to be subject to institutions that make deserving, solid individuals such as there have always been in France into apathetic, incompetent, or foolish people.

Composed at the age of eighty-two, Mauriac's text for "Friday, February 2, 1968" proves him still capable of subjecting the past to uncompromising scrutiny, moreover on one of the most painfully difficult subjects. The antisemitism so deeply rooted in the past of his own family, church, and country had manifested itself with unprecedented violence in the 1930s and '40s. Emmanuel Berl's book on Nasser thus prompts Mauriac to recall the vicissitudes of the Dreyfus affair and its many sinister implications on the enduring legacy of antisemitism in French politics, culture, and society.

Mauriac's birth on October 11, 1885, had made him a childhood witness to the stormy controversy over Alfred Dreyfus that played itself out so dramatically from Dreyfus's arrest on false accusations of spying on October 15, 1894, to his rehabilitation on July 12, 1906.[16] Mauriac not only sees the Dreyfus affair as symptomatic of a long tradition of Catholic antisemitism from which he himself was not exempt as a child, but also identifies the it as a political watershed that brought to the surface the major forces that would play themselves out in subsequent moments of crisis in France, including not only Vichy's persecution of Jews and collaboration with the Germans during the Occupation, but also the crimes committed by France during the conflicts in Morocco and Algeria.

Friday, February 2, 1968

What I like the least in this little book by Emmanuel Berl that is so dense is the title, *Nasser as He Is Praised,* which limits its significance. After reading this work, we must do nothing less than to question ourselves as to what subsists of antisemitism within us, if we were ever antisemitic in our lifetime. And who has not been, consciously or unknowingly, slightly or intensely antisemitic? It is an ailment which is never completely cured and which we must combat until the end. I even do so myself. At about the age of eighteen, I had to lash out against what people had made me swallow throughout the Dreyfus affair: it coincided with my childhood. It has often occurred to me that on the glorious day of my first communion, May 12, 1896, Alfred Dreyfus was suffering in his hut on Devil's Island.

What had people made me swallow? I am one of the last survivors of that generation of Catholic children in France who took great pleasure in the anti-Jewish cartoons of "the good press." But that wasn't the worst. As we progressively learned to use our reason, the "good paper" kept giving us some very good reasons to hate the Jews. Who did not admire Edouard Drumont at the time?[17] Even today, who has thought of holding

16. See "Dreyfus réhabilité, chronologie": http://www.assemblee-nationale.fr/histoire/dreyfus/dreyfus-chrono.asp.

17. Édouard Drumont, 1844–1917, was the most prominent author of the virulent antisemitism circulating in France at the end of the nineteenth century. After his two-volume book *La France juive* (*Jewish France*) became a huge bestseller, he founded an equally antisemitic newspaper,

it against Bernanos to have chosen Drumont as his most admired writer? He himself did not feel the slightest embarrassment, as if *La France juive* was not one of the sources of the bloody river of historical hate.

The daily newspaper *L'Action française* did not yet exist, but Bordeaux's royalist paper *Le Nouvelliste* was certainly not edited by fools. I remember articles by Oscar Havard and by a local journalist, Jacques Curieux, whose style seemed to me similar to the wonderful style of another man of that time from Bordeaux, the political cartoonist Sem, who had not yet gone up to Paris and who was sketching his first pictures out on the Cours de l'Intendance in Bordeaux. As one might suspect, not all of these nice people were on Dreyfus's side. Nor was I, but I suddenly remember what I have already written a few years ago as a preface for the republication of *Five Years of My Life* by Alfred Dreyfus, "The Affair as Seen by a Child."

The truth is that even before the outbreak of the Dreyfus affair, the Jew existed for us as a being apart from others. I don't remember if they told us anything specifically bad: there was no need to. The Gospel consisted of the Passion narrative for us: "May his blood be on us and on our children!"[18] It did indeed fall on us and it never ceased to fall. To this curse we added our own that corresponded to our little power as children as we walked through the Jewish market on the sidewalk of the Cours Victor Hugo in Bordeaux: making a pig's ear out the corner of our ponchos, we yelled "Pig's ear!" and ran away under the curses of poor old Mardochée. When I say "we," I am perhaps boasting and doubt that I ever did it myself.

It is certain that Jews in general are denounced particularly in the Gospel according to John: it's "for fear of the Jews" that the Lord hides. He himself was a Jew, his mother was a Jew, as was all of the first Church in Jerusalem along with the first martyr, Stephen, whose face was like that of an angel: how strange that this reality never at all disturbed the grown-ups that brought us up with their smug prejudices.

La Libre Parole, in 1892. See http://www.larousse.fr/encyclopedie/personnage/%C3%89douard_Drumont/117148.

18. Matthew 27.24–25 attributes these words to those responding to Pontius Pilate, who had declared: "I am innocent of this man's blood."

Poor Dreyfus thus found in us ground that had for a long time been made ready for the horrible story that would take root in it and grow a huge tree—a huge tree that could not be uprooted. Even today after every forgery has been discovered, the true culprit has confessed, Schwartzkoppen's diary has revealed the underpinnings, and the innocent man has been rehabilitated before the world, there are still some people protesting that we don't know everything. And it is true that we do not know everything, but we do know that Dreyfus was innocent.

How were my eyes opened? I fear that I might be arranging the story ex post facto. It seems to me that at the age of eighteen and under the influence of the Sillon,[19] I established a cause-and-effect connection between the grave misfortunes of the Catholic Church in France at that time and the sin against justice that, out of ignorance and due to being misinformed, it had committed in poisoning the conscience of children. From then on, in every instance whether in secret or in public, I never ceased to fight antisemitism without, in others, but also within, for my first inclination was not always free of it. And this time, I must admit that it seemed grounded in reason.

What happened in France with certain French people right after the Six-Day War is that what was in their own eyes an ill will that was repressed and kept in check but never completely overcome now found its justification. The outraged letters from Jewish friends and the insults directed at de Gaulle put our noses in something obvious which certainly does not in any way excuse antisemitism, but which gives one of its admitted keys. When we were children, we kept on repeating one of Bornier's verses: "Every man has two countries: his own and then France!" Every Jew has two countries: first of all, his own. That is what we were tempted to grant to the adversary and we had in part always believed: and the proof was this *numerus clausus* law that no longer exists,[20] but which continues to have an effect on many people: "Did you see in *Le Figaro* this morning," an alarmed friend said to me the other day, "there are 500,000 Jews in France. They doubled in number

19. A movement led by Marc Sangnier, who sought to reinfuse the themes of simplicity and social justice into French Catholicism at the beginning of the twentieth century.

20. A law setting a quota capping the number of Jews.

since the war. They are already invading everything ..." I made fun of him, but something within me was responding to his fear, something that I had nevertheless thought to have completely extirpated at the age of eighteen.

We knew and we have always known that the people of Bergson, Kafka, and Einstein were intellectually dominating, and we didn't wait until we had observed the miracle of Israel to know that they were also capable of having all the virtues that Christendom denied them throughout the centuries. We knew it already in 1914. I applaud Emmanuel Berl for reminding us of this fact without raising his voice: "I was a soldier in 1914 in the 356th Infantry Regiment. I was buried twice, I was cited to the order of the division, my uncle René Franck commanded a battalion of soldiers from August 1914 until the armistice, my first cousin Henri Lange was killed, and my cousin Raymond Berl was covered with numerous wounds and medals."

But that's the point of what I was saying: what is strange is that this wall should persist in separating us from this ingenious people who, for us Christians, have been elected for all eternity and are also a valiant people. That is a mystery that this little book *Nasser as He Is Praised* obliges us to look squarely in the face. Not that Berl is himself free of partisan views. He is not very fond of de Gaulle and loves the United States of America. And who can reproach him for it? But he is quite capable of giving a little nudge to history in order to make it go the way he wants: "I am not American, I am a Frenchman, but one that the Americans saved in 1917, liberated in 1945, and fed after 1945."

That's what you call a selective shorthand, where what has been left out is 1914, 1939, and 1940, the only times when the Americans would have been able to save Emmanuel Berl, but when it was out of the question, despite the calls for help. As for what weighed on the fate of Emmanuel Berl and that of France in 1917 and in 1941, Berl will grant me that American sentiment for France had nothing to do with it. Only "fed after 1945" remains true. I feel indebted to the United States for the Marshall Plan, not for the fact that the German torpedoes in 1917 and the attack on Pearl Harbor in 1941 forced them to enter into the war.

To return to the main point of this discussion, we know very well why the hatred that Israel inspires in Ismael is irreconcilable: Ismael knows that unless one of the two atomic empires gets mixed up in it, it will constantly get beat in six days by this little people of technicians, first in the class in all the lycées of the world.

American Symphonies: Uncle Sam or Big Brother?

Mauriac liked to quip that from a trip around the world, he wouldn't be able to bring back ten lines. Like most other French intellectuals, however, he never let his lack of empirical expertise keep him from penning the pithiest of opinions on subjects of interest and controversy, and to such unfailing audacity we owe a remarkable series of pronouncements on American culture and politics.[21] While Mauriac did often borrow certain themes already in circulation, his views cannot simply be dismissed as so much anti-American rhetoric. On the contrary, his commentaries provide a not-so-distant mirror of the specific historical circumstances and perspectives marking the time of their composition, while at the same time reflecting the two paradoxically inseparable cultures and nations (France and the United States) that inspired them. While often echoing the rather conventional French wisdom on America, he displayed an uncommon capacity to transcend the clichés, stereotypes, and ideological prejudices that were widely circulating in his time.

Mauriac's opinions on the subject, like those of his compatriots past and present, were highly charged: concerning the United States or things American, we find him awash in admiration, trembling with indignation, sputtering in exasperation, or smirking and "harrumphing" in smug condescension, but never indifferent. The metaphor of a "love-hate relationship" proves in this case quite apt.[22]

21. Philippe Roger has shown that French intellectuals were already dispensing with factual knowledge when delivering their definitive judgments on the United States in the years subsequent to World War I. See his book *L'ennemi américain: Généalogie de l'antiaméricanisme français* (Paris: Éditions du Seuil, 2002), 357.

22. Cf. Bracher, "A Not So Distant Mirror: Mauriac's Image of America," *Contemporary French Civilization* 30, no. 2 (Summer/Fall 2006): 17–43.

The Great War constituted an ordeal for Mauriac as for all of France. Studying Mauriac's personal correspondence, John Flower demonstrates that Mauriac was clearly shaken by the bloodshed that was to claim the lives of some 1.4 million French soldiers, including a number of personal acquaintances and close friends, such as the oft-mentioned André Lafon.[23] Though Mauriac indeed shuddered at the horrors of trench warfare, he nevertheless persisted in seeing the violence and destruction as part of a divine plan that had to be accepted.

He refused the prospect of a world governed by purely human values and, affirming that "the kingdom of God is within,"[24] he presented the war as an opportunity for a deepening or renewal of Catholicism. In accordance with the largely prevailing religious outlook of the time, Mauriac stressed the importance of sacrifice and suffering as means of expiation. He thus declared that Christians can accept the horrors of war because they believe in eternal life. The contrast with Mauriac's later views is nothing less than dramatic. In the wake of the Spanish Civil War, Auschwitz, and the atrocities of the colonial wars, Mauriac would vehemently refute the notion that events meted out divine justice. Such is notably the case in his "Bloc-notes" of "Monday, November 28, 1960," in which he declares, "I can no longer bear to hear some theologian give me his reasons on the subject."[25]

"The Americans in My Town," inspired by Mauriac's impressions of the throngs of American soldiers streaming into the port city of Bordeaux, his hometown, however, thankfully spares contemporary readers from such dreary, heavy-handed theology. We instead find a lively, colorful article that displays Mauriac's talent for deftly mixing personal memories and social observations with lyrical tableaus inspired by the painting of Claude Gellée ("le Lorrain") and Baudelaire's prose poems. Certain nationalist, even xenophobic views remain present in the young Mauriac's itinerant panorama of his venerable hometown invaded by Yankees and other decidedly nonwhite, non-Catholic groups visible on the quays of this port city now bustling with the newly augmented commerce of the war. He nevertheless sketches an admiring portrait of these easygoing, gre-

23. Flower, *François Mauriac, journaliste*, 44.

24. Ibid.

25. BN II, 508.

garious American boys who nonchalantly play baseball in the street and who, although prevented from visiting prostitutes by their military police, nevertheless ravish young French women as war brides. Indeed, Mauriac is clearly a bit disconcerted by the fact that these young women leave everything to follow their husbands to what, in the eyes of proper French families of the era, seemed the other end of the world. Yet the literary-minded young dandy who pens these often rather condescending lines quotes Pascal to encourage his readers, and no doubt himself, to empathize with these doughboys who, just like French soldiers, all have loved ones anxiously awaiting their safe return.

The Americans in My Town

La Revue hebdomadaire, September 28, 1918

In my town populated with Americans, the houses from the time of Louis XVI have not turned into skyscrapers, and ancient balconies are still suspending their exquisite swirls over the streets. But a World's Fair crowd clogs the sidewalks and Théophile Gautier would no longer, as he did while on his way to the Pyrenees, make fun of our thoroughfares, so excessively wide for the number of inhabitants in our city. Here, unlike Paris, the old quarters do not disappear, gutted in a few months by things like the Boulevard Raspail. Every façade is a familiar friend to me. Above the shores of the river filled with masts and sails, the upper floors of the Customs building stand out against the horizon like the architecture painted by Claude Gellée in his wondrous ports. Behind the high, golden gates, on the terrace of the public park, other children are enjoying the same games and chanting the same jingles that we used to use to see who would have to "be it." But there is no longer anyone to greet with a smile and the tip of the hat. None of the young women that I glimpse remind me of the little girl whose feet I trampled during my dancing lessons when I was seventeen. In the past, there was not a single young lady who, on an invisible tag, did not display the amount of her dowry and the value of her alliances: I knew her exact position in an infinitely hierarchical city. The street that you lived on, the sort of wine that you sold, and other more subtle elements determined your socioeconomic position between the ship owner and the trader, the wine merchant and the cod merchant. Where is the time when prominent businessmen used to humiliate civil servants with their insults? A huge wave of Americans and refugees has covered over this little world of yesteryear. In mourning, and often impoverished, old families rent out their country home and live off of potatoes and domestic rabbits while waiting for the war to end.

Camps full of Americans surround the city, and every evening trucks bring in their load of joyous, childlike giants jammed in so tight that they do not sway on curves. At the central town square, in front of the YMCA building, they get off. Young faces peer out of lighted windows. A band blares out music. Parisians might believe that they are staying in a holiday resort at the time when the seas washing up on France's shores during the warm season were strewn with gypsies, and when the waves of ancient ocean came to expire on the casinos' terraces. Coming from all around, women swoop down on this town where so many young men are gathered. Those who were properly educated and who speak English have reason to give thanks for the gift of tongues that was bestowed upon them. The American sailors, with their white caps and bell-bottomed pants, are similar to characters from Italian comedy and to those in Watteau's *Pilgrimage to the Isle of Cythera*. They drag all of these open hearts along after them and with their hands shoo them off like flies. These women stack up on street corners. These big boys with childlike faces must be protected against themselves. Policemen guard the entrance to certain quarters, armed with short sticks that are certainly less peaceful than those of our city police: held on the wrist by a leather strap, these billy clubs are an argument to which the wild Indians who receive it on the back of the neck will never find any response. Only Annamites, Moroccans, Chinese, and all the multicolored manual laborers on the docks freely invade the strange streets where creatures dressed in saffron, pink, and indigo show their faces painted like idols over their funny bodies of unbreakable dolls. But their sweet commerce is fortunately forbidden for our handsome allies, who console themselves by playing ball right out on the sidewalk. They throw it back and forth to each other in their gloved hands, with such vigor that any passersby struck by it would be sure to see stars. But these soldiers, who often have the movements and gestures of pelota players, are skilled and confident, and so are we, who walk around calmly amid their barrage of balls.

Oh my town, my overblown and slightly gloomy town, beyond your fever of today, I once again see you as did the adolescent who loved you while thinking he hated you. Out on the terrace of the Café de B., we pointed out the opera tenor Escalais from Toulouse, who was idolized by the gallery and who would belt out his renowned music that evening. The prominent socialites seated in the front rows were intent on giving him a cool reception and applauded with their fingertips, in this theater that the architect Louis built for a small audience: admirable columns separate basket-like balconies designed to hold no more than three or four hooped dresses. Does Madame Régina Badet remember that when she was still unknown, she danced the *Zingara* on the stage in my hometown? Why did she not ask the schoolboy that I was about her horoscope? At that time, a certain artist by the pen name of Sem took pleasure in tracing out silhouettes on one of our city streets. He has since made his way in the profession. To take a break from Le Trouvère and Le Pré aux clercs, the dilettantes sought out concerts in the circle of serious philharmonic music: Madame Georgette Le Blanc performed there one evening in bare feet. A silver-scaled belt held her Greek tunic under her arms: to no avail and with a timid, but quite skillful voice, she sang Schubert's "The Young Nun," but my fellow citizens of Bordeaux were shocked and judged these bare feet to be unacceptable.

I wanted to survey these places where we used to go on our gloomy Sunday walks along the muddy river toward the hills of L. There is nothing left of this sad countryside. Endless docks lined with American locomotives have covered it over. As far as the eye can see, there are giant cranes stretching out their arms over the heavy waters. Trucks keep kicking up a thick cloud through which one can see black, but handsome demons on top of mountains of anthracite laughing and biting into green fruit.

My town, you used to lie still in the river bend. Nonchalantly you waited for vessels to come to you through a difficult channel. You only accepted to offer them your best wines, your Graves that leave a taste of flowers in the mouth, and your Sauternes, a liqueur of the sun where the heat incubates torrid summers. You were turned into an industrial city against your will. But young men came from the West. They awakened you, a sleeping princess. You no longer let vessels come to you: you go out to greet the vessels. You passionately lay down your docks toward the estuary. You stretch out your arms to the ocean.

I came back in a gondola. I saw the town draw closer to me as I remembered how I used to return, when, after Sunday evening and the nocturnal rest, the following day would appear to me: clear, dry, full of traps and ordeals such as recitations and the reading of notes. A nameless melancholy would crystallize around these tiny torments. Here we see the wharf in the very heart of the town: delicate balustrades border an immense square, and two rostral columns form the two pillars of an invisible arch. The smoky sea of roofs carries its vessels of churches. The port is veiled in the pink vapors that Baudelaire speaks of in "Le Balcon," this poem that according to Claudel was composed here.

I disembark. I recognize every stone but not one face. An American steps aside to let a young woman pass by. Another fetches a little boy's ball. They have the desire to please us. They do indeed please us, these handsome foreigners for whom everything is simple, even getting married. One of them sees a girl at a skating rink, decides to marry her, and marries her two weeks later. She has no knowledge of English; he does not speak a word of French. Worried that she would no longer find a husband at the age of twenty-five, she accepts this mysterious destiny. The tender gaze of this young unknown giant reassures her. Where is he going to carry this little French woman off to? He came with his friends to his fiancée's house for dinner. Before the meal, the guests locked themselves up in the bathroom for endless ablutions. They were still singing and dancing at three o'clock in the morning.

Sunday evening, the trucks brought thousands of soldiers in khaki back to their camps. A huge crowd, a crowd of people in love washes up like waves on the long line of vehicles loaded with men. One by one, the trucks start up and head out amid the laughter, the shouts, and the farewells. Hands come apart. They have to tear away from each other. The singing cargo of men goes away toward the sad, sandy moors where, beneath a tent, more than one will gauge the frightful distance separating him from his loved ones. We say "the Americans" without it occurring to us that each of them has a mother, friends, a fiancée. The individual no longer exists. There only remain grains of wheat from a huge crop, the grapes from a unique harvest. Through the Dardanelles straits, in Salonica, Vladivostok, France, and Morocco, human cargoes in which all races are mixed together are being transported. "The culture of the self" and "the autonomy of the human person" are pretty words that I remember as I look at the endless procession of these trucks. The young men packed in them have but a collective existence there, carried thousands of leagues away from their dwellings, like dust in the night. And granted, we know that all of these individual destinies are being sacrificed to a cause that is well worth this immeasurable price. All the same, these faces pressed together and these eyes that I cannot distinguish from each other reflected the widest variety of landscapes, from the savanna of Florida, whose name means flowered Easter; Louisiana, the god-child of the kings of France; Indiana. Some loved one is waiting for them in a bedroom, at the end of this street in Astoria, Richmond, Raleigh, or Harrisburg, which are as familiar to them as are the street and the home where I am peacefully writing these lines. They are passing through, and how not to sigh with Pascal, "How many are the kingdoms that are unaware of us?"[26] The eternal silence of space that frightened the author of the *Pensées*, seems to me this evening less formidable than the silence of these thousands of inaccessible hearts.[27]

Why look so far away? Join in the crowd's acclamation of those who have come to support the living, replace the dead, and who will at least share with them the community of the grave. Listen: for the

26. Pascal, *Pensées* (42 Lafuma, 207 Brunschvicg).

27. Mauriac is alluding to one of Pascal's most famous *Pensées* (Lafuma 201, Brunschvicg 206): "Le silence éternel de ces espaces infinis m'effraie" (The eternal silence of this infinite space frightens me).

first time in four years, the clamors of celebration are filling the town. One truck is still there, full of laughter and singing. The band plays "La Marseillaise" and all these men suddenly stand still in silent respect. Their arms raised in military salute accomplish a religious gesture. Even those who are not departing and who are chatting in groups on the square throw down their cigarette and remain standing until the end of the anthem. How near these foreigners are to our hearts in this minute! One same hope, one same will, one same faith: there is now only one soul where, earlier, we were frightened of so many different races.

The crowd is breaking up and I hear a few reflections: "Just imagine, my dear! He was sitting across from me on the train. When I had finished reading my paper, he took it without saying a thing to me, and offered me two cents!" And someone else: "These Americans, people say that they throw off their coats to have freer movement when they charge."

A bit of daylight still remains. We must go see it die out over the river. An American ship is moored there. At the sound of a banjo, the thin sailors dressed in white are dancing and holding each other's waists, boyish and grave like Watteau's clowns. Several of them are stretched out on the back of the vessel and without saying a thing, look low in the sky where the sun hurried its way to the new world.

Life magazine's publication of a political cartoon depicting Marianne (the French equivalent of "Uncle Sam") tucking a wad of greenbacks into her stocking prompted a sharp reaction from Mauriac, whom we can almost feel shaking with indignation in "The Dollar Bills Stuffed into Marianne's Stocking." For all his willingness to expose the injustice and violations of human rights in France and its colonies, henevertheless remained fervently attached to his native land, especially since he had lived through the ordeals of the two world wars that had taken such a heavy toll on the French. Clearly, the derogatory image of France as a woman exercising the "oldest profession in the world" was hardly apt to suggest any American understanding of this traumatic history or of France's acute sense of honor and national dignity.

To gauge the intensity of Mauriac's anger, we should recall that the expression "delivered up" directly alludes to the passion of Christ handed over to Roman soldiers for mockery, scorn, and abuse.[28] For Mauriac and his compatriots, the notion of their country as a prostitute servicing financial interests is hardly a laughing matter, and Mauriac's rebuttal indicates that such vulgarity not only constitutes an affront to the French but also dishonors Americans who think in such terms. The well-known dictum sums it up nicely: noblesse oblige, and in this case *Life* magazine failed to exemplify its own honor even more than it failed to respect the honor of France.

Cultural stereotypes and insults of course reveal more about those formulating them than they do about their intended objects. Subjected to Mauriac's fierce rhetoric, the image of France as a call girl that *Life* magazine so flippantly tossed out to its readers thus becomes a boomerang that returns to embarrass the culture that produced it. Rather than exposing supposedly loose French morals, the image of the woman with the dollars instead underscores the vulgar materialism propelling the culture and politics of a people who assume that money is everything and that anything can be acquired if one pays the price. *Life*'s depiction of France as a submissive sex worker grateful for dollars tendered by a smug, cavalier American client moreover prompts Mauriac to offer a little history lesson to a people so oblivious both to the role of the past having shaped the present and to their own implication in it. He proceeds to point out to *Life*'s readers not only how much more than America France had suffered from World War I, but also how much the United States had compounded that suffering with its economic and military irresponsibility in the early twentieth century, and even with its reckless bombing of French towns and villages in World War II.

Such sharp criticism of the United States stems from a keen sense of national identity and from pride in France's heritage, as Mauriac's emphasis on his nation's rich past implicitly points to the shallowness of those either too ignorant or too indifferent to acknowledge its legacy. Should one wonder why Mauriac so often—but not always, as we shall soon see

28. In the original French, the text reads "livrée . . . aux outrages."

in his call to welcome Eisenhower to Paris—rejects the notion of France being beholden to the United States (as did most French intellectuals of the post–World War II period),[29] one reason in particular stands out: such indebtedness constitutes an insufferable affront to national pride.[30]

The Dollars Stuffed into Marianne's Stocking

Le Figaro, January 27, 1953

The French gladly make fun of themselves: they never stop talking about bad behavior in the political arena. But we do not easily suffer low-minded insults. This week, the magazine *Life* delivered to its readers and their scurrilous affronts the image of a Marianne stuffing dollar bills into her stocking. We look upon her as well, but she is not the source of our shame nor does she cause us to blush. We are in solidarity with the United States: they are taking on the defense of the West and of the spiritual values whose fate is at stake. That confers upon them a dignity that demands nobility. A people that holds the power to annihilate all life over huge areas should not be vulgar in its laughter.

If you measure the greatness of a nation by its material prosperity and the value of human beings by their bank accounts, my dear American friends, we will recall a few facts for you. It is not our bad political behavior that caused our financial ruin, since before 1914 we had been the bankers for Europe and the world, and the United States as well. We emerged exhausted from the first slaughter, in which about thirty French people died for every American death. Thanks to this sacrifice and thanks also to the initiative of President Wilson, the world was never closer than it was in 1918 to seeing the birth of a durable peace among nations. It is a fact that America's decision to torpedo the League of Nations is at the base of all the suffering of humanity today. If the United States had remained present in Geneva in this palace where they had been the founders, neither Mussolini nor Hitler would

29. Roger, *L'ennemi américain*, 430.
30. Cf. Bracher, "A Not So Distant Mirror," 27–30.

have become the masters of destiny. The internal history of the United States during those years provided a fine example of your political behavior to the rest of the world. "It is my friends who are tormenting me!" sighed President Harding. We will not here recall the story of the friends of President Harding.

We will recall another memory for the readers of *Life*: when France was precipitated into the Second World War, it had not yet completely pulled itself out of the ruins of the first, and was having to provide for the needs of a host of invalids, orphans, and widows. Twenty years had barely gone by. Among the thousands of new victims who were added to those already there (the readers of *Life* are entitled to forget this because we are too discreet to ever remind you of the fact), there were all the men, all the women, all the children of the towns and villages pulverized by American planes and who, according to many technicians, could have been saved.[31] We weren't technicians. We could very well differentiate between the methods followed by the Royal Air Force and those of our friends from America.[32] The least one could say is that we didn't put all our liberators in the same basket. But let's not belabor the point.

For the second time, our ruins were cleared up, our factories re-equipped, and our economy restarted. The readers of *Life* will admit that in spite of ephemeral teams of government ministers, there subsists here in France a permanent set of government offices that takes care of essential tasks. Only our army is still like a phantom entity, but that is because our officers and our men are being quietly killed from day to day in Indochina. I imagine that *Life* judges "this dirty war" harshly. But after all, the Pentagon sees it differently: it is not for France alone that French and Vietnamese are falling every day, and it is not just for France that the French and the Vietnamese, who like each other, are hurting each other so much. Meanwhile the German

31. Mauriac is citing a well-documented fact rarely mentioned by the American press and media: over the course of World War II, some 60,000 French civilians were killed by Allied bombings. In the summer of 1944, 14,000 died in Normandy alone following the D-Day landing.

32. The French have often criticized the American bomber squadrons for flying at higher altitudes than the British, which greatly reduced the accuracy of bombing and therefore produced significantly higher "collateral damage," including civilian casualties.

army is going to be revived under the knowing eye of our American friends: this German army will not, as is the case for our own, suffer an exhausting loss of blood and it will take advantage of Germany's excellent political mores.

Such is the historical reality of the Marianne who, with a vile gesture and to the delight of *Life*'s readers, stuffs a billion dollar bill from her client into her stocking. For this is indeed about France, this France that for us has the face of Jeanne d'Arc, or Charlotte Corday,[33] or the little Thérèse of Lisieux,[34] but for them is a bordello girl. That is what is hidden behind "this bedroom farce" which sums up French politics for the editor of *Life* and for the twenty million Americans who read the magazine. This may be a felicitous insult after all if it startles our nation, including both its leaders and those they lead, members of parliament and electors, into carrying out a rigorous self-examination. Just as the National Assembly is going to take up the subject of the proposal for a European army, may this billion dollar bill not be taken into account in a choice that will involve our national destiny?

In "Saturday, August 29, 1959," Eisenhower's impending visit to the French capital inspires Mauriac to pen one of his most eloquent and nuanced assessments of American culture and politics. Admonishing his compatriots to throng to the streets for a fervent welcome to the leader of the Free World who was also the military architect of the Liberation of France and victory over Nazi Germany, Mauriac nevertheless explains why he finds American culture so alien and Washington's interventionist foreign policy so unsettling. His candid commentary is in fact highly symptomatic of France's uncomfortable position as one of America's allies in the late 1950s, and equally emblematic of the mixture of fascination and apprehension with which the French were greeting the massive influx of American culture into everyday French life.

33. Outraged by the Reign of Terror, Charlotte Corday stabbed to death one of its most outspoken proponents, the journalist Marat, when he was in his bath. See http://www.larousse.fr/encyclopedie/personnage/Corday_dArmont/114643.

34. Saint Thérèse of Lisieux, 1873–1897, is known for having transformed the provincial Norman town of Lisieux into a site of pilgrimage.

To fully appreciate Mauriac's ambivalence toward the United States and things American, we must situate it within the larger context of cultural history that he so vividly chronicled in his "Bloc-notes" of the 1950s and 1960s. On the one hand, thanks in no small measure to the Marshall Plan that provided the backdrop for the 1948 cartoon in *Life* magazine, France managed to emerge from the tremendous material devastation of World War II and return to prosperity even while having to face the trauma of colonial war in Vietnam and Algeria. On the other hand, the postwar years brought radical transformations that eroded France's cultural self-assurance and blurred its sense of identity: within two decades the largely agrarian, rural, Catholic nation that had prevailed up until the 1940s changed into a highly urbanized consumer society no longer even hostile but simply indifferent to religion. The preeminence of an elitist culture of arts and letters was yielding to the youthful appetite for popular culture imported from or inspired by American film and music. For writers and intellectuals steeped in literature and history as was Mauriac, these trends seemed to threaten the contemplative life they held most dear. Like many other French writers, Mauriac recoiled in horror from the standardization so antithetical to their desire for unique, distinctive individuality.[35]

Saturday, August 29, 1959

May God grant that on September 2, on the sidewalks of Paris, there should be as many Parisians to acclaim the president of the United States as there were Londoners on the sidewalks of London. In spite of certain indications, I hope and believe that it will be so. Our people's instinct is by nature attuned to politics. Once again, they will understand that the wisest and true political course consists of giving in to reasons of the heart.

On September 2, the wounded pride and bitterness that we feel as a nation that had been the greatest (which had even been the only great nation, since "la grande nation" for a long time designated France) must all give way to the esteem and respect due the president of the

35. Cf. Roger, *L'ennemi américain*, 493–94, 506, 520. My commentary on the article has been adapted from Bracher, "A Not So Distant Mirror," 31, 33.

United States of America, and above all, to the admiration and the gratitude that General Eisenhower, the premier artisan of our deliverance, inspires in the French people.

I am thus preaching to others, but what are my true sentiments on the subject? What do I really feel? The reason why I am publicly asking myself this question at this time is that I am certain of the answer. I am sure that if I were among the crowd on the Champs-Elysées, I would not be the least fervent of those who will acclaim our illustrious guest. That constitutes a contradiction that I would like to clarify.

For indeed my affection goes out to this leader of a great people that I do admire. In many aspects of its cultural character, however, the American people is more foreign to me than any other. I have never visited the United States. What good would it do? They have done much more than visit us: they have transformed us. The pace of our daily life has been synchronized with theirs. Through millions of records, their music orchestrates our days. Thousands of their films screened in Paris and in the provinces impose on us their ideas on every subject: a certain type of stereotypical woman, the interchangeable star that any Brigitte or Pascale from les Batignolles can become,[36] but above all, the worship and idolatry of technology, of all the technologies invented by humans and to which humans are enslaved, the craze for speed, this dizziness that affects all the sheep in the West, and an agitation that none of us can escape. Such excess in all things is what is most alien to our own cultural character.

"We will understand nothing about modern civilization," wrote Georges Bernanos in 1945, "if we do not first admit that it is a worldwide conspiracy against every sort of inner life." Yes, against everything that has become precious for French people like me: a contemplative life in an old house where before us lived those from whom we have descended and whom we loved, and from which we wish to distance ourselves as little as possible, for it is there and nowhere else that they are in communion with the earth and where the wind in the branches speaks to them with a human voice. I hate everything that

36. Les Batignolles was a working-class neighborhood in Paris.

interrupts reflection, all that violates silence, except for the music that does not disturb silence because it is born from silence and is nourished by silence (the opposite of what proceeds from jazz).

Of course, Americans are not all of the same type. Many react as I do to today's world, its noise and its stupid fidgeting. There is doubtless no lack of contemplative souls among them (Julien Green is American). And all of their literature should be studied from this perspective. The development of Catholicism in the United States nevertheless does not seem to be leading to the inner life. But then again, what do I know? I had the honor, one day, of dining at the same table as Cardinal Spellman. He was so nice, but my entire being tended to recoil: I would have probably felt closer to the Dalai Lama.

I concede that the world would have scarcely experienced any progress if it had only been populated with mindsets of people like me. They go forward facing backward, their eyes fixed on the past that enchants and enchains them, prisoners of their childhood, from which they have never freed themselves: they remain above all prisoners of themselves and their own enigma. I admire and I like the president of the United States even though nothing within me is attuned to the civilization that he represents: I struggle against it, even as it invades my own life and even though I depend a bit more each day on its technology. That is the contradiction which astonishes me and that I would like to unravel.

For I will not have to force myself to acclaim the American president. What attaches me to him is difficult to define. It is easy to criticize the politics of the United States. The behavior of their political leaders has not always enjoyed good press in the world. And yet, as realistic as their politics may be, they are imbued with a certain moral element, a preoccupation of a spiritual order. The will to power of this nation that dominates the West is no smaller than that of its giant of an adversary or than that of the old nations of Europe. But this will to power is filled with an anxious concern and a sense of responsibility for the weaker and the have-nots, and at the same time a great patience, a manner of closing its eyes, of letting itself be relieved of its dollars. Now I will not claim that this is a nation of innocent lambs.

Here I am thinking less of the atomic bomb than of the methods that allowed them to obtain it and from which we ourselves have suffered. I quote once more from Bernanos: "The machinery is charged with burning, crushing, and leveling. After that, the troops go through." That is all true. The Puritanism permeating American politics from their beginnings nevertheless remains visible and effective. One has the impression that the leaders of this nation are at each instant aware that they will be held accountable for their deeds. They doubtless believe that question which will be asked of each of us, "What have you done with your brother?"—and we will be judged on that score—will also be put to the dominating nations who from one age to the next have imposed their will on the world.

Compared with the other world power that only cares about efficacy, American scruples carry both a weakness and an advantage: to my mind, the weakness is obvious, while the advantage is real. We have seen with our own eyes that those who believed only in force ended up yielding to force. The sign of the true power of the United States is not being in a frenzy but having scruples. Their obsession with gigantic size and dancing mania would create doubts about the health of this nation if they did not have this spiritual heritage, this sense of responsibility that they have inherited from their forebears.

In France, we are too inclined to judge the United States on their Hollywood magnates. I myself have indulged in that simplification here. General Eisenhower embodies another America much closer to us than we imagine in Europe, since, after all, Americans come from here and they remain tied to us by their faith in humanity and in what surpasses humankind.

When on March 7, 1966, de Gaulle sent French Foreign Minister Couve de Murville to the American embassy to announce the withdrawal of French military forces from the central NATO military command, Mauriac saw his hopes for a return to French grandeur fulfilled and was nothing short of jubilant. What follows in his article "Monday, March 7, 1966" is a textbook exposition of his sense of national honor as conferred by a long history and noble character that demand recognition of France's rightfully preeminent role in international affairs, now overshadowed by a nation of upstarts. Insisting that his fervent support for de Gaulle has nothing to do with nostalgia for the French grandeur of yesteryear, Mauriac simply cannot contain his euphoria, and his savory remarks suggest precisely the opposite. Nowhere does Mauriac more openly express his contempt for the United States as a superpower having gained its status from recently acquired untempered military and economic force. At the same time, his resentment of American influence and low opinion of American society and culture are clearly indissociable from his own sense of national identity. Or to put it more bluntly, his anti-Americanism is simply the flip side of a chauvinism exacerbated by the underlying insecurity that comes out so clearly elsewhere in the same piece, when Mauriac reminds his readers that France was known as "*the* great nation."

This article thus expresses the frustration that Mauriac shares with his compatriots at seeing France's rightful place of honor, prestige, and influence on the international scene usurped by a nation of *nouveaux riches* that seemingly exemplifies the opposite of all that the French pride themselves in: a rich legacy of history and tradition, distinguished accomplishments in the arts and literature, a keen sense of measure and moderation, and a preference for the qualitative over the quantitative.[37]

Monday, March 7, 1966

The title of today's entry, if I gave it one, could be "The Miracle." What a miracle, when we think of what the French people are today, having come out of two parliamentary republics (I am only counting the Third and Fourth Republics, under which a person of my age has lived). Yes, what a miracle that these French people who were confronted with so many catastrophes due to a political strategy inspired by London, and who, thirty years ago passively watched Germany give birth to Hitler without attempting to thwart it in any way that might have offended its major and minor allies, what a wonder that these same French of today—for they are the same people—accept the idea of annoying all

37. Cf. Bracher, "A Not So Distant Mirror," 25–27.

the leaders of the West, but without any bravado, nor out of rancor or pride, nor by anything temperamental.

That is because we have come upon good fortune: by grace, it has been granted us to see the remedy emerge from the very ills stemming from our atrocious institutions. In order for the French to consent without flinching to see one single man irk the United States of America and all its clientele within and without—in other words, all of Western Europe and a virtually unanimous French press—they had had to undergo the atrocious experiment that was conducted on the body and soul of their nation from 1945 until 1958.[38]

Thank God, our nation cannot yet reflect on these years without shuddering. That is de Gaulle's strength, but for how long? The other day I asked the students who had come from the Institut des Études Politiques to interview me how old they were: they were born in 1944.[39] They had no experience of Hitler, and even the war in Algeria and the Organisation de l'Armée Secrète correspond to their childhood. How quickly one wave covers another! De Gaulle is the only one to stay above them, but the water is already reaching his shoulders.

That is the tragic (as in tragic theater) aspect of the personalization of power, of the embodiment of a people in one man: as great as he may be, this mortal being is only ephemeral. He knows that the nation, with which he is mingled as long as he is there, will outlive him, not as does a body after the soul has escaped, not as a corpse, but as something different from what it was before, and forever marked by the one who will no longer be there.

France without de Gaulle is entitled to the entire legacy of de Gaulle; that is why he is going all out in this brief span of time remaining for him. I imagine that he asks God every evening to leave him yet one more day for the pursuit of this grand project: a France that is once

38. Mauriac is referring to the years in which France was governed by the parliamentary regime established according to the constitution of the Fourth Republic, which was instituted at the end of 1945 and replaced by that of the Fifth Republic, which laid the foundation for a presidential regime shortly after de Gaulle's return to power in 1958.

39. Most often referred to as "Sciences Po" or the IEP, the Institut des Études Politiques has, since it was founded at the outset of the Third Republic in 1871, trained students for eminent careers in administration and public service. See http://www.sciencespo.fr/stories/#!/fr/frise/.

again sovereign, a faithful ally for its friends, yet independent of all of them, particularly the friend whose policies in Asia and Latin America are what we see as most surely absurd in their effects, if not criminal in their intent.

This France, with its fifty million inhabitants, is the flagship of Europe. With its new well-adapted army, this France is not, as Americans accuse it of being, nostalgic for its past grandeur. We do indeed love our history, but in the heart and mind of de Gaulle, and thus also in our hearts and minds, this history is continuing, in spite of the shadow that the enormous power of the United States casts over us. If I were Belgian, I would doubtless be resigned to the idea of seeing my little bilingual country that is incurably divided against itself break up and dissolve like a lump of sugar. If I were Italian, I would perhaps be nostalgic for the Florence of the Medicis, or the Rome of the popes, or the Venice of the doges. But it is not reasonable to demand that France, whose history began more than a thousand years ago, be dissolved and overwhelmed.

Just as someone about to venture out on a great journey without knowing if they will return puts all their affairs in order so that their loved ones may be sure of receiving the inheritance that has been prepared for them, de Gaulle could not have done anything other than what he undertook to do this week. What is tragic is that many of his heirs are already refusing the inheritance: they are perhaps not the most numerous, but they occupy all the avenues of the press in Paris, the provinces, and big business. They are everywhere, even in the palace of the Quai d'Orsay, where today a political strategy that they hate is being elaborated: they are like priests who have lost faith and who hate and despise the faith of simple souls.

For it is indeed a matter of faith. It did not take any virtue to believe in France when France was a great nation, when the United States did not count, when our army was the premier army of Europe, and when we were dominating so many peoples in Africa and Asia. The honor of de Gaulle and those who did not lose heart at the time was to have believed in France with the same faith when it lay wounded with a broken back in 1940. Today, this France that has been reduced to more modest proportions and that is overwhelmingly dominated economically by America, nevertheless occupies a place of privilege: it is the unique flagship state for Europe and for millions of hearts in the Third World. For them, France nonetheless remains the land invoked by Du Bellay: "France, mother of the arts, of arms, and of laws!" It is not possible to conceive of France without the history it has had. A history is not some past frozen in words: it continues, proceeds, and lasts, together with that of other friendly nations, but without losing its course. France remains free to choose its way and to refuse to take part in the folly of a political strategy that it condemns, be it that of an enormous, disproportionate power that might have the capability of occupying and colonizing it against its will. I imagine that today nothing counts more in de Gaulle's mind than to arrange everything ahead of time so that after he leaves power, these French who have lost faith in France do not once again hitch it back up to the American wagon, along with other docile nations.

In "Sunday, December 18, 1966," Mauriac explains that he has declined to sit alongside Jean-Paul Sartre on the Russell tribunal and pass judgment on the United States because of the log that he had not removed from his own eye: namely France's long record of colonial abuses in Asia and Africa.

Sunday, December 18, 1966

Several people have asked me "Why do you remain silent about Vietnam?" Yes, why? I refused to sit with Sartre in judgment of the Americans, as I have also been explicitly invited to do. Besides the fact that I feel myself as a person to be too minuscule on such a scale of problems, the reality is that as a French citizen, I remain implicated in all that was done in our name in Asia and Africa. I have this log that I have never taken out of my own eye.[40] But here is another reason for

40. Mauriac is alluding to one of Jesus' well-known teachings, found in Matthew 7.3–5: "Why do you see the speck that is in your brother's eye, but do not notice the log that is in your own eye? Or how can you say to your brother, 'Let me take the speck out of your eye,' when there is the log

my silence: American policy is undecipherable for me, whereas de Gaulle's is a delight to my mind: I follow it like a well-built speech verified by results. As for American policy, I have a hard time believing that it has only those motives that are immediately visible. What are they waiting for? What are they hoping for? Raymond Aron or André François-Poncet can tell us what they think of the matter. As for me, I have no thoughts on the matter on this sad Sunday so luminous and pale over these roofs in Auteuil: I love the chimneys, pink like the pink of cow teats that I used to receive as a New Year's Day present and which were also used to populate the nativity scene. But I will refrain from delving into such nostalgia. I won't serve you up another Christmas jingle. Ah! all has been drunk, all is eaten, nothing more to say.[41] There are days in this area in which not one single book is a must and any music would be intolerable, and the life that we have led suddenly becomes, when we survey it, a story that no longer looks like us. But I know well that all it will take for peace to well up again is an instant of prayerful meditation.

"Sunday, January 28, 1968" displays a remarkable level of intellectual and ethical honesty on the part of the aging Mauriac, now eighty-two. Even though his discourse on the United States is informed by a longing for a return to French preeminence, an overweening pride in France as "le flambeau de la civilization" (the torchbearer of civilization), and a concomitant disdain for a youthful new culture hard for a man born in the nineteenth-

in your own eye? You hypocrite, first take the log out of your own eye, and then you will see clearly to take the speck out of your brother's eye."

41. To convey a certain melancholy, Mauriac is citing a line from the third strophe of Paul Verlaine's poem "Langueur":

> O n'y vouloir, ô n'y pouvoir mourir un peu!
> Ah! tout est bu! Bathylle, as-tu fini de rire?
> Ah! tout est bu, tout est mangé! Plus rien à dire!
> [Of death, perchance! Alas, so lagging in desire!
> Ah, all is drunk! Bathyllus, hast done laughing, pray?
> Ah, all is drunk,—all eaten! Nothing more to say!]

French text is found at http://poesie.webnet.fr/lesgrandsclassiques/poemes/paul_verlaine/langueur.html. Translation is by Gertrude Hall, http://www.gutenberg.org/files/8426/8426-h/8426-h.htm.

century Catholic bourgeoisie of the Bordeaux region to appreciate, Mauriac has the courage to expose the most vital and ticklish nerve in the entire network of his cultural and political sensibility, namely the one inextricably linking him and his nation to America and everything America does.

Already visible in his article urging readers to extend the warmest of welcomes to President Eisenhower, all the while explaining his distaste for things "made in America," this close connection between his cultural sensitivities and his political views becomes the specific focus of the January 1968 reflections on "the American challenge," the subject of a best-selling book published in 1967 by Mauriac's former colleague and publisher, Jean-Jacques Servan-Schreiber, chief editor of *L'Express*, who argued that Europe had to defend its character against the risk of virtual annexation by the United States.[42] Voicing once again his misgivings about the arrogance of American power and its simplistic, heavy-handed approach to international politics, Mauriac nevertheless faces the reality that at the end of the day, the plight of the United States will ultimately be that of France as well.[43]

Sunday, January 28, 1968

The American challenge? And what if it were the challenge to the conventional wisdom of nations posed by a certain boundless energy and ambition? What is striking in all that has been and continues to be written on this subject is this faith in an absolute technological preeminence that would have nothing to fear from some miscalculation as long as the error was not linked to some mechanical function. One gets the impression that once they achieve a certain level of power, everything, even false reasoning, is permitted. But I stop here to object right away to the idea that some readers will express. No, I do not take pleasure in that which threatens the United States: what I feel is exactly the opposite, especially since I have just read a series of articles on racism and its virulence, the upheavals it is producing in the greater metropolitan areas of the United States, and the ghettos that are forming there.

42. Touzot in BN IV, 549n1.

43. Cf. Bracher, "A Not So Distant Mirror," 37.

I imagine that, whatever he may do, de Gaulle knows quite well that our wise disengagement from the United States will always be only relative, and that we remain tied to them for better and for worse. At least as far as I am concerned, I have never doubted the fact. It is therefore not malevolence, but rather fear that leads me to what I am saying here. In some quarters, of course, nobody will believe it, since they have decided that I am an old partisan fool. Again this week, an extreme right-wing journalist has condemned me as having ideas "that have determined against all comers to rush headlong into idolatry."

In reality, I am trying now as always to understand. And while it is true that with de Gaulle events almost always confirm or at least elucidate the reasons for a policy pursued in the face of any and all opposition, I nevertheless harbor no illusions as to the possibility of a total disengagement: the ordeal of the United States cannot fail to be ours as well. What ordeal? That which, as stated yesterday evening in *Le Monde*, consists "of having unilaterally decided to be the policemen of the entire world. No power has ever been able to claim such a role without making a large number of enemies." And yet these policemen have as their mission to protect law-abiding people from those who do not respect the law. Are those who are protected by the United States in South America and Asia the good guys and their adversaries the bad guys? Is the Pentagon nowhere at the service of fierce special interests embodied by the power of the United States? What is sure is that, anywhere in the world and whatever rabbit is being hunted down, be it Régis Debray or Ben Barka, in the end one is going to meet up with the American intelligence services.

Everything that opposes them must be taken out by these "incorruptibles" that have done so much to corrupt the youth of the entire world. The politics of espionage and policing on the scale of continents ends up becoming a show and a game and creates the myths of these haggard adolescents.

Appalled by the story of the horrific My Lai massacre published by the *New York Times* two weeks earlier, "The First Sunday in Advent, 1969" nevertheless underscores Mauriac's attachment to America. When all is said and done, Mauriac's various assessments of the United States stem from a genuine concern for the plight of both nations, the democratic, humanist values both claim to defend, and the image that they ultimately project to the world community. Paradoxically, this deep concern for the United States finds its most powerful expression when Mauriac contemplates the horror of the crimes committed at My Lai. Penned at the age of eighty-four, less than a year before Mauriac was to die, the piece testifies once more to the eloquence and uncompromising honesty that made him one of France's greatest editorialists.

Just when one could expect the most stinging indictment, Mauriac not only refrains from sermonizing, but even goes on to explain why the French could take a lesson from the Americans on the subject of transparency and self-criticism. He shares his apprehensions over the political repercussions of this scandal, which in all likelihood will make the United States and its South Vietnamese allies more vulnerable and peace less attainable. Just as he lashes out most vehemently when confronting the arrogance of American power that seems to deny if not deliberately humiliate France's venerable historical legacy or when enduring the avalanche of American culture that seems to inundate and possibly drown out the voices of French art and literature, so he displays his greatest intellectual honesty, moral courage, and political loyalty when he sees the United States experiencing an ordeal.

If indeed noblesse oblige, what demonstration of moral nobility could be more impressive? Yet something more is operative here. In fact, Mauriac abstains from throwing the first stone in this instance for the exact same reason that he declined an invitation to sit with Bertrand Russell and Jean-Paul Sartre in judgment of America's alleged war crimes in Vietnam in 1966: "I have this log that I have never taken out of my own eye."[44] Although he had fiercely denounced torture and oppression in Algeria, the log of French colonialism still irritated his mind's eye, and he assessed American and French atrocities in terms not of national allegiance or cultural preference but of a common humanity. Concluding his remarks on the My Lai atrocities, Mauriac contemplates both countries' difficulties in

44. BN IV, 367.

reconciling ethics and politics. In the final analysis, he rises above his nationalist bias to analyze American conduct in light of the ethical vocation that, in Mauriac's view, the United States historically shares with France and to which both countries must submit.[45]

The First Sunday in Advent, 1969

On the radio, I am listening for the first time to the new *Ordo Missae*.[46] I find it disconcerting at first, but I immediately regain my composure. This ordinary rite of Mass as we see it here has been proposed to us by Paul VI. He assumes the role of fatherhood for it, so to speak. It would be absurd to agree with the Holy Father every time that his words and deeds follow our preferences, and to be opposed to a reform that he has approved but which we do not like. As difficult as it is to disconnect it from all that it has meant to me throughout my life and to push myself to understand the reasons for these changes and what has made them necessary, I have therefore resolved to bid farewell to the old order of Mass.

The main thing is to place oneself in the everlasting liturgy which does not change and to acquire today the spirit of waiting specific to this first Sunday in Advent. This is certainly not the folklore surrounding Christmas, the tender, moving memories of childhood, and all that the world has made of this holiday. No, that is not what stirs up my impatience. I am on the contrary anxious to have made it through these holidays, but the Lord is before us: although we carry Him within us, we walk before Him.

It is strange that, far from making America odious, what is apparent to me from the My Lai massacre is what makes them better than us. At the time when in France we were denouncing the use of torture, the culprits had nothing to fear: they always got away with it. I remember that when I was summoned to testify before a parliamentary commission in the National Assembly, I appeared to them as a culprit. No widespread movement of public opinion supported me.

45. Cf. Bracher, "A Not So Distant Mirror," 38–40.
46. *Order of the Mass.*

Whatever it may cost them, the United States gives a very different example. It is an established fact that this type of war, a war of subversion involving an entire people, gives rise in all armies to the same monstrosities and reveals the potential monster lurking in young men who otherwise would have remained respectable citizens all their lives.

The American people do not cover up their nasty crimes as we do: they demand that justice be done. And yet, if this movement gains strength, it will be a powerful boost to the adversary. Once the peace is signed, it will allow the Vietcong to lash out to their hearts' content against those who have collaborated with the Americans and thus implicated themselves in these murders.

Moral law sometimes concurs with the demands of politics. Such was the case for France, at the time when the good Christians in power ordered the bombing of Haiphong and the deposition and deportation of the sultan of Morocco: in violating moral law, they did the opposite of what our national interest would have required. But moral law does not always nor often concur with political necessity. The United States is caught in the contradiction between the people, who react according to the requirements of legal justice, and their political leaders, who, at all costs, must win the peace if they have not been able to win the war.

The March of History and the Sermon on the Mount

From the time of the Spanish Civil War until his death in 1970, Mauriac's status as one of the most widely read and highly respected voices in the public arena was due in no small part to the eloquence and integrity of his urgent appeals for justice, outspoken condemnations of torture, and deep remorse over the seemingly unending bloodshed that characterized the history of France and of humankind. But he was also recognized as one of the most fervent—and in Parisian intellectual circles, increasingly rare—proponents of the Christianity that was moreover intimately involved in the perceptions and positions articulated in these editorials.

Mauriac's sense of the infinite value of each person, and therefore of the inestimable importance of each moment and each gesture of our lives, was firmly rooted in his Christianity, as he so clearly and powerfully explained in a long editorial penned for Holy Week in March 1948. As suggested by the title, "A Human Story of History," Mauriac presented the suffering and death of Jesus as the ongoing presence of Christ both in everyday human life and in the drama of human history:

> The story of Christ's suffering and death continues and each of us plays in turn one character after another. . . .
>
> For those who believe that Christ's suffering and death is ongoing, their every deed takes on tremendous significance. Unable to sleep in the dead of this holy night, I peruse one book after another (it's one way of questioning the dead), open at random a collection of the sermons of Bossuet, and receive this terrifying answer that goes right to my heart: "Everything is either infinitely useful or infinitely harmful to us: every moment of our lives, each breath, each heartbeat, every flash of thought has eternal repercussions."
>
> We can well understand just how much those who exploit humans as raw material hate this doctrine that gives the ephemeral creature an infinite value.[47]

For Mauriac, only the Christian view of each person as a unique creation endowed by the Creator with an immortal soul fully responded to what, in his editorial "All Saints' Day 1950," he termed the "frightful depreciation of the human person" brought about by the history of the twentieth century. Thus, he contended, "the Christian lends value and gives meaning to that supreme anguish [death] and believes that it has an Everlasting witness."[48]

Mauriac's poignant reaffirmation of the human in the face of the devastation of the twentieth century and the pathos of the nascent Cold War is thus of a piece with his eloquent profession of Christianity. In these timely reflections, Mauriac returns to the good news of the New Testament as humanity's inalienable title to dignity and worth, not in spite of, but because of the historical despair both as conveyed by Sartre, Camus, and Adamov on the most prominent stages of Paris, and also as produced by the confrontation of Stalinism and capitalism. In the following editorial, appropriately titled "All Saints' Day 1950," he embraces the promise of eternal life not as a pretext for disregarding the agonies of the present but rather as a mandate for infusing value and meaning into the here and now.

47. Mauriac, *La Paix des Cimes*, 27–28.

48. Ibid.

We would do well to avoid giving these lines any sectarian tenor. Mauriac was first of all articulating an explicitly Christian response to his times. While he was indeed interested in drawing his French readers back to the Church that so many of them had long since rejected or disregarded, his Christian humanism proves profoundly ecumenical and universal, in that it adamantly defends the dignity, value, and autonomy of all persons against the myriad principalities and powers seeking to transform human beings into mere instruments for achieving economic or political ends.[49]

All Saints' Day 1950

Le Figaro, October 31, 1950

On this All Saints' Day of 1950, I am reflecting on the relation that the human species is maintaining with death: how things have changed over the last thirty years, perhaps even more than over the thousand years that had come before. For a good number of people, death has ceased to be this portal opening onto unknown, hoped for, and dreaded heavens. How would they believe that they will be asked to render their souls since they do not know that they have a soul? No idea is more foreign to them than the notion that they will one day have to be accountable to a merciful justice. The death of the soulless individual has become something without importance.

At the heart of a civilization still permeated by a Christian mindset, even the nonbelievers and the atheists found in the thought of death the subject of a metaphysical meditation on being and nothingness. Today, death interests philosophers less than it does hygienists and statisticians. It has lost its terrifying, romantic aspect. It no longer gallops through the heavens, armed with its scythe, as in ancient prints. "This empty skull and this eternal laugh" have become reassuring ever since death dressed itself in the uniform of a social worker and the hat of a nurse, and since instead of a scythe it holds a euthanizing syringe or a needle. The Christian notion of death that had outlived Christianity in many hearts is about to die out. As long as there remains a breath

49. See Bracher, "The Cold War Christian Humanism of François Mauriac," 398–99.

of life, our duty is to maintain it, even if it be in the most tortured body, and even if no chance of a cure exists. Let's admit it: only Christians are logical when they forbid themselves from interrupting this last fight between the flesh that is almost vanquished and the throbbing soul about to spring out into unimaginable light, because Christians attach value and meaning to this supreme anguish, believing that it has an everlasting witness.

But here is the strangest thing: economists, or at least some of them, are inclined to think that we have vilified death, that it is a necessary and benevolent fairy that we have excessively resisted. Old people are not dying any more, and some candidates for the Académie française are not alone in complaining that certain "immortals" (as academicians are traditionally called) are taking their immortality too seriously. One statistician dared say to me the other day that ever since the discovery of penicillin, there reigns over the entire surface of the inhabited world a threat of overcrowding all the more formidable now that infant mortality has been brought in check and natural selection no longer plays itself out.

Deep within a humanity that has lost its soul, everything thus turns against humankind. Slaughters, mass destructions, and maybe even gas chambers intended for displaced persons could ultimately appear as necessities on a planet that is too small and threatened with overpopulation. But we reject such an outlook with horror, and however weak our faith or fragile our hope, we turn to the sole power in this world that is fighting against the frightful depreciation of the human person: above the chain gangs, labor camps, and work bureaus, that power is holding up the promise that all succeeding generations have received and kept since it was heard by twelve obscure Jewish men and one Samaritan woman.

This promise that resounds on All Saints' Day in all the churches in the universe, the promise that those who hunger for justice shall be satisfied, the promise of an unmitigated joy and an unending love confers right here on this earth an eminent dignity on those who receive it, even if it were not to be fulfilled. In a materialistic society, no other force in the world could possibly protect individuals against the use and abuse that nameless powers, faceless bureaucracies, and state police make of them.

But do we Christians really believe in eternal life? As disconcerting as it may be for many minds (and I admit it is for me), the doctrine of the Assumption that the Holy Father is going to lay out on All Saints' Day directs our attention on this most mysterious, most incredible article of the Apostles' Creed that rarely receives commentary in church and which constitutes a wild and marvelous hope: the resurrection of the body. This body of the Virgin now already risen and glorified (if I understand the new doctrine correctly) reminds us that all bodies, ever since there have been bodies in the world that were loved, all faces, all eyes, all hands, all bosoms on which heads rested themselves, will experience on that day among all days the same resurrection and the same glory, and that we will forever and ever see, from such and such eyelid that we remember, the tear that on one evening of our adolescence our lips had received.

Contemplating the unspeakable horrors of the Holocaust as underscored by Erwin Leiser's film *Mein Kampf*, Mauriac's article for "Monday, November 28, 1960" points to the long series of historical crimes perpetrated by a host of nations, ideologies, and social groups in Europe, beginning with those closest to him, the French Catholics. Refusing theological "explanations" of evil, he nevertheless points to the Cross as the sign of the divine love crucified in all human suffering.

For Mauriac, history ultimately represents a moral drama in which humanity plays out its ideals and passions, a story of occasional triumph and redemption (as with de Gaulle), but with seemingly endless crime and retribution. Hence the many allusions to the story of Cain and Abel, to which Mauriac frequently returns when characterizing human history in general, as in the lines decrying "this interminable massacre of innocents that, ever since the murder of Abel, has been perpetuated through so-called sacred history."[50] Throughout the 1950s and '60s, Mauriac's overriding preoccu-

50. BN IV, 556.

pation is the criminal violence manifest in every epoch and perpetrated by groups of all ideological, national, and religious persuasions, beginning with those most intimately linked to his own identity, the European Christians. We find the clearest expression of this perception in the lines written in response to unspeakable historical crimes depicted by Leiser's film on Hitler. The parallels that Mauriac draws between Nazi crimes and various chapters of French history are as uncompromising as they are ahead of their time, since it was only in the 1970s that a general reflection on the Holocaust as a cataclysm calling into question European history and culture in general was undertaken in France, as elsewhere. Mauriac's conclusion to this article proves unsettling to any and all conceptions of history, including his own.[51]

Monday, November 28, 1960

One must say everything, and say also that I would not have distanced myself so easily from the film, perhaps, and that I would not have so gladly left the cinema hall where the show was continuing, if it had not boiled down to a gloomy accumulation of crimes. These crimes have reached such an extreme degree of abomination in our time that we can now contemplate them with our eyes at the movie theater in *Mein Kampf*, the film that Erwin Leiser made from documents taken from the official archives of the Third Reich. Granted, I no longer have the strength to go see what was happening in the Warsaw ghetto. I will rely on the testimony of my oldest son: "Returning from a perilous hunt for food, the children were searched and caught, and had to abandon their supply of five rutabagas concealed under their ragged shirts. The children looked up at their uniformed tormentors with a gaze more distant than despair and deeper than revolt, a scarcely surprised, sad, and empty gaze, that does not judge and which judges us." And there is this: "Here we see a Mom in a camp. As they have done with her friends, they have taken all her clothes off. She holds her infant, who is also naked, against her bosom. Such maternity no artist has ever paint-

51. Cf. Bracher, *Through the Past Darkly*, 214.

ed: what a moving back, what a light and graceful neck, what a trusting head on this condemned baby. In that manner, this naked woman walks among her naked friends to the showers with her child in her arms. There she knows (or perhaps does not know, that depended on the camp) that it is not at all water but gas and death that will gush out."

That the generation having witnessed these things has not fallen to their knees while beating their breasts and that, on the contrary ... But why go on? I am standing at the heart of a contradiction that I know will not be resolved here and now. There is no use in trying to make this world of *Mein Kampf* (which in our sweet France was also that of the war against the Albigenses[52] and Caboche,[53] that of the Saint Bartholomew Day massacre, of the revolutionary slaughters, the insurrectional days of June,[54] the uprising of the Commune, and the repression by troops from Versailles) with the New Testament dictum *Deus caritas est.*[55] I can no longer bear to hear some theologian give me his reasons on the subject. The conformity of the Cross with human suffering is enough for me. I have never forgotten what someone said to me one day: "What we have crucified is love, and we will keep on crucifying love until the end of the world." That is the story of history, and there is no other.

"Malagar, Friday, October 16, 1964" was written on the eve of Mauriac's return to Paris from an extended stay at his country estate. He again de-

52. Over the first three decades of the thirteenth century, the Albigensian Crusade was, with the approval and encouragement of the pope, mercilessly conducted in the south of France by nobles from the north intent on stamping out the Cathar heresy and establishing Capetian dominance. The crusade involved a number of massacres of civilian populations in cities of southwestern France.

53. In 1413 Simon Caboche led a group of Parisian merchants to riot in protest of corruption. His men formed a faction that blamed King Charles VI and favored his rival, the duke of Burgundy, known as John the Fearless. See George Childs Kohn, *Dictionary of Wars* (New York: Routledge, 1999), 92.

54. Mauriac is referring to the bloody events that marked the month of June 1848, when riots protesting a harsh crackdown on workers, who were forced either to join the army or leave Paris, were met with even more fierce and violent repression that left some 1,500 workers dead and some 11,000 to 15,000 imprisoned. See http://www.larousse.fr/encyclopedie/divers/r%C3%A9volution_fran%C3%A7aise_de_1848/140734 .

55. God is love.

cries the inhumanity of the brave new world of technology and consumerism springing up amid rapid urbanization and taking a heavy toll on France's wildlife and rural landscapes. The unbridled urbanization transforming the Paris region not only signifies a break with the past and the destruction of the rural habitat, but, in Mauriac's eyes, also marks a more general dehumanization. Hence his apprehension about returning to the "city of lights." For him, the methodically impersonal expanses of concrete emblematic of modern urban development in Brasilia and Paris echo the banishment of the human element from contemporary literature and art. Conversely, the animals, crops, and edifices of his rural dwellings at both Malagar and Vémars connect Mauriac with a vibrant network of human activity transmitting a tangible legacy of the past.

Hay fields abandoned by harvesters, streams choked with dead fish, heirlooms and walls damaged by sonic booms: all signal the violation and seemingly inexorable destruction of a venerable human habitat, breaking down the web of human relations embedded within it. The disappearance of the agrarian society and physical environment not only creates an abrupt discontinuity and a sense of loss, but also constitutes an acute crisis of personal, social, and human identity. In the end, affirms Mauriac, Christianity's insistence on the worth and dignity of every person holds the best hope for preservation of a truly human manner of dwelling within nature and society.[56]

Malagar, Friday, October 16, 1964

Tomorrow I return to Paris. I am tired of this rain, this threatening sky, the lost grape harvest, and this house full of the dead, or rather (for if the dead were there, I would not wish to distance myself from them) the house is too full of their absence. This absence is not as awful as the oblivion that already covered even the closest among them. That's what makes me freeze. I keep pondering this verse from Leconte de Lisle: "Voiceless multitudes, empty names, extinct families."[57]

56. Cf. Bracher, *Through the Past Darkly*, 156–57.

57. Mauriac is citing a line from the first strophe of Leconte de Lisle's poem "Aux Morts" ("To the Dead"):

I will leave here without looking back, not that I should feel the attraction of this Paris where I have interviews waiting, and where I will have to repeat the gestures and the words for the role that I began to play forty-five years ago. I am so accustomed to this clamor of praises and insults that I scarcely hear it anymore. On October 11, my birthday, I was thinking that I should be able to claim the title of "oldest object of insults in France."

I go without regret for what I am leaving behind, without being attracted to what I am going to find ... I do not dread humans (as dreadful as they may be) as much as I dread the sort of world we see developing in its accelerated mutation: this world is inhuman.

What is striking is the inhuman character of the world. It was not enough to call it absurd, for what is absurd is still of human proportions, as are all forms of madness. What could be more human than the madmen who have been our masters: Baudelaire, Verlaine, Rimbaud? The city being built under our very eyes, this termite colony, on the other hand, is logical and reasonable. The Brasilia that I contemplated with terror on television is the conception of a mentally balanced technician, not the nightmare of some wildly unreasonable man, as are the chateaus in Bavaria.

The reference to humanity is the secret that has been lost not only from architecture and all that is connected with urban development. The absence of humanity is being celebrated everywhere as a victory, in novels, poems, and art galleries. There is no longer any face anywhere. Not a single heart beats in any book.

But even the material world is being destroyed. Distances have been overcome, as they say, and humanity stupidly thinks that this

---

Après l'apothéose après les gémonies,
Pour le vorace oubli marqués du même sceau,
Multitudes sans voix, vains noms, races finies,
Feuilles du noble chêne ou de l'humble arbrisseau;
[After the apotheosis, after the pillory
Marked with the same seal for voracious oblivion
Voiceless multitudes, empty names, extinct families,
Leaves of the noble oak or the humble shrub.]

French text is found at http://poesie.webnet.fr/lesgrandsclassiques/poemes/charles_marie_leconte_de_lisle/aux_morts.html. The translation is mine.

is a victory when it is a suicide. Anatole France had sensed and announced this world that he found repugnant: "An enormous and consistent ugliness." It sprang up more quickly than he had predicted.

I walked into the stable, where there is still a steer. There used to be four of them. I could see his large eye in the shadows; a ray of sunlight streaming in through a hole in the door touched his reddish brown hide. I listened to that calm sound of rumination as I breathed in this strong, sweet smell which had permeated the obscure lives of my forgotten ancestors. And all of a sudden, in a procession of images born from what had been saddening me recently, I saw again around my house in the Seine-et-Oise these prairies for which there are no longer any reapers. And when the grim reaper had come for them, we had to burn the hay that used to be so valuable, that used to feed the cattle, turn into manure, return to the earth, and enrich the soil after having nourished the birds, following a law that is perhaps sacred. And then I saw again in my mind the thousands of dead fish floating down the Adour river (and many other rivers) a few weeks ago. Finally, I remembered the heavy Venetian mirror from my mother's home. It fell off the wall of my study at Malagar and would perhaps have killed me if it had hit my head instead of grazing my leg. Rightly or wrongly, this mishap was blamed on the shaking caused by planes breaking the sound barrier over Malagar. For my part, I believe it, for there are a good many other signs that these cracked, age-old walls will not hold up forever as this law is repeatedly violated.

I went to thank one of these farm workers who had sent roses to me and my wife for our anniversary. I sat down at the side of the hearth where a fire of vine branches was burning. I once again found the same semi-darkness as in the barn. I recognized a world dear to my childhood, but from well before my childhood. There one finds the holy shadow out of which I emerged. In the Landes region where my ancestors used to tend their flocks, how I loved kitchens similar to this one during the vacations of yesteryear! While having me admire the slightly ornate fireplace in a home almost as poor as that of the peasants, they would tell me that in her adolescence, my grandmother in her adolescence would sit near this hearth and read the novels of Alexandre Dumas by the light of a pine resin candle. This house became that of a sharecropper and burned along with the ancient oak trees that shaded it during the great fire fifteen years ago. Nothing remains of this place, which in its humility was one of the most beautiful that it has been granted to me to cherish in this world.

The feeling that I experienced in this farmworker's kitchen in Malagar is the same that I had had the day before in the stable where I had entered: the anxiety of a lost secret, an essential secret forever lost by a humanity that is so proud of orbiting the earth and taking scarcely more time to reach New York or Rio from Paris than my grandfather took in his horse-drawn buggy to go from Langon to Villandraut.

I was speaking of a holy shadow. Yes, I wrote one day that every stable makes one think of the Nativity. A little poor child is forever lying in the straw, next to a steer exhaling over him. And similarly in this farmer's kitchen where I had come to sit down and whose inhabitants are hardly pious, the Holy Family was sitting in silence around the bare, heavy table. It is strange to think that there is nothing more human than the supernatural and that there is nothing more inhuman than a world without God. To the extent that Zarathustra was right and that "God is dead," humanity is dead as well. If I had not remained in the faith, because I believe that the Church has the words of eternal life, it seems to me that I would have remained faithful out of an instinct of conservation, because it alone, in this inhuman world, remains human.

This meeting of God and humanity in the bread and in the wine, this unending, yet down-to-earth mystery which has become so familiar caused these countless churches to spring up throughout the Christian West. I am not thinking of the cathedrals but of the most humble churches. The poor in these peasant kitchens that I was speaking about would in the past come to worship under their vaults because, being straightforward, unsophisticated, and ignorant, they were capable of God. If the atheistic world is interested in what is now happening in Rome, perhaps it is because it senses obscurely that what subsists of Christianity on earth constitutes, even in the most physical sense, its last chance of survival.

Amid the heated controversy surrounding the film production of *La Religieuse*, Diderot's iconoclastic narrative of feminine sexuality in a convent, Mauriac's reflection for "Maundy Thursday, April 7, 1966" focuses on what he considers to be the most troublesome scandal facing Christians: that of the historical crimes perpetrated by those claiming to further divine will on earth. Poring over the legacy of Christendom and the Church, Mauriac finds not triumphant grandeur, but a tragic co-existence of sainthood and criminality. As devoted to the Catholic Church as he certainly is, Mauriac refuses to mitigate historical crimes by assimilating them into some divine plan or providential dialectic. On the contrary, to truly proclaim the message of the Gospel in the contemporary world, submits Mauriac, Christians must confront these painful episodes of the past with honesty and courage.[58]

Maundy Thursday, April 7, 1966

I will refrain from entering into a quarrel like the one over *La Religieuse*, on which I feel I agree with no one. I do not agree with the government minister who has thrown this unexpected sardine to the sea lions of the opposing parties: he of all people should know that ever since Charles X's "justice and love" law,[59] censorship makes those in power odious to the people of France and favors postures that are advantageous to the knights of the writing table (and today of the screen) who stand up bravely to face the censuring monster. Nor do I agree with these good apostles of freedom who, among the thousand and one true or imagined scandals that have played themselves out in this old country, choose precisely the Albigensian crusade or Diderot's toxic novel, whereas they would never dream of butting heads with the children of the Prophet, the Huguenots, or the Jews: against the Catholics, everything is permitted.

58. Cf. Bracher, *Through the Past Darkly*, 217.

59. The law dubbed "Justice et amour" was promulgated on June 24, 1827, in an attempt by King Charles X to silence the press, but was quickly rejected, even by the ultraconservative Chambre des députés. See http://www.linternaute.com/histoire/categorie/evenement/58/1/a/53051/rejet_de_la_loi_justice_et_amour.shtml.

I nevertheless do not agree with these clergymen either, who, without knowing what the film is really about, have declared war on something they haven't seen. To these pious petitioners, but also to myself (and I have not recovered from the hurt that I suffered from the program on the Cathars), I would like to recall a reality that we Catholics don't like to confront, and that the Church itself has only really confronted since Vatican II.

How shall I articulate this reality? Of all animals, humans are the most ferocious: they have displayed their ferocity in every period of history. From one century to another, only the form of this ferocity has changed, not its virulence. Simon de Montfort is covered with less blood than, I won't say Hitler and Stalin, but less than the great Churchill demanding the destruction of Dresden or Truman that of Hiroshima and Nagasaki.[60] What assigns a special place for Christians in this museum of historical horrors is not that they were worse than the others, but the fact that the burnings at the stake and the destruction of cities were done in the name of Christ. In the New World, the Spanish perpetrated their deeds with the cross in their hands. The very word crusade, whose story was told like a sacred epic when we were children, sums up the frightful misconception that has prevailed ever since Constantine: the Spanish Civil War constituted the final episode of this legacy.

Since intolerance is the most widely shared thing in the world,[61] one could easily find persecutions and auto-da-fé to inscribe on the record of all religions and all ideologies. But that is the tribute that even her adversaries pay to the Catholic Church: what comes from her echoes farther and falls from higher up. Perhaps some of the nuns who have felt hurt and indignant that *La Religieuse* was screened have meditated and applied to themselves these words that the Lord spoke to his disciples as he was about to leave them: "If the world hates you,

60. Simon de Montfort, leader of the Albigensian Crusade, allegedly told his crusaders in reference to the men, women, and children who had sought refuge in a church in Béziers: "Kill them all, God will recognize his own."

61. Mauriac is once again alluding to the famous phrase from Descartes's *Discourse on the Method* affirming good sense to be the most commonly shared thing in the world.

know that it has hated me before it hated you. If you were of the world, the world would love its own; but because you are not of the world, but I chose you out of the world, therefore the world hates you."[62] Now these words were directed toward "pre-Christians," so to speak, to those who had not yet entered into the fray. They are not directed to the constituted Church, to the Church that, precisely, has been of the world, to such an extent that for several centuries it claimed to have dominance over all nations. The Lord's words are directed to the everlasting Church, to the Church of the saints whose exact boundaries are known only to God and which perhaps includes the Cathars, who sought perfection, and the strictly observant Franciscans, who were also persecuted. The Church of the saints silently takes on itself the hatred that the political Church has stirred up in the world.

This silence of the saints is what we must imitate. There would certainly be a film to shoot on the life of Antoine Chevrier, the founder of the Prado, who is also the subject of a book that Jean-François Six has published with the Éditions du Seuil. What is striking in this admirable story of a priest in Lyon during the Second Empire is that he was on the side of the poor, as are the disciples of today: not only did he live the same life, he was one of them, at a time when all of the clergy were on the other side of the barricade helping the powerful maintain the established order and making themselves odious.

The Church is holy, and it is holy deep within: that is why the politicians who have exploited it have not destroyed it. After two thousand years of fratricidal wars, but also of sainthood, we the contemporaries of Vatican II must assume responsibility for everything, even the worst, in our past, but without separating it from the best.

I have met more than one priest like Father Chevrier in my life. In my childhood, the clergy was still like that of the Second Empire described by Jean-François Six. The fact remains that even in a family as traditional as mine, people were interested in the apostolic mission of Abbot Naudet, who from his pulpit in Bordeaux thundered out his criticism of the Catholic bourgeoisie. At the age of eighteen I was at-

62. John 15.18–19.

tracted to Marc Sangnier and the Sillon, and I became the friend of Abbot Desgranges: that's because I had already experienced certain influences and the way within me had been prepared.[63]

Today, the stakes are higher, and there is nothing to gain from concealing a history in which certain chapters make one shudder. We have to take responsibility for this entire legacy of the Church and draw the lessons as did the saintly Father Chevrier, and as do his present-day disciples and the priests of the Mission of France (to which Jean-François Six belongs) and the working priests.

The swing of the pendulum may have led today's priests to take extreme positions opposite of those taken by the clergy of a hundred years ago, but they are allowed every excess in the direction of poverty. We must trust them, especially those of us who have been the beneficiaries of a religion that had become the fiefdom of a social class: we must agree to no longer occupy the first place in their lives, and to let the poor precede us in their hearts.

And then, too, we must consent to the world's judgment on the history of these bygone years, to the extent that this judgment is right. If I am to believe the article published here in these same pages last Thursday about the film *La Religieuse*, the filmmaker, out of conviction or caution, depicted Diderot's heroine as having enough faith and love to make our contemporaries who are the farthest from those qualities stop and think about this wrenching debate within a naturally Christian soul, in a fierce world that utilizes everything and even the Gospel to dominate others.

Having come from all folds and beginning to unite, we Christians of 1966 have nothing to fear from a past for which we have taken responsibility. I write this while waiting for Maundy Thursday Mass, this meal of an evening among all evenings when words were spoken over a piece of bread, over a cup of wine: after two thousand years, we who have believed are still living from this meal.

63. Jean-Marie Desgranges, 1874–1958, was a Catholic priest, author, and member of the National Assembly known for his oratory and his work for social justice. See http://www.assemblee-nationale.fr/sycomore/fiche.asp?num_dept=2434.

"Tuesday, September 27, 1966" constitutes one of Mauriac's most lyrical articles, as he observes an approaching storm, reflects on the tumultuous episodes of collective and individual history that he has witnessed in the span of his life, and finally articulates his own understanding of "this promise of eternal love." On one level, he weaves the motifs of the storm, dust, and ashes into a veritable prose poem meditating on mortality. On another level, he situates the individual with respect to history. Not only does history always have a human (if often barbaric) face in Mauriac's eyes, this human face tells a story of history. If often full of sound and fury, it is a tale that never signifies nothing, and that moreover cannot be summed up by any Hegelian prose of the world nor any saga of national grandeur. Embroiled in the "tangled mess of errors and violence" that is history, answerable for the plight of others as was Cain for Abel, each human being remains distinct and autonomous. For Mauriac, this inalienable status is grounded in the divine.[64]

Tuesday, September 27, 1966

A gathering storm. "It's within me that the storm is gathering," I noted in one of my teenage poems. And it's always within me that I experience the storm before it raises its dark forehead above the hedgerows. The storm does me in, but no more so at the age of eighty than when I was eighteen. The big difference is that the overwhelmed young man was given over defenselessly to desires and dreams, whereas the overburdened old man has to hold up against the dust and ashes that the winds of the storm stir up and carry into his face at the very end of his spent life, covering him to the point of snuffing it out.

Such is the temptation of despair that thought turned toward God keeps at bay, although the temptation remains as long as the storm lasts. There is in the storm, at least for me, an almost unbearable capacity to conjure up the past. Indeed, such is the very atmosphere of the vacations when I was an adolescent: everything recalls these equi-

64. Cf. Bracher, *Through the Past Darkly*, 220.

> noxes of yesteryear. This long stretch of a human life will have lasted but an instant, yet it has reflected an infinite number of faces that not even a faithful heart keeps in mind, for a man of my age has seen entire families die out: the last one to die was the last to remember. Now there is nothing left of them other than the flies that kept buzzing around the dark living rooms of those years during nap time. It is at this point that faith—the virtue of faith if we put it into practice—comes to our aid. Each of these persons who are now but dust and ashes had a story, and it continues: it is a singular itinerary that cannot be confused with any other, no more than their faces, which are also unique, different from all the faces that existed before them and that will exist after them. Just as they were, they were loved, they are loved, not by others who are no longer, but by Him who is from everlasting to everlasting. It was not I who invented this, though I do believe it. I believe in this promise of eternal love. I am surprised that the Catholic liturgy uses so rarely John's Epistle, where this tremendous hope is expressed.

In "Friday, December 15, 1967," the killing of a seven-year-old child by a fifteen-year-old boy spurs Mauriac to reflect once again on the unsettling and seemingly unending episodes of cruelty and violence committed by "ordinary" human beings, including Christians. Refusing to formulate any justification for the destruction of human life, he points out that the murder of a seven-year-old boy by a fifteen-year-old was sadly just the latest illustration of all that was criminal in humanity and history. Depicting predatory violence as "the law that governs relations between living things, from plant life to the most highly evolved animal," Mauriac even formulates the neologism "*l'entre-dévorement*" (mutual devouring) to designate the phenomenon. Decrying murder as "the obviously absolute negation of the Love in whom we have faith," Mauriac rejects not only all attempts to invoke a metaphysical absolute, namely the Deity, in support of a group or nation at war, but also the notion that the will of God is immanent in historical events. Mauriac thus rejects "explanations" tending to justify violence by integrating it into some grandiose plan or dialectic. Instead, he insists that the role of Christians must be to affirm divine love not by seeking escape from the world, but on the contrary by participating fully in the story of history, showing solidarity in word and deed with all who are afflicted.[65]

Friday, December 15, 1967

To those who are surprised at my silence over the incident in which Abel is seven and Cain fifteen, I have no other answer than to claim that we who have condemned ourselves to a life of perpetual writing have the right to remain silent. It is we who have inflicted this life of forced labor upon ourselves. We retain the liberty to break it off at any moment without having to be accountable to anyone. Everything that taints or injures the childhood within us, everything that presses our nose down over the proof that this last refuge of childhood, this last recourse against what is criminal in life is but a myth, that it does not exist, that evil is a primordial reality, and that the wellspring of life, so pure in appearance is already fouled at the source, that is what I have not been able to face. That has been the case ever since I have come of age, and I remain impervious to the arguments of theologians who have an answer for everything.

And yet, and yet … "Emmanuel was an angel!" So said the child who murdered him, if I am to believe the reporter for *Le Monde*. That is true as well: Emmanuel was an angel, he is an angel forever. His mother and father believe that he is eternally alive, that he has not had to become like a child once again, as the Lord says we must, since he is forever that child whom we ourselves have been, whom we resemble, and whom, to say the least, we must revive in us if we want to partake of the Kingdom of God.

That is what I believed, and that is what I believe now; but now I am believing it at the heart of a creation given over to murder, founded on murder. As horrible as the present case of murder may be, given the age of those involved, it does not in the least run counter to the law governing the relations between all living things, from the realm of plants to the most highly evolved animal, and which is the law of

65. Cf. ibid., 207–10.

"mutual devouring." This word cannot be found in any dictionary, as if human language had shirked the necessity of giving a name to that which is in appearance the absolute negation of the Love in which we believe.

The particularity of humankind is to have become aware of this organized murder, to use it for entertainment, to orchestrate it, and to broadcast it using all the technical means at our disposal. And perhaps also to make it more virulent than it ever was in the past? That remains to be seen. Mme de Sévigné tells gaily of the king's soldiers in occupied Brittany who skewered a small child for fun and then put it to roast. We must abandon this claim that progress has also been evident in crime. Even Hitler falls well short, it seems to me, of the Spanish and Portuguese conquistadors who destroyed entire races: they win out over him because they did it with the cross in their hands and in the name of Christ, which is the crime of all crimes.

That reminds me of the elderly hunting ladies, who were wearing such strange hats when I saw them not so long ago on television, in a feature about Saint Hubert's Mass. They were holding on tightly to the lamb of God that some wretched priest was lifting up in his hands without trembling; and then we were treated to the agonizing death of the deer and to the dogs' disgusting feeding frenzy. And then, without even thinking to hide his face, one of these gentlemen came up to explain to us that the raison d'être for hunting with dogs is to provide an outlet for the killer instinct within us, and that we kill deer for lack of anything better. If François, who is in an infinitely more miserable state than Emmanuel, had seen this feature on hunting instead of the one on "In Your Heart and Soul," which reportedly gave him the idea for his crime, perhaps he would have contented himself with killing a dog or a cat.

I'm sorry if I give the impression of joking, for I have a heavy heart and I should be speaking of these matters as the saddest thing in the world. What grips our throat in such a strange crime is the fact that it is actually not strange. It is just the most horrible tragedy in the news. It is one more tragedy in this interminable massacre of innocents that, ever since the murder of Abel, has been perpetuated throughout so-called sacred history, every time a city was plundered ("they spared neither the women nor the small children ..."), just as it has been perpetuated throughout history in general, particularly during the Crusades and religious wars, the most ferocious of all, in which both sides had mobilized the Eternal Being for their cause.

If I am "letting off steam" in this "Bloc-notes," it's because throughout all these years that the mystery of evil has tormented me, I have after all had the remedy at hand. Not an answer that could satisfy my mind, but like a man whose clothes were on fire would throw himself into the sea, I throw myself into this ocean of goodness that the story of human history nevertheless remains: a story that is criminal, yet sacred. From generation to generation, countless men and women have found within themselves this Emmanuel that they had been at the outset.

It is about them that I, as a Christian, think first: this Little Sister of the Poor or of the Assumption, this Brother of Charles de Foucauld, this vicar, this worker priest. Charity is actually the most widely shared thing in the world. I remember this illustrious atheist that one of my friends was telling me about yesterday: "He who made so much money gave it all away, he no longer has a thing." Good and evil are mixed up together closely in the same person. All living persons, regardless of what they may have done, are potential saints: the wretched child who bears the same first name as I do and who wanted to die should be told again and again that, as for each one of us, only a sigh separates him from forgiveness.

In the night that is soon to come, it is a child that the faithful will bring back to the holy table, hidden under their coats: it is a little Emmanuel that they will hold warmly in their arms without asking him the reasons behind this incomprehensible world: this dirt, but also this little mustard seed that germinates in it, this bloody dough of humanity, but also the yeast that penetrates into it and makes it rise.

BIBLIOGRAPHY

Albert, Pierre. *Histoire de la presse*. Paris: Presses Universitaires de France (Que sais-je?), 1996.

Balzac, Honoré de. "Sur Catherine de Medicis." In *Oeuvres Complètes*, vol. 16: *La Comédie Humaine*. Paris: Calmann-Lévy, 1879.

Baratta, Joseph P. *The Politics of World Federation*. Vol. 2: *From World Federalism to Global Governance*. Westport, Conn.: Praeger Press, 2004.

Barré, Jean-Luc. *François Mauriac. Biographie intime, 1. 1885–1940*. Paris: Fayard, 2009.

———. *François Mauriac. Biographie intime, 2. 1940–1970*. Paris: Librairie Arthème Fayard, 2010.

Baudelaire, Charles. *The Flowers of Evil*. Translated by William Aggeler. Fresno, Calif.: Academy Library Guild, 1954.

Benjamin, Walter. *Illuminations*. New York: Schocken Books, 1969.

Bennett, Scott H. *Radical Pacifism: The War Resisters League and Gandhian Nonviolence in America, 1915–1963*. Syracuse, N.Y.: Syracuse University Press, 2003.

Bracher, Nathan. "Facing History: Mauriac and Lévinas on Nazism." *Journal of European Studies* 23 (1993): 159–77.

———. "The Cold War Christian Humanism of François Mauriac." *Christianity and Literature* 52, no. 3 (Spring 2003): 387–408.

———. "A Not So Distant Mirror: Mauriac's Image of America." *Contemporary French Civilization* 30, no. 2 (Summer/Fall 2006): 17–43.

Burrin, Philippe. *La France à l'heure allemande*. Paris: Éditions du Seuil, 1995.

Châteaubriand, René de. *Aben-Hamet, the Last of the Abencerages*. Open web source: http://books.google.com.

Cohen, Daniel. *Lettre à une amie allemande*. Paris: L'Harmattan, 1998.

De Gaulle, Charles. *Mémoires de guerre. L'appel, 1940–1942*. Paris: Plon, 1954.

Finkielkraut, Alain. *L'humanité perdue*. Paris: Éditions du Seuil, 1996.

Flower, John. *François Mauriac, journaliste. Les vingt premières années, 1905–1925*. Bern: Peter Lang, 2011.

François Mauriac un journaliste engagé. Jean Daniel, Jean-Claude Guillebaud, Francis Jeanson, Jean Lacouture, René Rémond, Jean Touzot. Propos recueillis par Gilbert et Nicole Balavoine. Centre François Mauriac de Malagar: Éditions confluences, 2007.

Fourastié, Jean. *Les Trente Glorieuses, ou la révolution invisible de 1946 à 1975*. Paris: Fayard, 1979.

Gordon, Bertram M., ed. *Historical Dictionary of World War II France*. Westport, Conn.: Greenwood Press, 1998.

Gyles, Mary Francis. "Nero: Qualis artifex?" *Classical Journal* 57, no. 5 (February 1962): 193–200.

Jammes, Francis. "Élégie." *Mercure de France*. October–November 1898, 338–39.

Judt, Tony. *Past Imperfect: French Intellectuals, 1944–1956*. Berkeley: University of California Press, 1992.

Kaufman, Michael J. "Jacques Massu, 94, General Who Led Battle of Algiers." *New York Times*, October 31, 2002.

Kohn, George Childs. *Dictionary of Wars*. New York: Routledge, 1999.

Lacouture, Jean. *François Mauriac 2. Un citoyen du siècle*. Paris: Éditions du Seuil, 1980.

Lacretelle, Charles. *Histoire de la Convention Nationale*. Vol. 2. Paris: Treutel & Wurtz, 1825.

Lamartine, Alphonse de. "La Marseillaise de la paix." In *Oeuvres complètes*, 1173–77. Paris: Gallimard, 1963.

Lesenko, Valentine. "Une lecture pascalienne du *Noeud de vipères*." In *Pascal-Mauriac: L'oeuvre en dialogue*, edited by Jean-François Durand. Paris: L'Harmattan, 2000.

Lévinas, Emmanuel. *Difficile liberté: Essai sur le Judaïsme*. Paris: Albin Michel, 1963. Available in English as *Difficult Freedom: Essays on Judaism*, translated by Seán Hand. Baltimore, Md.: Johns Hopkins University Press, 1990.

Lévi-Valensi, Jacqueline, ed. *Camus at Combat: Writing, 1944–1947*. Translated by Arthur Goldhammer. Princeton, N.J.: Princeton University Press, 2007.

Mauriac, François. *Nouveaux mémoires intérieurs*. Available in English as *Inner Presence: Recollections of My Spiritual Life*. Indianapolis, Ind.: Bobbs-Merrill, 1968.

———. *Bloc-notes 1952–1970*. 5 vols. Edited and annotated by Jean Touzot. Paris: Éditions du Seuil (Points-Essais), 1993.

———. *La Paix des cimes*. Edited and annotated by Jean Touzot. Paris: Bartillat, 1999.

———. *D'Un Bloc-notes à l'autre*. Edited and annotated by Jean Touzot. Paris: Bartillat, 2004.

———. *Journal: Mémoires politiques*. Edited and annotated by Jean Touzot and Laurence Granger. Paris: Robert Laffont, 2008.

———. *"On n'est jamais sûr de rien avec la télévision": Chroniques 1959–1964*. Paris: Bartillat, 2008.

Nora, Pierre. "Entre mémoire et histoire: la problématique des lieux." In *Les Lieux de mémoire*, vol. 1: *La République*, edited by Pierre Nora. Paris: Gallimard, 1984.

Petitier, Paule. "Introduction." In *Histoire de France: choix de textes présentés par Paule Petitier*, by Jules Michelet, 7–31. Paris: Flammarion, 2008.

Philonenko, Alexis. *Essai sur la philosophie de la guerre*. Paris: Vrin, 2003.

Roger, Philippe. *L'ennemi américain: Généalogie de l'antiaméricanisme français*. Paris: Éditions du Seuil, 2002.

Sainte-Beuve, Charles-Augustin. *Histoire de Port-Royal*. Paris: Eugène Renduel, 1840.

Sartre, Jean-Paul. "Qu'est-ce que la littérature?" In *Situations II*, 55–330. Paris: Gallimard, 1948.

———. "La République du silence." In *Situations III*, 11–14. Paris: Gallimard, 1949.

Sirinelli, Jean-François. "Mauriac, un intellectuel engagé sous la IVe République." In *François Mauriac entre la Gauche et la Droite*, edited by André Séailles. Paris: Klincksieck, 1995.

Stokes, Lawrence D. "Historical Introduction." In *The Silence of the Sea / Le Silence de la mer*, by Vercors, edited by James W. Brown and Lawrence D. Stokes, translated by Cyril Connelly, 1–23. New York: Berg Publishers, 1991.

Texcier, Jean. *Écrit dans la nuit*. Paris: La Nouvelle Édition, 1945.

Todorov, Tzvetan. *Nous et les autres: la réflexion française sur la diversité humaine*. Paris: Éditions du Seuil, 1989.

———. *L'homme dépaysé*. Paris: Éditions du Seuil, 1996.

Touzot, Jean. *Mauriac sous l'Occupation*. Paris: La Manufacture, 1990.

Vercors [Jean Bruller]. *Le Silence de la mer*. Paris: Albin Michel, 1951. Available in English as *The Silence of the Sea / Le Silence de la mer*, edited by James W. Brown and Lawrence D. Stokes, translated by Cyril Connelly. New York: Berg, 1991.

Verlaine, Paul. *Selected Poems*. New York: Oxford University Press, 1999.

Winock, Michel. *Le Siècle des intellectuels* . Paris: Éditions du Seuil, 1997.

Wylie, Laurence, and Jean-François Brière. *Les Français*, 3rd ed. Upper Saddle River, N.J.: Prentice-Hall, 2001.

INDEX

François Mauriac on Race, War, Politics, and Religion: The Great War through the 1960s was designed in Minion Pro and composed by Kachergis Book Design of Pittsboro, North Carolina. It was printed on 60-pound House Natural Smooth and bound by Sheridan Books of Ann Arbor, Michigan.